Rosslyn Chapel

An Icon through the Ages

ROSSLYN CHAPEL

AN ICON THROUGH THE AGES

ANGELO MAGGI

BIRLINN

First published in 2008 by
Birlinn Limited
West Newington House
10 Newington Road
Edinburgh
EH9 1QS

www.birlinn.co.uk

ISBN13: 978 1 84158 724 0
ISBN10: 1 84158 724 9

British Library Cataloguing-in-Publication Data
A catalogue record for this book is available from the
British Library

Typeset at Birlinn in Perpetua with headings in ITC Galliard
Printed and bound in China through Worldprint

Dedication

Without Bianca neither this book nor I would be

CONTENTS

ILLUSTRATIONS

Details of the sources of illustrations are given in their captions and in the list of photographic credits, p. 173.

Illustrations

Illustrations

PREFACE

Seeing ruins can make us fleetingly aware of the existence
of a special time: it is not the time encountered in history
books nor one that can be brought back through a process of restoration. It is a time which is 'pure' and which
we cannot date. It is distinct from this modern age of images, cults and virtual reality, apart from our violent world
where architectural debris may no longer be dignified by
the concept of a 'ruin'. It is a lost time which only art can
retrieve.

Marc Augé from the introduction to *Le Temps
en Ruines*, 2003.

For many people and for many centuries the Collegiate Church of St Matthew in
Midlothian, known commonly as Rosslyn Chapel, though never completed and
surviving now only after a history of neglect, near ruin and restoration, stands as the
most romantic and picturesque monument of late medieval Scotland. In a sense the
building has become an icon of its age, yet it is a monument which, as a piece of
architecture that is unique, has been interpreted and understood in different ways at
different times.

The primary intention of this book is two-fold: to examine and record the range
of historical and visual evidence that exists to sustain the perception of Rosslyn as
a uniquely valuable and evocative structure; and to evaluate, through the discussion
of this evidence, the changing cultural climate and understanding of the 'meaning of
architecture' as expressed by the images that the building has generated as an historic
monument.

This study examines as precisely as possible the changing visual language of the
many representations that have been made of Rosslyn Chapel from 1693 to the early
twentieth century. It aims to explore their varied and changing meanings as historical
and artistic documents, and to evaluate the growing status of the building itself as an
icon of Scottish mediaeval architecture. Each painting, drawing, print and photograph
has its own integrity as a work of art, while at the same time it expresses its creator's
convictions as to the value of the structure in itself and in its setting.

In the development of the argument of the book I have elected to follow a thematic
rather than a chronological approach, as I believe our understanding of the building
and of its cultural context is better served by focusing on the specific approaches of
different critics and artists at different times. Several themes are here identified: one
is associated with light and illumination; another with the picturesque and antiquarian
interest of the site; and yet another with the practical considerations of building
conservation and the related issues of authenticity and replacement.

The opening quotation by Marc Augé is one which resonates with my own understanding of an historic monument. I do not consider Rosslyn as an example of a picturesque ruin but primarily as a living building. Augé's perception of 'pure' time, to be gained from looking at a ruin, is interesting because it seems to be independent from past and present, yet somehow to be made up of both. My approach to the history of Rosslyn Chapel is essentially similar. Thus, the act of looking at an image, which by its very nature is open to alternative readings, can become the source of an architectural understanding. It is the unfinished feeling that a viewer has which interests me. It is a tension which also relates to human beings across time, or in Augé's words: "a lost time which only art can retrieve".

ACKNOWLEDGEMENTS

This book has a long history. Its origins lie in the time I spent as an Erasmus exchange student at the School of Architecture in the Edinurgh College of Art. At that time, the Principal, Alistair Rowan, suggested that I might prepare a catalogue of the published views of Rosslyn Chapel which had interested architects for 300 years. In this work I was ably supervised by Roger Emmerson and Professor Rowan, and it provided the starting point for the much more detailed investigation which this book represents. One person who was crucial to the outcome of my initial work was Janet Skidmore in the Department of Prints and Drawings in the Victoria and Albert Museum, who introduced me to the methodologies of academic catalogues and taught me a great deal.

I also owe a great debt to my colleague and co-author Lady Helen Rosslyn, with whom, while working on this project, I collaborated in the production of a research exhibition, *Rosslyn Country of Painter and Poet*, held in the National Gallery of Scotland in 2002. Inevitably the research for the exhibition and this work could not be separated, and much of the material and the analysis included here is a result of many discussions between us. In the exhibition Helen had responsibility for the family and the Castle while the Chapel was my concern.

In conducting my research many people have given me help: and to all those who have readily answered my numerous enquiries, or shown me how systems worked, I am extremely grateful. In the British Library Peter Barber of the Topographical Collections was extremely helpful, as were the staff in the Manuscript room. I received similar courtesies from all the staff in the Print Room at the Victoria and Albert Museum in London, and from the Bodleian Library in Oxford. Stephen Wildman of the Ruskin Library at the University of Lancaster, was particularly helpful in tracing material in the library's collection and Julie Milne of the Mappin Art Gallery in Sheffield helped me with a curious painting which is now identified as by George Cattermole. Sheila Millar of the Loanhead Library, Midlothian, has given invaluable assistance on the history of the Chapel in all its local significance.

I owe a special debt of thanks to Margaret Richardson, former curator of Sir John Soane's Museum, whose interest in my work has been constant, who kindly drew Gandy's sketchbook to my attention and who, as President of the Society of Architectural Historians of Great Britain, awarded me the President's Commendation in the essay prize of 1998. At the Soane Museum I would also like to record the helpfulness of Susan Palmer and Stephen Astley.

My subject is Scottish, and it is from Edinburgh's cultural institutions that I have received regular, at times almost daily, support. Here I would particularly mention Jane Thomas and Veronica Steele of the Royal Commission on the Ancient and Historical Monuments of Scotland; Iain Gordon Brown and Kenneth Dunn of the National Library of Scotland; Alison Lindsay and Susan Corrigall in the National Archives of Scotland, Register House; Joanna Soden of the Royal Scottish Academy;

Elaine Greig in the Writers' Museum; Katrina Thomson, former assistant keeper, and Valerie Hunter, present curator of the Prints and Drawings Collection at the National Galleries of Scotland, and Susanna Kerr, Sara Stevenson and Helen Watson of the Scottish National Portrait Gallery. I would also like to pay tribute to Janis Adams and Christine Thompson.

Robert Cooper and Bob Brydon helped me through the mysteries of Masonic lore; George and Marcelle Blancett flew from Memphis, Tennessee, to bring a painting of the Chapel for me to view, and P.A. Campbell-Fraser brought several pictures of the Chapel for me to examine.

In investigating the fabric of the Chapel I was greatly helped by the support of James Simpson, senior partner of Simpson & Brown Architects. I would also like to record my gratitude to the Rosslyn Chapel Trust which has always been welcoming and helpful.

While I was working in the Edinburgh College of Art many colleagues and friends were supportive. I would mention particularly Leslie Forsyth, Rosie Hall, Alison Murison and Moira Seftor in the School of Architecture; June Cormack, Valerie Hawkins, Heather Hillman, Alan Shipway and Wilson Smith in the Library.

I should like to acknowledge the kindness of Sir Howard Colvin, the examiner of my Ph.D. thesis on Rosslyn, who was always receptive to my ideas and who encouraged me to continue with an approach to architectural history which he described as innovative.

I hope my ideas are clearly expressed, and if they are that is due very largely to the kindness of my friends Dr Scott Cooper and David P. Hemmings who, at different times, have read large sections of my text and have helped me with my English. I should also record the essential support offered by several bodies: the SAHGB which awarded me the Dorothy Stroud bursary in 1999; the RIAS from which I received the Thomas Ross Award in 1999; the Edinburgh College of Art for an Andrew Grant research bursary in 2000 and 2001, and the Italian Cultural Institute in London for a further 'Borsa di studio per l'estero'.

In the preparation of this book I have been greatly assisted by Mrs Joan B. Taylor and her son Charles, who kindly gave me permission to borrow the album 'Documents Relating to Roslin Chapel' and to reproduce images in order to complete my research. The book's publication owes a great deal to the special efforts of Tom Johnstone and Seán Costello in Edinburgh and of Luca Chiavegato in Verona. Their organisational skills and commitment to this project have been invaluable.

My parents, Vito e Palma, gave me unfailing support from the far south of Italy, and my sister Mariafrancesca is largely responsible for the index.

To my wife Bianca I owe the incalculable example of good humour and intelligence, of versatile industry and domestic equilibrium that formed the day in, day out environment in which this work was produced.

Finally, I wish to thank, above all, Alistair Rowan, whose contributions have been not only fundamental, but also so varied as to be unlistable. He kept me in a good humour at a difficult time and I could not have finished this book without his caring and supportive interest.

1
ROSSLYN CHAPEL[1]

No person can enter into it, who has the smallest degree of solid
thinking, without being struck with reverential awe at its august
appearance.

Robert Forbes, *An Account of the Chapel of Roslin*, 1761.

1.1. History and Description

DURING the fifteenth century it became common practice for wealthy families to endow
and establish colleges of secular canons in Scotland. They were called *Praepositurae*, or
Collegiate Churches, and were governed by a dean or provost, who had jurisdiction
over them. They were institutes for performing divine service, and the singing of
masses for the souls of the founders, their relations and benefactors. These churches
consisted of prebendaries (*praebendarii*), or canons (*canonicii*), who had several degrees
or stalls where they sat for singing during the canonical hours and, with their dean or
provost, made up the chapter. The ritual was much the same as that of the cathedral
church, so that almost any form of plan was suitable, provided that provision was
made for a number of different altars in appropriate positions. The most simple way of
providing for a college was by making an addition to an existing church; however most
collegiate churches were built on a larger scale even when the college grew from small
beginnings. In fact most patrons chose to provide an appropriate architectural setting
for their foundations, particularly since the collegiate churches that they founded were
usually also family burial places. Of about fifty collegiate churches founded in Scotland,
many continued in use after the Reformation as parish churches, and over thirty still
survive today.[2]

A number of these Scottish collegiate churches were cross-shaped and T-shaped
in plan, presumably both because of the symbolism and for the convenience of the
additional altar space.[3] The choir was the essential part. It provided everything necessary
to enable the service to be conducted, and since this was so it sometimes happened that
no attempt was made to continue the building westwards of the transepts. As a result
many collegiate churches were left in an unfinished state. A further possible reason why
few plans were fully completed may be linked to the process of construction. This was
achieved in successive building phases and stopped when funds dried up, which affected
the progress of the work. One of the most ambitious collegiate foundations was the
church at Roslin in Midlothian, where the great magnate, William Sinclair, built one
of the finest gems of Scottish late gothic architecture. Although it was never more than
half completed, Rosslyn Collegiate Church, commonly called Rosslyn Chapel because
of its small dimensions, is unique both as a plan in the context of Scottish architectural
history and as a veritable Mecca which has fascinated antiquarians, historians, painters

1

and poets. No other building in Scotland has been more studied than Rosslyn and it may be useful before we turn to the cultural significance of the building to describe its layout and to set out its subsequent history.

Rosslyn Chapel, or the Collegiate Church of St Matthew the Apostle, is situated a short distance from Rosslyn Castle, on a high bank overlooking the valley of the river Esk. It is said to have originally been called Roskelyn, a Gaelic or Erse word meaning 'a hill in a glen',[4] which describes exactly the position of the Chapel, and is easily recognisable in the modern Rosslyn or Roslin.[5] According to the *Genealogie of the Sainteclaires of Rosslyn* compiled by the Rev. Richard Augustine Hay, the Chapel was commenced in the year 1446, by William Sinclair, Earl of Orkney.[6] At the time of foundation, Sinclair was a wealthy man and it seems clear that he must have expended considerable sums on the fabric of the church. Recently it has been shown that he was experiencing financial problems in the late 1450s and 1460s, which may have caused delays in the construction of the building.[7] These problems came to a head between 1468 and 1470 when he lost the majority of his Orkney earldom, which must have placed considerable financial limitations on the realisation of his dream in stone.

Nevertheless in late medieval society Sinclair, who wished to combine a collegiate establishment with a place of interment for himself and his successors, seems to have been an unusually enlightened employer for those working on the Chapel. He is said to have assembled a skilful workforce with men from all parts, and to have rewarded their work generously 'with a munificence well calculated to give energy to their operations'.[8] As the building is evidently incomplete, and as there is no record of the demolition of any part of it, it is most probable that work came to a halt following the death of the Earl in 1484. At that time only the choir or east end was finished, and the transept existed simply as an external wall; once stopped the work was never resumed. The whole building is remarkable for the peculiarities of its style, and for the richness of its ornament which once led commentators, quite incorrectly, to imagine that the unique nature of the design indicated that it had been built by foreign masons.[9]

The plan of the Chapel [fig.1] takes the form of a long choir with a five-bay arcade down each side supporting a clerestory and pointed barrel vault. The east end is a closed rectangle, unusually only two bays wide, and the entire choir is surrounded by a vaulted single-storey outer aisle or ambulatory which returns at right-angles across the east end. Here it becomes a double or inner and outer aisle with a second row of piers which mark the end of the choir. The external elevation is remarkable for its succession of square-sectioned buttresses projecting boldly from the aisle walls and topped by crocketed pinnacles. These have a geometric precision almost like Gothic obelisks. They contain niches for statues, though whether these were ever filled is doubtful, despite the fact that both John Slezer [fig.2] and Father Hay [fig.4 and 5] chose to illustrate them thus.[10]

Entry to the Chapel is provided by two doors, exactly opposite each other, one on the north and the other on the south side. A segmental arch, thrown across from one buttress to the other, forms a porch to these entrances, with a segmental triangular window above. The interior is planned as a high central space with two side aisles, separated by clustered piers, arranged in two rows, and supporting Gothic arches. Though the piers are no more than eight feet high, their capitals are adorned with foliage and curiously wrought figures, so that they produce a very imposing effect. Above them stand the clerestory windows, also beautifully carved. The pointed barrel vault of the choir is divided into five compartments, each decorated with shallow

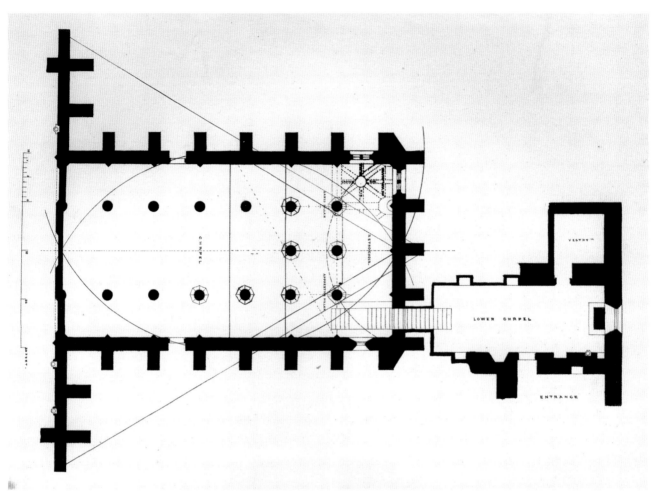

1. Plan of Rosslyn Chapel from Proceedings of the Society of Antiquaries of Scotland, 1878.

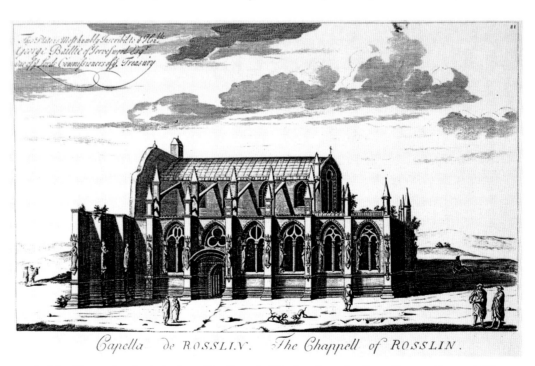

2. John Slezer, *Capella de Rosslin – The Chappel of Rosslin*. Engraving from *Theatrum Scotiae*, 1693.

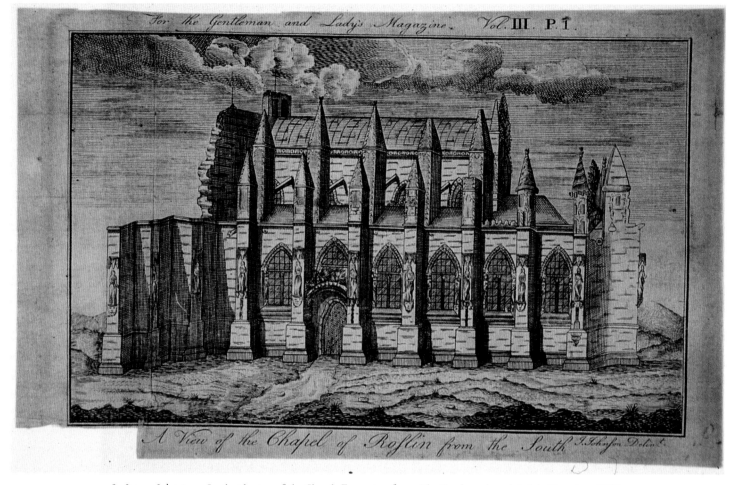

3. James Johnston, *South side view of the Chapel*. Engraving from *The Gentleman's and Lady's Magazine*, 1780.

coffers whose individual panels are filled with different flowers. The entire ceiling, the bosses of the vault, the capitals, the architraves – indeed it seems the whole interior – is covered with sculptures representing flowers, leaves, passages of sacred history, texts of scripture and grotesque figures, all worked with extraordinary precision. The effect is rich and bizarre.

At the south-east angle of the Chapel one pier stands out from the rest, wreathed with ascending spirals of foliage; this is known as 'The Apprentice's Pillar'. The legend, which is surely apocryphal, tells of an apprentice who proved a better workman than his master. In this story the master-mason of Rosslyn was unable to interpret the design of this pier from the plans furnished to him, and had to go to Rome to take an accurate drawing of a similar one there. On his return he found that his apprentice had, in his absence, overcome all difficulties and that the work was already finished. Instead of being delighted at having trained such a workman, the mason was so overcome by jealousy that he immediately killed the apprentice with a blow of his hammer, and was thereafter hanged for the murder.[11]

The double aisle across the East end of the Chapel served as a separate Lady chapel. The floor of the outer aisle is one step higher than in the other parts of the building and here, according to the charter of Lord Sinclair, were four altars dedicated respectively to St Matthew, St Andrew, St Peter and the Virgin Mary.[12] The burial-place of the Sinclair family is in a vault underneath the chapel, the entrance being under a large flagstone between the north wall and the third and fourth pillars, while a straight stair in the south-east corner bay leads down to a long crypt located outside and below the main building.

The crypt, also known as the sacristy, is a long rectangle covered by a simple barrel vault decorated by transverse and ridge ribs which have enlarged edges. The ribs are supported by figurative corbels, some of which are painted. There is a modern altar against the east wall and a piscina in the south wall. Some of the corbelled figures, most representing angels, appear to be turned towards the altar. The east wall has a single chamfered lancet window, flanked by statue corbels, which have shields of arms. There is a round-headed doorway in the north wall leading to a small chamber. A similar door in the south wall leads to the outside, and on the same wall appears a square-headed fireplace with a roll moulding on the surround. Incised on the stone surface of the north and south walls of the crypt there are some full-sized drawings that have survived from the period of construction. These original delineations of architectural details – such as the eastern chapel's vault ribs and a pinnacle – are extremely interesting and valuable evidence of how accurately portions of the building were designed. This also suggests that the room functioned during the building of the Chapel as a mason's office.[13]

Barbara Crawford suggests a chronology of the work at Rosslyn based on the appearance of three different coats of arms.[14] The first, on the south side of the window in the crypt, shows the arms of Sinclair's first wife, Elisabeth Douglas, daughter of the fourth Earl of Douglas. Her death in 1451 may indicate that the crypt was built before this date. The second, above the central pier over the high altar, depicts the Sinclair coat of arms alone, which might indicate that it was built before William Sinclair married his second wife Marjorie Sutherland. The third, on the north wall, combines the arms of Sinclair with those of his second wife. It is important to mention the fact that Lady Elisabeth Douglas is said to have taken a great interest in the building of this church, especially in matters of style.[15] In fact, a difference in style occurs between the crypt and the upper building, which changes suddenly from simplicity to the ornate elaboration of the arcades in the main Chapel. Though the greater simplicity of the architecture of the Crypt may well be the result of the minor role which this part of the building played within the structure as a whole, it may, perhaps, not be unreasonable to infer, as Crawford suggests, that the building had only proceeded as far as the Crypt when Lady Elisabeth died and her influence ceased.

When William Sinclair died, his dream of a church worthy of God's praise was only partly realised. It fell to his son and heir, Oliver Sinclair, to continue the work. His work at the Chapel, consisted of roofing the choir with a stone vault.[16] In 1523, William's grandson, upon his succession to the family seat, although not making any alterations to the Chapel did grant land to the provost and prebendaries for dwelling houses and gardens.[17]

During the last three decades of the sixteenth century there was a struggle in Scotland between the Protestants and many important families which remained Roman Catholics. These years of religious strife are reflected in the history of Rosslyn Chapel.[18] In February 1571 the provost and the prebendaries resigned following the violent confiscation of their endowments. The Presbytery records of Dalkeith reveal that eighteen years later Rosslyn Chapel was a 'kirk' full of 'images and uther monumentis of idolatrie',[19] which implies that the Sinclairs had not yet succumbed to the Reformation and remained Roman Catholics. In 1592 the family was threatened with excommunication unless the

4 and 5. Anonymous, *Rosslyn Chapel Ante 1700*. First and second versions of a pen drawing in Richard Augustine Hay's manuscripts *Genealogie of the Sainteclaries of Rosslyn*. National Library of Scotland, Edinburgh.

altars in the family church were destroyed. At the end of August of the same year it was recorded that the altars of Rosslyn Chapel had been demolished.[20]

From 1610 until 1638, the Episcopal Church was the established form of religion in Scotland. In this period Rosslyn Chapel lay abandoned, worship in the Chapel having ceased after the destruction of its altars. It remained unused until 1650 when Cromwellian troops, under the command of General Monk, stabled their horses in the Chapel after attacking the Castle. Despite this secular use, the building was to be violated once more at the establishment of Presbyterianism in Scotland in 1688 when a mob, raised in Edinburgh, ransacked the Chapel destroying whatever was considered as idolatrous adornment. Fortunately, most of the damage caused by attacks over a hundred-year period left the main structure of the church relatively unscathed, as we can see from the first iconographic record of the building by Captain John Slezer (c.1645-1717) whose engraved view of the *Capella de Rosslin* was published in 1693 [fig.2].

Nothing more is known of the Chapel until 1736, when General James St Clair removed the shutters from the outside of the windows and replaced them with clear glass. It was Sir John Clerk of Penicuik (1676-1755), one of the most respected and endearing personalities among the early eighteenth century antiquaries in Scotland, who promoted the preservation of Rosslyn Chapel, encouraging General Sinclair to carry out repairs between 1738 and 1742. One of his major contributions to the history of the Chapel was the addition of a high sloping side roof made by the architect and carpenter John Baxter the elder (d.1770). The same roof was removed almost one hundred years later, when the architect William Burn was asked by the third Earl of Rosslyn, James Alexander Sinclair, to replace it by a new lower one 'rendering the appearance of the roof more in conformity with the original plan'.[21] In 1861, Lord Rosslyn decided that Sunday services should resume at the Chapel, and to make this posssible he employed Burn's one-time assistant and partner, David Bryce. In contrast to Burn, Bryce seems to have undertaken a more thorough repair, understandably, as he had to make the church habitable whereas Burn had only to try and halt its decay. These operations raised storms of protest and much hysterical rhetoric. The numerous disparaging reports that were written on the restoration works at Rosslyn highlight the Victorian attitude towards the preservation of the building. Nevertheless the restoration works were carried out and in April 1862 the Chapel was rededicated by the Bishop of Edinburgh.

In 1878 the fourth Earl of Rosslyn, Francis Robert Sinclair, planned an extension to the Chapel at the west front. The new structure was designed by Andrew Kerr: an Edinburgh architect who had made himself well known to the Earl thanks to a very detailed essay on the medieval history of the Chapel published the same year.[22] In its external elevation this structure shows two storeys surmounted by a cornice and parapet. Each side has two Gothic windows, one above the other, arched by hood mouldings. At each corner there are two buttresses, terminating in pinnacles with ornamental finials, and provided, like the wall spaces left between them, with niches for the reception of statues. The west end is pierced on the ground level by a doorway, flanked with two small lancet windows, and in the upper storey by a rose window. The ground floor of the new building became the baptistery, which could be reached from the Chapel by the old transept entrance. The upper portion was set apart for the accommodation of the organ and a small choir.

In 1913 the architect Robert Lorimer (1864-1929) was asked to undertake a survey of the Chapel, but unfortunately the only record of his involvement with the building is a letter in which he reported details of his findings and made various proposals for action.[23] No further documentation exists to prove whether Lorimer's recommendations were acted upon and if so by whom. The major repairs undertaken during the twentieth century were carried out by the Ministry of Works in the 1950s. On this occasion the roof on the baptistery was re-covered in copper and a new oil-fired heating system was installed, including the construction of a new boiler house and a tank room. This system replaced the previous coal-fired system, added during Bryce's intervention. Extensive work was also undertaken on the ornate carved stonework on the interior and a 'cementitious wash' applied, that unfortunately sealed the surface of the masonry with an impermeable coating, leading to a very high level of humidity in the Chapel in recent years. In 1997 Simpson and Brown Architects, who were engaged in the Rosslyn Chapel Conservation Plan, Historic Scotland and other local bodies decided on the use of a free-standing steel structure to cover the building. The 'canopy' was erected to enable the stone fabric of the roof vaults to dry outwards away from the carved interior surfaces. This superstructure, still on site, provides modern visitors with an opportunity to appreciate the building from a high vantage point. As long as this protective structure exists, Rosslyn Chapel, one of the finest examples of Scottish architecture, might be said to have become a 'pocket cathedral in an earthly paradise'.[24]

Countless writers have described the visual glories of Rosslyn Chapel and much has been written on the spirit that animated its erection. Some historians have dealt with economics and the politics of financing the building,[25] while others have analysed the geometrical layout of this late medieval structure, both in plan and elevation, thereby seeking to uncover the 'secret' of its design.[26] In seeking to account for its unusual richness and finish it should be remembered that this 'unfinished thought in stone' is very much a personal creation, reflecting the mind and tastes of its founder.

We will probably never know the precise detail of the construction processes carried out at Rosslyn Chapel. We can however review and clarify what is definitely known; we can differentiate between speculation and hard fact; we can assess the assumptions of previous writers and draughtsmen, and consider the premises on which they based their arguments and at what point they were content to leave off both investigation and theorising.

Having set out briefly the factual story of this Chapel, perhaps the most celebrated architectural Icon of late medieval Scotland, we must now move on to consider developments within the context of the building itself and to examine the flux of opinions and reasoning through which William Sinclair's masterwork captured the imagination of writers, poets, architects, photographers, painters, antiquarians and scholars in different ages and for many generations.

2

INSPIRED BY LIGHT

Every phenomenon of nature, or extraordinary effort of
art, was formerly the parent of some strange legendary tale,
or romantic story. In the gloomy ages of ignorance such
occurrences were always deemed marvellous. The castle,
chapel, and lairds of Roslyn were certainly calculated to
amaze the illiterate, and intimidate the weak.

John Britton, *Architectural Antiquities*, 1812.

2.1. Gandy's Visions.

IN his article entitled 'Gandy and the Tomb of Merlin', published in 1941, John
Summerson brought to light one of the most introverted figures in the history of
early nineteenth-century architecture.[1] The essay, which begins with an analysis of
one of the finest watercolour perspectives [fig.6] by the English draughtsman Joseph
Michael Gandy (1771-1843), shows how the scene represented in the painting could

6. Joseph Michael Gandy, *The Tomb of Merlin*. Watercolour, 1815. Library Drawings Collections, Royal Institute of British
Architects, London.

7. Henry William Pickersgill, *Portrait of Joseph Michael Gandy*. Pencil on paper, 1822.
National Portrait Gallery, London.

be associated with a passage from Ludovico Ariosto's chivalric poem *Orlando Furioso* (1516).[2] Some years later, the same author described the architecture of 'Merlin's Tomb Chamber' as 'a version of Anglo-Norman, with some reminiscences of Roslin Chapel which Gandy had measured and drawn'.[3]

Referring to the analysis conducted by Summerson, Brian Lukacher clarifies the similarities between the painting *The Tomb of Merlin* (1815) and Rosslyn Chapel, not only in some of its architectural aspects, but also for its legendary associations. According to Lukacher, the imaginary burial chamber which Gandy portrayed has a noteworthy source: the Scottish legend that the night before a Lord of Rosslyn died, the chapel appeared to be in flames, without sustaining any injury. He writes that 'such an unconsuming fire, a supernatural radiance prescient of life beyond death, must have been associated in Gandy's mind with the spectral glow from Merlin's tomb'.[4]

This superstition, as with so many others, takes its origin from the pen of Sir Walter Scott (1771-1832), who in *The Lay of the Last Minstrel* (1805) recounts, in poetic tones, how Rosslyn Chapel seemed to be on fire when a death drew near for a member of the Sinclair family.

> Seem'd all on fire that chapel proud,
> Where Roslin's chiefs uncoffin'd lie;
> Each baron, for a sable shroud,
> Sheathed in his iron panoply.
>
> Seem'd all on fire within, around,
> Deep sacristy and altars pale;

Shone every pillar foliage bound,
And glimmer'd all the dead men's mail.

Blaz'd battlement, and pinnet high,
Blaz'd every rose-carved buttress fair –
So still they blaze, when fate is nigh
The lordly line of high St Clair.[5]

A later text by Robert William Billings (1813-1874), which accompanied the plates of Rosslyn in *The Baronial and Ecclesiastical Antiquities of Scotland* (1845), gives us a logical explanation for this eerie effect. Billings explains how he was rendered speechless 'by the appearance, through the branches of the trees, of what seemed a row of bright-red smokeless furnaces,'[6] but which was only 'a fine setting sun shining straight through the double windows of the chapel... The phenomenon had a powerful effect on the vision; but it was more that of ignition than of sunlight, from the rich red which often attends Scottish sunsets'.[7] It is probable then that this remarkable 'supernatural' effect was determined by the position of the building: 'the most appropriate that could be chosen, had its builder desired to produce this effect'.[8] Although the Chapel is located halfway down the side of a hill, there are no obstacles on the west to interrupt the lowest rays of the setting sun.

It was, no doubt, a combination of the emotional quality suggested by such phantasmagorical light effects, of the association of rich architectural forms and of the events of which they were supposed to be a testimony, which captured Gandy's visionary imagination, and persuaded him to travel from London to Scotland in September 1806 where he spent a few days preparing a detailed survey of Rosslyn Chapel.[9] Three years later, Gandy presented at the Royal Academy of London summer exhibition a large watercolour depicting a corner of the choir and Lady Chapel with the stair leading to the crypt. This painting reminded the reviewer of an old woman called Annie Wilson [fig.13] – a 'venerable damsel of Caledonian nativity'[10] – who guided visitors around Rosslyn Chapel pointing out the prominent enrichments with the aid of a long mysterious divining-rod which Gandy shows leaning against the Apprentice Pillar.[11] Unfortunately Gandy's painting has disappeared, but a copy of it made the same year by George Shepherd (fl.1800-1830) shows the extent to which he was intrigued by the decoration [fig.9]. The massive pillars and vaulted arches, with a variety of foliate mouldings and chevrons, emerge from the darkness as various light sources illuminate them to create an ethereal atmosphere. Yet not everyone was sympathetic to Gandy's visionary interpretation; for instance the writer of *Monthly Retrospect of the Fine Arts* for that year declares that 'Gandy's Roslin Chapel in the Exhibition of the Royal Academy of London is beautifully drawn, but too ideal in colouring and finishing for a real view'.[12] It was, however, important for Gandy to idealise all of his architectural compositions, imbuing them with an evanescent and mysterious air, which made him one of the most favoured draughtsman in Sir John Soane's *atelier*.[13]

It seems probable that the fame which Gandy achieved with this picture brought him to the attention of the architectural publisher and antiquarian John Britton (1771-1857), who invited him to draw the fourteen plates of Rosslyn Chapel for the third volume of *The Architectural Antiquities of Great Britain* published in 1812.[14] Britton's historical analysis of Rosslyn Chapel dwelt on the building's anachronistic style, which he thought was shown in its unclassifiable combination of overcharged ornament and

8. John Burnett after Joseph Michael Gandy, *Interior view of Rosslyn Chapel*. Engraving from J.Britton, *The Architectural Antiquities of Great Britain*, 1812.

9. George Shepherd after Joseph Michael Gandy, *Interior view of the Chapel from the south aisle looking towards the Lady Chapel*. Watercolour, 1809. Victoria and Albert Museum, London.

primitive solidity. He also discussed the Masonic lore surrounding the building: the master-mason reputedly murdering his apprentice in envy over the design of the pillar, and the hallowed lineage of the Lords of Rosslyn in Scottish Freemasonry.[15]

Gandy's interior view of Rosslyn Chapel [fig.8], an engraving of the watercolour exhibited at the Royal Academy, has many key elements that were to be reworked in his painting of *The Tomb of Merlin*. These are the same viewpoint, the pervasive luminosity and the definition of the architectural details.[16] The other drawings executed by Gandy, that were published by Britton, ranged from an accurate plan of the building [fig.10] to an extremely detailed outline section [fig.11]; from scaled drawings of single architectural elements to beautiful interior perspectives and a detailed view of the pinnacles. Though printing processes tend to weaken the effects of light on stone, Gandy managed to reproduce them and make them visible even when printed. The way Gandy manages to render the subjects of his drawings is unique and his work became a source of inspiration and factual information for future illustrators.[17]

According to Britton the Chapel 'awakened the enthusiasm' of Gandy's genius; and it was 'highly creditable to this artist, that he did not leave the spot till he had stored his sketch book with all the architectural parts of the chapel, as well as general views of the surrounding scenery'.[18] If we think of the difficulty of executing a detailed survey of a building which is so rich in its ornament, the comment seems more than

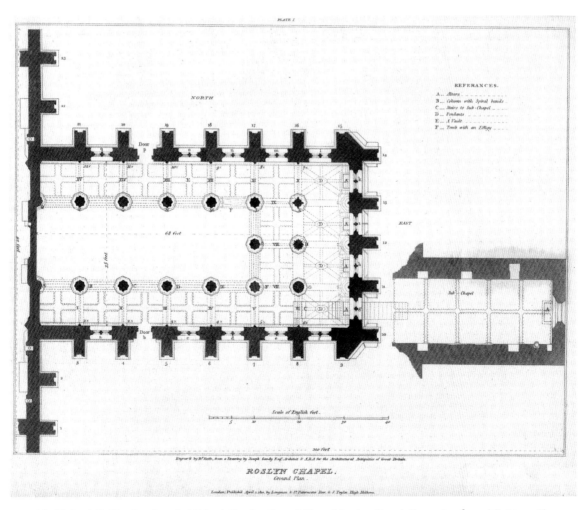

10. Richard Roffe after Joseph Michael Gandy, *Ground Plan of Rosslyn Chapel*. Engraving from J.Britton, *The Architectural Antiquities of Great Britain*, 1812.

13

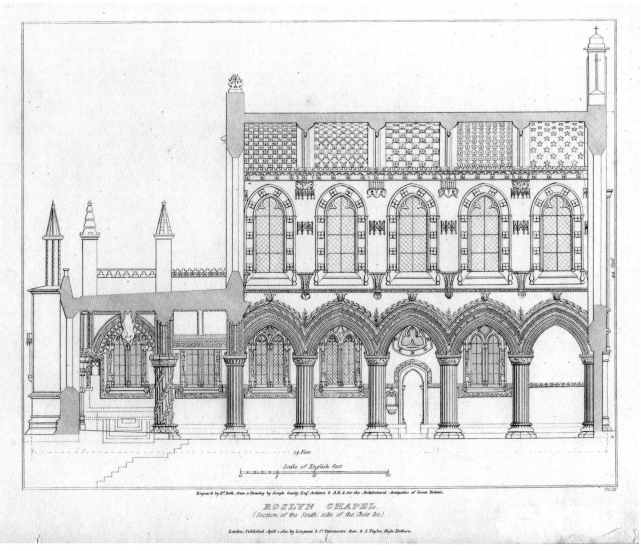

ROSSLYN CHAPEL.
(Section of the South side of the Choir &c.)

11. Richard Roffe after Joseph Michael Gandy, *East to west section of the Chapel.* Engraving from J.Britton, *The Architectural Antiquities of Great Britain*, 1812.

justified. The sketchbook which Britton mentions, recently acquired by Sir John Soane's Museum,[19] is a wonderful demonstration of Gandy as a 'scientific antiquary' in his approach to the building and provides, within its modest format, the source material both for his illustrations for the *Architectural Antiquities*, and also for his magnificent 'Rosslynesque' watercolour, the celebrated *Tomb of Merlin*. Through a comparative analysis of the plates published in 1812 and the sketches made six years before, it is possible to understand the key elements that struck Gandy's imagination, and above all to follow the evolution of his plates.

For Gandy, the need to revisit the sacred and mystical traditions of this building clearly involved a search for authoritative sources for his visionary works. It is exactly this visionary style which influences his exterior views: here the result is that the artist decides to concentrate in one single illustration the most striking parts of the Chapel. Thus the observer is made to appreciate the splendour of the work even if the illustration does not correspond precisely to the truth. Some of the plates, in fact, are a conglomeration of striking elements, far removed from modern ideas of

14

architectural accuracy. We should not blame Gandy however for over-embellishing his prints of the building, or for having changed part of its essence, especially when we consider the taste of the collectors for whom the plates were intended. It is the genius of Gandy that in fact the whole process of embellishment, or fakery, in the image is almost imperceptible. Only the closest attention to detail can allow us to unravel the architectural illusion that he presents. As a good architect, Gandy studies every single detail, fusing all together by a taste which, with a graceful logic, though inaccurate, respects the historic identity of the building. In the view entitled *Roslyn Chapel, Elevation of part of the South side* [fig.14], for example, Gandy inserts a small window that interrupts the base course in order to show us an interesting architectural feature that appears three bays further on. Also in the same view he chooses to crown the south wall with architectural finishes: a delicate stone cresting and cusp, and arched battlements, both of which come from a different location on the East end walls.

This architectural *collage* characterises also the measured drawings contained in the sketchbook where the artist, guided by the refinement of the most elaborately carved parts of the Chapel, sketches different details that he was to assemble later on. One of the most interesting elements with which he seems to play is the circular finial. In the Chapel there are three of them and they are all positioned on the north wall. In the published view there appears only one which is positioned by Gandy on the arch over the south door.[20] In the sketchbook, however, this motif is accompanied by two

12. William Dunn, *Inside view of the Chapel*. Watercolour, 1816. Scottish Library Edinburgh City Libraries.

13. Anonymous, *Annie Wilson*. Etching from *The Gentleman's Magazine,*
September 1817.

others in a single crowning decorative element [fig.16]. Once again the composition of
the details on paper does not correspond with the reality in stone [fig.15]; rather this
capriccio helps us to understand the overall content of the Chapel.[21]

Gandy therefore organises every object and episode inside a balanced visual
construction, in order to be able to arrive at the best solution. Nothing is impossible,
so long as every alteration is pursued with clarity and is consistently based on an actual
object. The high-pitched roof on the aisle, for example, despite being in place when
Gandy visited the Chapel in 1806, is not shown in any of his views.[22] For this reason,
at times, he also omits the clerestory windows, as the presence of the roof made it
impossible to verify the measurements of what was hidden below. The only suggestion
that the roof was in place was in the pencil sketches that were never redrawn in
pen.[23]

When Gandy described the building as a 'combination of Egyptian, Grecian, Roman,
and Saracenic styles,'[24] he did not intend to reduce Rosslyn Chapel to a bizarre eclectic
agglomeration of parts, but rather to extol it as one of the most astonishing architectural
compositions ever realised. And it is for this reason that his rendering of the facts, even
if they are not archaeologically precise, can be considered as an interpretation of the
original appearance of the building and of the functionality of all its parts. In contrast
to this way of depicting the architecture, Gandy's work is topographically accurate in
his series of five plates representing the pinnacles, pedestal columns, canopies, brackets
in front of the buttresses, and the tracery and mouldings of different windows. All
of them are rigorously numbered and indicated in the general plan of the Chapel,
permitting the reader to position and reconstruct exactly every single part of the
building through a simple comparison of the plates. This graphic correlation between
plan, section and details is even more accentuated in the sketchbook, where the artist
appears to have superimposed his measured annotations one on top of the other, almost
like acetate transparencies. In the page devoted to 'The Apprentice Pillar' [fig.17], the
section of the pier, with an elevation and details of mouldings, are intermingled, while
they appear with greater order in the published plate [fig.18].[25]

An album entitled 'Documents Relating to Roslin Chapel',[26] which came to light during research for the Rosslyn exhibition at the National Gallery of Scotland, offers a unique collection of papers related to Britton's involvement with Rosslyn and the publication of the plates of the Chapel by Gandy in *Architectural Antiquities*.[27] In a recent article on the Gandy Sketchbook Ian Goodall and Margaret Richardson voiced their concern that there are insufficient drawings in the sketchbook to serve as basis for all fourteen plates published in *Architectural Antiquities*.[28] The album 'Documents Relating to Roslin Chapel' goes further towards supplying the missing information and sheds new light on other planned images which, in the event, were not to be published by Britton. There is no doubt that twelve of the drawings contained in the album are by Gandy's hand. Further comparisons with what he recorded while at Rosslyn in 1806 clearly identifies their source. For instance the album contains an ink over pencil drawing – apparently the preparatory design for a supposed engraved plate – of the west end elevation of the Chapel [fig.19], which corresponds with the measured drawing Gandy made of it on the reverse side of page 27 in his sketchbook [fig.20]. Another comparison can be made with the sketchbook drawing of the *piscina* near the south door entrance [fig.22] and the measured drawing of what Gandy records as 'Window No.13' [fig.23]. In the album these two images become clean and neat ink drawings ready to be

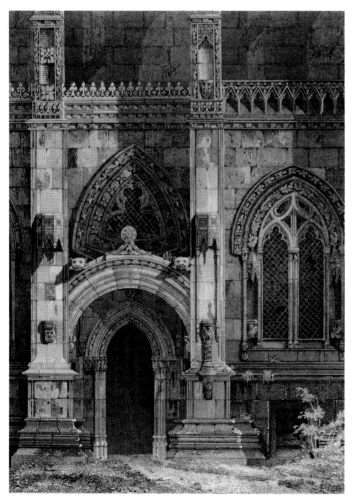

14. John Burnett after Joseph Michael Gandy, *Elevation of a part of the Chapel's south side.* Engraving from J.Britton, *The Architectural Antiquities of Great Britain*, 1812.

15. *Contemporary photograph of the south porch of Rosslyn Chapel.* (Author's photograph)

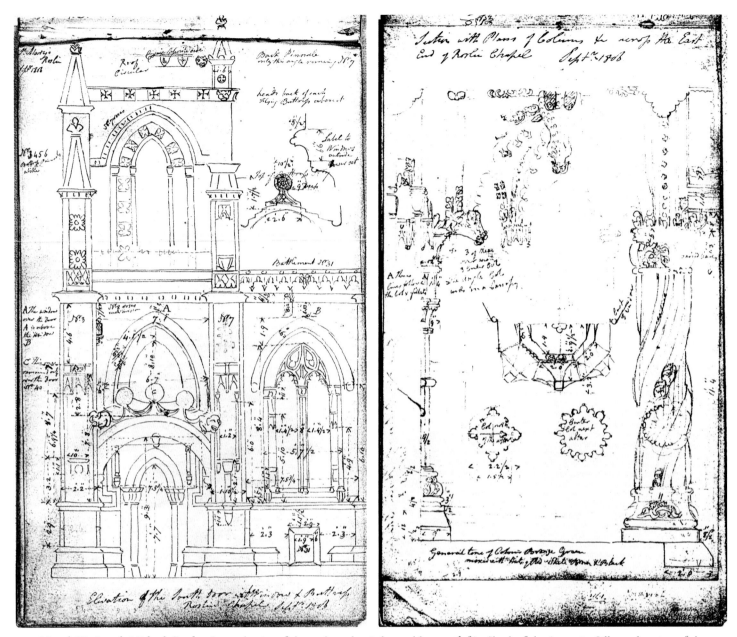

16 and 17. Joseph Michael Gandy, *Survey drawing of the south porch, window and buttress* (left). *Sketch of the Apprentice Pillar and sections of the other columns in the Lady Chapel* (right). Pencil and pen, 1806, from Gandy's sketchbook, Sir John Soane's Museum, London.

engraved. When such careful preliminary work had been undertaken for these designs, it seems important to ask why these drawings were never published?

The drawings executed by Gandy that were published by Britton ranged from two plans of the Chapel, an elevation of the south side and two interior perspectives, to several drawings of architectural elements numbered according to a survey sequence. We can note that the style of the first nine plates and that of the last five plates are slightly different. It would appear that at a certain point the engraving of the architectural plates was stopped, then replaced by a rather odd collage of numbered architectural details which the last five plates represent. Some of these details appear in the sketchbook with a different set of numbers, but most of them do not. This suggests that Britton may have gone back to Rosslyn on his own account, possibly accompanied by another draughtsman. Indeed the only letter in the album by Gandy confirms that

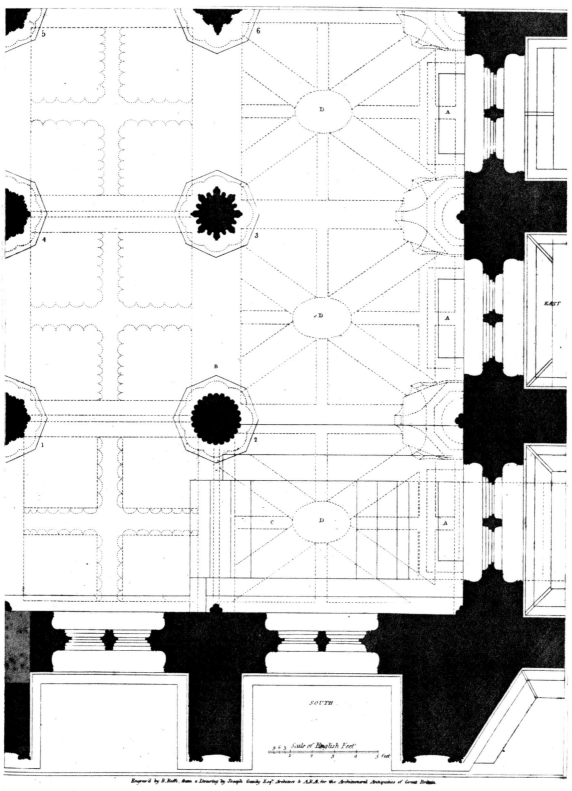

Engraved by R.Roffe, from a Drawing by Joseph Gandy Esq. Architect & A.R.A. for the Architectural Antiquities of Great Britain.

ROSLYN CHAPEL,
Ground Plan of Columns, Wall &c. at the East end.

London; Published April 1.1812. by Longman & C° Paternoster Row, & J.Taylor, High Holborn.

18. Richard Roffe after Joseph Michael Gandy, *Ground Plan of the south east part of the Lady Chapel.* Engraving from
J.Britton, *The Architectural Antiquities of Great Britain*, 1812.

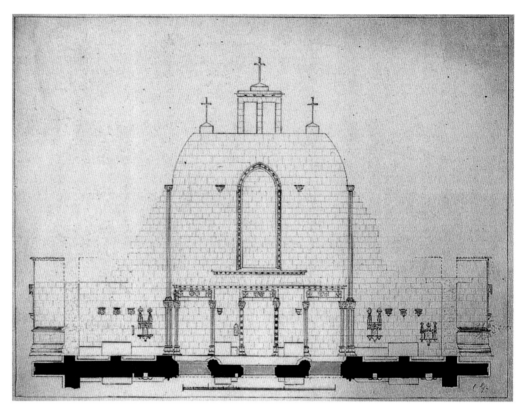

19. Joseph Michael Gandy, *West end elevation of the Chapel.* Pencil and pen, c.1810. From the album *Documents Relating to Roslin Chapel*, Private Collection.

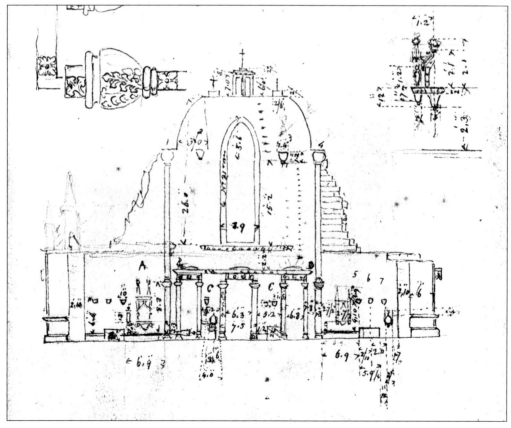

20. Joseph Michael Gandy, *Survey drawing of the west end elevation.* Pencil and pen, 1806, from Gandy's sketchbook, Sir John Soane's Museum, London.

21. Joseph Michael Gandy, *South wall cresting and moulding sections; plan and elevation of piscina in the south aisle.* Pencil and pen, c.1810. From the album *Documents*, Private collection.

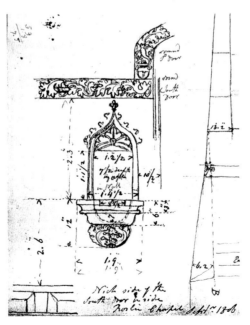

22. Joseph Michael Gandy, *Survey drawing of the piscina in the south aisle.* Pencil and pen, 1806. From Gandy's sketchbook, Sir John Soane's Museum, London.

21

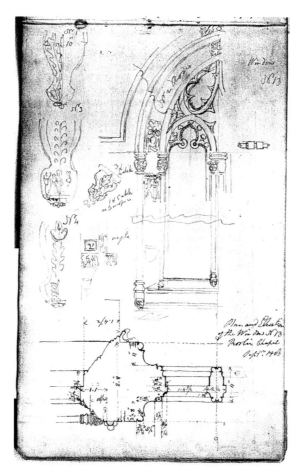

23. Joseph Michael Gandy, *Plan and elevation of a window, boss details of the Lady Chapel*. Pencil and pen, 1806, from Gandy's sketchbook, Sir John Soane's Museum, London.

he never managed to complete the survey and, in referring to his perspective view of the interior, he suggested that Britton should make a rubbing on the architrave joining the Apprentice Pillar to the south wall.

> The form of the letter on the Ribbon of the Beam seen in my perspective view of the inside has more of the Saxon or Saracen character, the letters being interwoven. I had not time to copy them when at Roslin but I hope you will be able to obtain their correct forms by getting someone to press paper over them using black chalk to rub on the paper on the parts which project.[29]

That the survey was not completed cannot entirely explain why some fine quality drawings by Gandy did not appear in the final edition of the work. For example it is odd that the east elevation was published while the other three elevations, which were prepared as drawings, were never engraved. A letter to Britton recently discovered by Brian Lukacher, clearly written at least six years later than the aforementioned letter by Gandy, suggests some friction between the artist and the publisher. On a visit to Liverpool Gandy had spent some time with 'the Gentleman who bought the view of the inside of the Chapel' exhibited at the Royal Academy in 1809. He had been at a dinner, where the Mayor of Liverpool was present, and the assembled company had looked at the plates of Rosslyn published in Britton's book of 1812. No doubt it may have been the wine talking, but on this occasion the people of Liverpool were not slow to point out the very superior qualities of Gandy's draughtsmanship, presumably present in the drawing which this 'Gentleman' had purchased, over its transcription in the published plates. Someone even suggested that its publication 'would ruin a reputation'; subsequently Gandy naively asked Britton whether it would be possible to remove his name from the plates since he was 'ashamed to see it so much disgraced'.[30] Since the book was published and the plates already issued, the request was impossible and Britton can hardly have been pleased by Gandy's observation. Nor will he have been gratified by the following detailed complaint:

> The section has not been much attended to, the twisted column has not the character of the view, it represents laurel leaves instead of rich carved work of another figure, the upper windows are totally wrong and mistaken. They were originally like the lower windows.[31]

However, *Architectural Antiquities* had already been published, so it was far too late to remedy the mistaken parts; but although this was the case, Britton returned to Rosslyn, and Gandy, who writes in a demanding and uncompromising way at first, ends the letter in surprisingly friendly terms:

> I am glad to hear you are going to Roslyn. It will be a high treat, do not forget to make a drawing of… the inscription on one of the Stone Beams inside the Chapel, the letters in the shield on the uppermost cornice outside North, and if you have time take some sketches of the Castle which is very curious and of the same style and date with the Chapel in a plainer manner, the doors and windows being singularly ornamented. You had better take a draftsman with you for it. For if I mistake not [you] will be so fascinated, you will leave the spot reluctantly and not have time to finish your intentions.[32]

It is intriguing to consider that after suffering a 'ruined reputation', Gandy kept in touch with Britton and exchanged ideas about his other 'intentions', perhaps a separate publication on Scottish architectural features, in which Rosslyn Chapel was set to become a key reference point. It may therefore be suggested that there is a hitherto unknown and still unrecognised aspect to their relationship. If so, it demonstrates that Britton's approach to the building was entirely subject to Gandy's influence. The visionary architect was astonished by the unexpected beauty of the intricate ornament at Rosslyn. The *lumière mystérieuse* advocated by his patron John Soane was a tangible reality in the legends of the Chapel. The result is not mere antiquarian reproduction, but visual synthesis of a profoundly original character.

2.2. The Daguerre Diorama.

According to John Britton, Rosslyn Chapel was certainly 'calculated to amaze the illiterate, and intimidate the weak'.[33] Exactly these sentiments might be said to have inspired Louis-Jacques-Mandé Daguerre (1789-1851), another person who was to promote the extraordinary interest of Rosslyn to the British public, when contriving the construction of his celebrated and popular *tour de force*, the Diorama of Rosslyn Chapel. Daguerre was famous for his stage sets, and especially for his lighting effects, long before he was to be immortalised by his experiments with photography and the daguerreotype. He believed that the Chapel, with its phantasmagorical effects, offered an ideal subject for a dioramic illusion and that the legends linked to the Chapel would be sure to attract large numbers of visitors.[34]

The Diorama, first presented to the public in 1822, was a form of visual and almost theatrical public entertainment that reached the peak of its popularity in Britain in the late Regency period.[35] It was an ideal medium for dramatic visual presentations and depicted scenes by colour applied to a large transparent screen which was lit by a variety of different sources. The illusion of reality and of a changing spectacle was produced by lighting effects.[36] One of its most interesting features, apart from the complicated lighting arrangements, was the proximity of the audience to the enormous screen, which could be as much as 22 metres wide by 14 metres high. The pictures had to remain stationary while the auditorium, a cylindrical room with a single opening in the wall like the proscenium of a stage, was slowly revolved from one picture to another.[37]

Daguerre's Diorama of the interior of Rosslyn Chapel, entitled *L'Abbaye de Roslyn, effet de soleil*, was exhibited at Paris in 1824 and in London in 1826.[38] At both exhibitions it was accompanied by a second Scottish subject, a view of the 'Nave of Holyrood Abbey in Edinburgh by moonlight'. Press comments in France evoke the experience: '*Monsieur Daguerre nous donne un effet de soleil ravissant... les rayons du soleil qui paraissent par intervalles en dessinant sur le corps les ombres portèes, le reflet qui règne dans l'intérieur, sont si justes que nous avons cru un moment qu'ils étaient produits par la nature*'.[39] The first mention of the Rosslyn Diorama in a Scottish journal appears in *Blackwood's Edinburgh Magazine* in 1826. Here a correspondent from London describes for a friend his experience of the building seen only with the aid of 'mechanical contrivance' and without any knowledge of the actual edifice.

> The Diorama pictures, opened only about a week since, are interesting. One of them – a view of the interior of Roslin Chapel, by Daguerre – is decidedly the best that has been exhibited. Independent, indeed, of any aid from mechanical contrivance, it is a most finished and extraordinary painting. The effect of the trees, seen through the windows on the right hand of the Chapel, sparkling when the sun bursts out upon them, is absolutely magical. And yet, perhaps, this is inferior as a work of art – as every thing I ever recollect to have seen is in execution – except Rembrandt – to the side opposite, where the building is in shade, the

eye absolutely, upon deliberation, seems to penetrate into darkness, and to discover objects, after a time, which at first were not visible. From your acquaintance with the reality, I am sure you will be delighted when you see it.[40]

An important visual record to survive of the Rosslyn Diorama is an engraving [fig. 32] in a magazine of the time, *The Mirror of Literature*, for March 1826. Enthusiastic comment on the extraordinary effects of the scene runs as follows:

> The view of Roslyn Chapel was painted by M. Daguerre, and it surpasses every representation of an architectural structure we ever saw – a Scotchman would drop on his knees before it, and no person would believe that the variety of light and shade – the management of the rays of the sun reflected through a half opened door, the cobweb tinge of the window – the beam of timber and the loose cord, together with the mixture of light and shade which it displays are the mere effect of art; yet such is the case, and we are sure it requires no prophetic ken to say, that Roslyn Chapel will be one of the most attractive features of the most fascinating exhibition ever opened in London within our knowledge.[41]

The article that accompanies the illustration contains a detailed architectural description of the Chapel and is written in tones of high praise:

> …of the view of it at the Diorama it is more difficult to speak for we can scarcely expect our readers to believe that persons who have seen this chapel and observed it well, on viewing the Diorama might think themselves transported by some magic spell to the scene itself – so perfect is the illusion; indeed we know an artist though eminent not in one branch, but in a general knowledge of the arts, who declared that had he not clearly ascertained that the view of Roslyn Chapel was a painting on a flat surface, he would not have believed but the effect was produced by more than one position of the scene, or rather by many scenes placed in different positions, yet such is not the case; the illusion, however, is so extraordinary that connoisseurs and even artists may be excused for scepticism on the subject.[42]

What caused most amazement and interest was the extraordinary illusion and brilliant illumination of the show: the building, flooded by intense sunlight, appeared suddenly in the dark hall, the Diorama being accompanied by an ancient Scottish tune played on bagpipes. The popularity of the subject was certainly enhanced by the success of Walter Scott's *The Lay of the Last Minstrel*. There are in fact strong connections between the techniques used by a Diorama and Scott's literary style. Like a Diorama, Scott's literary descriptions are constructed with a visual conception. In them the variation of light is strong, unexpected and often has supernatural overtones. Thus architecture has a fundamental function in establishing the identity of place, in the definition of local character and in fluctuations of weather.[43]

Much of the impact of the view of Rosslyn was, no doubt, due to the fact that the

London Diorama had been closed for some months and was reopened in February 1826 with Daguerre's view as its principal exhibit. The *Times* too dedicated a lengthy article to the splendid effect of *The Interior of Roslyn Chapel*:

> The beauty of this elegant ruin is very much heightened by the manner in which the light is introduced from an open door and ruined window, on the right side of the picture. From the window the sunlight issues in a bright stream, but is intercepted in some degree by the foliage of some shrubs growing without, and is reflected upon the jamb of the arch in which the window is built. The sparkling brilliancy of the leaves is imitated in a manner which seems to go beyond the power of painting. The door beyond it is standing open, and a broad mass of sunshine falls through it upon the broken floor of the chapel. By one of the contribances [sic] peculiar to this species of exhibition, this light is made to fade and disappear, as if caused by a cloud passing over the sun; but the effect of the delusion, which it produces, surpasses every thing of the kind that has been yet attempted; – it is perfectly magical. An open door at the extreme end of the chapel, looks into a small garden, and is so disposed as to convey an idea of the length of the chapel. The feature we have just mentioned is the most striking, and will be the most popular in this diorama; but it is not its greatest excellence. As a painting alone, the scene is entitled to great praise, and in this respect the left aile [sic], which is in total shade, possesses extraordinary merit. The dim light which, obscured by the decayed and overgrown window, falls in a thin cold stream upon the more distant side of the pillars, is painted with the utmost fidelity and nicety. The *chiaro'scuro* of the more distant parts of the same ailes [sic] has been expressed in a manner which must astonish as well as delight every one who can appreciate the great difficulty of the subject. To descend to less important parts of the picture, all the circumstances which accompany ruins of this kind are given with sticking accuracy. A basket, some broken stones, the fragments on the floor, a scaffold and some ropes, with the abrupt and scattered lights that fall upon them, aid the notion of reality which the rest of the scenes excites. The ruin is in itself remarkable for being one of the most elegant specimen of florid architecture, in its internal decorations, which our kingdom contains… Upon the whole we consider this view to be decidedly the best that has yet been exhibited, and so good, that for excellence of painting, for force of illusion, we cannot believe it will be possible to surpass it.[44]

A Diorama building opened in Edinburgh in Lothian Road at the end of 1827. The building, which also housed a lithographic establishment, was designed for programmes showing only one Diorama picture at a time. Scottish people had to wait almost ten years to appreciate the Rosslyn entertainment before it reached Edinburgh. And even then it was never confirmed that the Lothian Road Diorama of Rosslyn was the one painted by Daguerre in Paris and exhibited in London.[45] In 1825, in fact, a reviewer in the *Caledonian Mercury* reported on an unnamed young artist of Edinburgh, who 'has not to boast of the borrowed name of a French artist to procure visitors,' and that he was 'engaged in bringing out a View of… the Interior of Rosslyn Chapel; for the exhibition

24. Andrew Bell, *Diagramatic section and interior perspective view of Rosslyn Chapel*. Engraving from *The Edinburgh Magazine*, 1761.

of which an appropriate building will be erected'.[46] According to the historian R. Derek Wood, the Edinburgh artist involved in painting a diorama of the same subject as that done in Paris could only have been David Roberts (1796-1864). Roberts seems to have been commissioned to produce copies rather than bring the original painting up from London. This 'rival version' of the Rosslyn Diorama painting was also exhibited in Dublin in 1828 and in Liverpool in 1829.[47]

Debate centres around the sources influential on Daguerre's spectacular depiction of Rosslyn Chapel. It seems likely that he studied Gandy's views and measured drawings which had been published fifteen years earlier, and that in devising his own work he made use of their accuracy and studied their lighting effects. Another source available to the artist was *An Inside Perspective view of the Chapel of Roslin* [fig.24] drawn by the engraver Andrew Bell (1726-1806) and published with Forbes's 'Account of the Chapel of Roslin' in 1761.[48] Daguerre could also have had access to a series of drawings, executed in the same year as the publication of Bell's engraving, by the French artist and scene painter William Delacour (d.1768).

Between 1760 and 1767 William Delacour [fig.25] held the first appointment as Master of the Trustees' Academy in Edinburgh, the school newly established by the Board of Manufacturers to improve the quality of design in Scotland and ultimately the forerunner of Edinburgh College of Art.[49] After a period working in London, Delacour settled in Edinburgh in 1757 where he produced landscapes for use in stage scenery and architectural settings. John Adam commissioned a series of landscape panels in 1758 for Lord Milton's house in Edinburgh. In 1761 Delacour painted his most complete surviving decorative scheme for the fourth Marquess of Tweeddale in the Saloon at Yester House, where he provided seven large landscapes painted in distemper upon

25. William Delacour, *Self portrait*. Oil on panel, c.1765. Scottish National Portrait Gallery, Edinburgh.

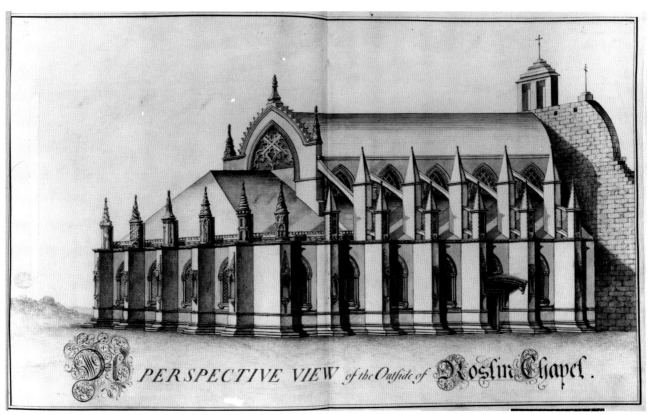

26 and 27. William Delacour, *Perspective view of the outside of Rosslyn Chapel* (top). *Section of Rosslyn Chapel from North to South* (bottom). Pen and wash, c.1761. British Library, London.

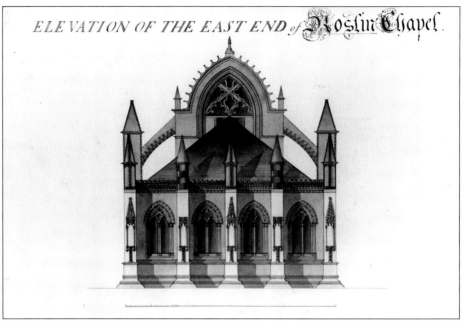

28. William Delacour, *Elevation of the east end of Rosslyn Chapel*. Pen and wash, c.1761. British Library, London.

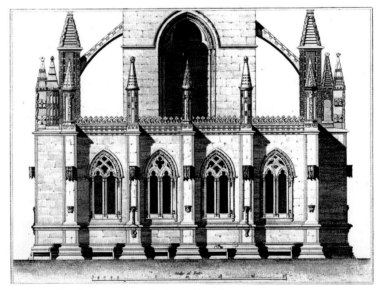

29. John Roffe after Joseph Michael Gandy, *Elevation of the east end of the Chapel*. Engraving from J.Britton, *The Architectural Antiquities of Great Britain*, 1812.

cloth, which are signed and dated: 'W. De la Cour 1761'. Delacour also worked in watercolour, using a broad style and a rococo interpretation of landscape, although he was equally capable of precise topographical views, especially when intended for engraving.[50]

Delacour's drawings of Rosslyn Chapel exhibit a certain rigidity in their graphic definition, so much so that every elaborate ornament in the original is eliminated. While this simplification makes the architectural structure of the building clearer, the process of elimination has also led to some mistakes. For instance, in the drawing titled *Elevation of the East end of the Chapel* [fig.28] the French painter eliminated the side buttresses together with their pinnacles, but they reappear incorrectly in the North to South Section [fig.27]. Delacour's pictorial simplification becomes more topographically

30 and 31. William Delacour, *The prospect of Rosslyn Castle and Chapel from south east [sic for north west]* (top). *The prospect of Rosslyn Castle and Chapel from north west [sic for south east]* (bottom). Pen and wash, c.1761. British Library, London.

precise in his picturesque views of the Chapel and the Castle [fig.30 and 31]. It is evident that drawing, as an instrument, not only has the function of preserving a record of the building, but also of contributing immeasurably to the image of the place. All the elements in the landscape are recorded accurately; for example the bridge of the Castle on the river Esk, the ruined arch in the distant view of the Chapel through the foliage, all bear great significance, and they are skilfully used by Delacour to create a picturesque scene.

A comparison between Delacour's *Perspective View of the Inside of Roslin Chapel* [fig.33] and the woodcut of the view of Rosslyn Chapel taken from Daguerre's Diorama

31

32. Anonymous, *View of Roslyn Chapel at the Diorama.* Woodcut from *The Mirror of Literature, Amusement and, Instruction,* 1826.

33. William Delacour, *Perspective view of the inside of Rosslyn Chapel.* Pen and wash, c.1761. British Library, London.

[fig.32], reveals similarities: both the wood-engraver of Daguerre's Diorama and Delacour show the interior of the Chapel in a perspective which greatly exaggerates its actual length. Since the drawing by Delacour was part of the collection of George III, transferred to the British Museum after the king's death in 1820, it would seem likely that the anonymous London engraver had access to it there and was able to base his own design on it. This would go some way to explaining the close similarities in the two views; however this element is not, in itself, sufficient to prove that the one is based on the other or that Daguerre had made use of Delacour's perspective view for his own representation. The Diorama *Roslyn Chapel, effect of Sun*, being addressed

34. Louis Jacques Mandé Daguerre, *Rosslyn Chapel effect of Sun [Diorama subject]*. Oil on canvas, signed and dated 1824. Musée des Beaux-Arts, Rouen.

to a mass audience, had the important and particularly effective function of arousing curiosity about the place itself, thanks to the stunning new sense of reality created by the manipulation of the image of a building. Is it possible then that Daguerre, though based in France, or perhaps someone working for him, visited and recorded the Chapel in person?

Daguerre started his career as a painter of stage scenery. He did not abandon traditional pictorial techniques completely. Despite the success he achieved, he made only a few oil-paintings representing Diorama subjects. The oil-painting *The Interior of Roslyn Abbey* [sic], which was on display at the Salon of 1824, seems to have followed the Diorama in Paris, and for this reason cannot be considered a preparatory study for it. Paintings of this type constituted a sort of exercise in representing identical subjects with different techniques, either for the artist's own use or it may be that they were sold in the wake of the success of the views exhibited at the Diorama itself.

Yet a nagging suspicion remains that Daguerre must have visited Scotland. Helmut Gernsheim, in his *History of Photography*, has argued that the precise detail in the Diorama and in the oil painting of the *Ruins of Holyrood Chapel, by Moonlight* (1825) is

35. Louis Jacques Mandé Daguerre, Detail of *Rosslyn Chapel effect of Sun* showing the opening of a doorway on the east end wall. Oil on canvas, 1824. Musée des Beaux-Arts, Rouen.

36. Louis Jacques Mandé Daguerre, Detail of *Rosslyn Chapel effect of Sun* showing the holes in the piers. Oil on canvas, 1824. Musée des Beaux-Arts, Rouen.

37. Thomas Vernon Begbie, *Stereophotograph of the Interior of Rosslyn Chapel*. From the original glass negative n.128, City Art Centre, Edinburgh.

only to be explained by Daguerre's use of a camera obscura while working at Holyrood itself.[51] However Daguerre is not known to have been in Scotland, and by 1816 the tracery in the east window which he shows ruined had in fact been repaired. However the writer of the pamphlet describing the Diorama in Regent's Park, entitled *Two Views, Holyrood Chapel etc.*, observed that Daguerre choose to show the tracery unrepaired to give a more picturesque effect.[52] If Daguerre's visit to Holyrood Chapel is doubtful, the question arises as to how he could paint and create a Diorama from it. The same question can be posed about Rosslyn Chapel: how could Daguerre paint it in such detail and arouse such enthusiasm in his London audience, without ever visiting it or making a drawing of it?

As presented earlier the only visual evidence, until now, of the Rosslyn Diorama was the engraving that appeared in London papers in 1826, where the discrepancy with the reality of the structure itself cannot prove Daguerre's presence at the Chapel. The answer could only be hidden behind the history of the execution of the Rosslyn oil painting exhibited at the Salon in 1824 and for many years considered lost. Architectural historians and lovers of pioneering photography are fortunate that the very oil painting by Daguerre representing the Rosslyn Diorama has recently come to light [fig. 34]. As Helmut Gernsheim would have said if he had known this painting, it is 'remarkably realistic', and in a reproduction might appear 'at first sight be taken for an actual photograph'.[53] The whole canvas in fact displays astonishing 'photographic' detail, lighting, and perspective treatment.

An intricate and detailed perspective painting of a complex building such as Rosslyn Chapel cannot be achieved without a great deal of careful planning. Daguerre in this oil painting subtly manipulated the building's real dimensions to make the scale more impressive, raising the pointed arches in the foreground while making the distant arches lower and shortening the height of the figures. The intended effect succeeds in making the Chapel seem vast, dwarfing the three Knights Templar contemplating the stone flags laid by two workmen.[54]

These 'liberties' taken by Daguerre in his painting of the interior reflect a dual concern: first, for perspective – the convincing depiction of three-dimensional space – and second, for the effectiveness of the picture as an aesthetically satisfying composition. Each of the elements is persuasive, and in combination provide a virtually comprehensive understanding of the building as it stands. Although wishing to record the salient features of the Chapel and to capture its subjective 'feel', Daguerre added to the composition a few imaginary architectural features which never existed in the actual building. One is the 'North' doorway shown open at the east end [fig. 35] which, together with the exaggerated cusping of the transverse ribs of the roof, gives added variety to the spatial patterns and effectively emphasises the sense of height and depth.

New evidence on the 'Daguerre problem' is provided by the Scottish Victorian photographer Thomas Vernon Begbie (1840-1915), who took many photographs of Rosslyn Chapel, both before, during, and after the building's restoration in 1860-61.[55] Begbie's photographs of the building, more than forty exposures, were taken to record the progress of the restoration works. Now, in some of these negatives – Neg. 128 for example – a series of rectangular holes in the piers appear at the same height [fig. 37]. Though these holes were to be filled by new masonry during the restoration, they are clearly shown in the right arcade in Daguerre's painting of the interior of Rosslyn Chapel, just as they appear in the photographs taken more than thirty years later. No artists before Daguerre ever showed this detail in their pictorial compositions. The visual evidence is irrefutable: either Daguerre went to Scotland himself or made use of a draughtsman sent to the Chapel specifically to record its existing state.

The intricate and mysterious decoration, together with the poetic manipulation of the masonry, which is Rosslyn Chapel in its very essence, is celebrated by Daguerre – in an imaginary and transfigured fashion – as a work of supreme art in which the artist can exhibit and explore to the full his particular interests as revolutionary scene-painter. His interpretations are not limited simply to its physical representation, but equally are intended to invest the monument with new and unexpected meanings. With these dynamic and allusive images, the remarkable vision of Rosslyn Chapel, in all its light effects, power of attraction and architectural freedom, is set before us as an architectural creation which, from its very origins, must be considered as existing and extending beyond the bounds of any actual or limited reality.

2.3. Captured Lights of Early Photography.

EARLY in the second half of the nineteenth century, when painters were still fascinated by the extraordinary artistic potential of Rosslyn Chapel, the simultaneous discoveries of William Henry Fox Talbot (1800-1877) and Louis-Jacques-Mandé Daguerre in 1839 were to revolutionise how we perceive and represent architecture. Photography was able to make an exactly repeatable pictorial statement about the shapes and surfaces of things, and for this reason it became a medium which competed directly with the realism pursued by many artists of the period. An article dedicated to early photographic discoveries published in *The Scotsman* reported that the photographer – described as an artist – 'cannot fail to tell the truth; he can neither flatter nor detract from the appearance of the object which is presented to him; he is merely a secondary agent, and the work is painted with a pencil of light'.[56]

38. David Octavius Hill and Robert Adamson, *West wall of Rosslyn Chapel*. Calotype, c.1843-8. Scottish National Portrait Gallery, Edinburgh.

With the discovery of the etching processes of light on a prepared chemical surface, Daguerre, who had earlier exhibited the Rosslyn diorama in 1826, developed the 'daguerrotype': a photographic process which gave a single image. In a daguerrotype there was no way, except by copying the original, that duplicates could be made. The process was complicated, but the quality was high. The uniqueness of the picture was proclaimed as one of its advantages: it was as much a peerless work of art as a miniature painting. The daguerrotype's chief rival in the race to become the established process of photography was the British calotype. Invented by Fox-Talbot, the calotype produced a negative from which any number of prints could be made. The image was of cruder quality, but the benefit of multiple printing from a single negative would establish it, and not the daguerrotype, as the basis from which all modern photographic techniques were to evolve.

A curious historical circumstance was to promote Scotland as a country in which early photography developed. This was the existence of patents to limit the use both of the daguerrotype and calotype in England which did not apply north of the Border. In England the rights to Daguerre's discoveries were purchased by a certain entrepreneur, Richard Beard, who patented the process and required a licence fee from any person who made use of it. In Scotland, where Beard's patent did not apply, all photographic processes were free. As a result, Scottish amateur photographers had a unique opportunity to play an important role. It is one thing for a professional to pay a licence fee to secure a means of earning his living, but quite another for an amateur to be faced with high costs merely to enjoy a hobby. Later in the nineteenth century patent restrictions on amateur use were lifted, but the only way a professional could avoid this cost was to work in an area not covered by the patent. Fox-Talbot, like Beard, had patented his calotype discoveries in England but not in Scotland. These factors favoured the development of photography in Scotland generally, and Edinburgh was destined to become the city where the practice of this art developed to the highest level. In these developments the romantic architecture of Rosslyn had a significant part to play.[57]

The main contribution of the calotype to the art of photography is in the work of two Scottish photographers, David Octavius Hill (1802-1870) and Robert Adamson (1821-1848). Their topographical views of Scotland and their documentation of early Victorian Scottish life, particularly in their portrait work, mark the high point which this early photographic process could achieve. Hill was a pupil of the Edinburgh painter Alexander Nasmyth, and later became secretary to the emergent Royal Scottish Academy. Whereas Nasmyth made the transition from a portrait painter to a landscape specialist, Hill's career developed in something of the opposite direction, as he began experimenting with photography primarily as a direct form of reproduction on which he could base his painting. Adamson, whose background was more technical and scientific, was responsible for the photographic processes, leaving the artistic arrangements of the sitters to Hill.

Capturing with the camera a 'motionless architectural scene' was easier than dealing with the result of an exposure which included a living subject. It should be remembered that in these early days of the calotype, exposures of ten minutes or more were common, and although Hill gives his images an air of immediacy, like a snapshot, we can see that his figure subjects are carefully posed to reduce the physical strain the exposure would subject them to. Rosslyn Chapel appears in no less than ten calotypes. In one of these views, for example, a figure who may be identified as the architect William Burn is shown with his right arm supporting his head, leaning against the south doorway

39. David Octavius Hill and Robert Adamson, *Great east window with figure from the upper storey*. Calotype, c.1843-8. Scottish National Portrait Gallery, Edinburgh.

[fig.77]; in another an unknown man is seated in the unglazed East-end window, and has wobbled his head which appears as a fuzz [fig.39]; and in two views which include two small boys, Hill poses the group with the children's arms either close in to their bodies, in their laps or supporting the head – never pointing in dramatic painterly fashion or outstretched [fig.40 and 41]. They are leaning on each other for support, but Hill does this so well that the effect seems completely natural, while the Chapel itself becomes part of the picture that he presents. We should also recognise that essential aspects of the artistic effect of the images are due to the manipulation of technical processes by Adamson. It is significant that Hill's later photographic endeavours achieve nothing like the same artistry. The partnership between the two men, a true pooling of talents, ended in January 1848 with Robert Adamson's premature death.[58]

What was often regarded as a weakness of the calotype by comparison with the Daguerrotype was its lack of definition. Hill, as a painter, was had the sensitivity to exploit the calotype as a medium in its own right and not as an inferior substitute for the Daguerrotype. The graininess and limited tonality inherent in the calotype imposes a unity on the composition which invites the viewer to regard each work in its entirety, whereas with the pin-sharp Daguerrotype it is easy to lose this sense of the whole by becoming preoccupied with the details. This is quite evident in the *West wall of Rosslyn Chapel* taken in 1844 [fig.38]. This photograph shows the west wall and part of the north transept, which marks the end of the building. The contrast between the highly finished carving of the wall, the green foreground and the sky is too great for the paper to handle, transforming this calotype into a surreal, veiled composition in which leaves and grass are recorded as featureless and the architectural details are difficult to focus. It is clear that Hill came to regard the calotype as an interpretative rather than a descriptive medium. Whether he considered it as a worthy alternative to painting is difficult to say. He only admitted that his connection with this 'art' was purely that of

40. David Octavius Hill and Robert Adamson, *Group of three figures at Rosslyn Chapel: west wall with piscina.* Calotype, c.1843-8. Scottish National Portrait Gallery, Edinburgh.

an artist, and astonished by its powerful effect he declared: 'I know not the process though it is done under my nose continually and I believe I never will'.[59]

According to the photographic historian and photographer Richard Pare, in Hill's view of the *West wall of Rosslyn Chapel* there is a meaning of space that would not be displaced even by the stunning clarity of later photographic processes. His 'rhapsodic and romantic interpretation' of this private and contemplative image runs as follows:

> The photograph of Roslin Chapel is only nominally a picture of the chapel. Though the building takes up almost half of the area of the picture's space, the extremely oblique vantage point impacts the architectural information to such a degree that the picture is not so much an examination of the ruins of the building as it is a meditation on the nature of the place, its past and its present. We see it enshrouded in creeping ivy and sheltered by an ancient stand of trees.[60]

The exterior of the Chapel was one of the sites of Hill and Adamson's early experimental work, and a location ideally suited for photography. The ornate pinnacles

41. David Octavius Hill and Robert Adamson, *Group of two figures at the west wall with piscina*. Calotype, c.1843-8. Scottish National Portrait Gallery, Edinburgh.

42. Thomas Keith, *South porch of Rosslyn Chapel, c.1855*. Contemporary print in the Edinburgh City Libraries from a negative in the International Museum of Photography.

and the charming segmental arch on the south side well exposed to the noonday sunlight provided a truly romantic setting for another of Edinburgh's pioneer photographers, Dr Thomas Keith, who worked intensively at his hobby between the years 1845 and 1857.[61]

The comparison between Hill and Adamson's work and Keith's early experiments does more than just suggest a link. There can be little doubt that in these photographs Keith is simply imitating two established masters of photography for whom he doubtless had a considerable respect. The opportunity to repeat the Rosslyn Chapel experimental image, coupled with the romantic potential of this ancient church, made it an obvious choice for his early work. The fact that he could also copy the work of Hill and Adamson, and thus experience many of the problems which they must have encountered, would have made the exercise doubly beneficial. In a comparison, the strong Keith image evokes different reactions from the slightly oblique, more distant view of the Chapel by Hill and Adamson.

The approach is totally direct and clearly ahead of its time. The figures are gone and the image relies for its success solely on the lighting conditions and the framing of the subject to produce a more descriptive account of the place itself. Keith's pictures, at first unspectacular and yet attractive, involve the viewer more and more – the mysterious blackness of the interior of the Chapel, the small entrance seen through the heavy gloom of the nave, the strong angular shapes, all combine to produce a fascinating study.

Keith's photography, which made use of the new waxed paper process – a later variant of the calotype process in which the negative was made clearer by waxing the paper before treating it with chemicals – was capable of finer detail and therefore better quality. Furthermore this process gave the photographer the facility of being able to pick up a small amount of equipment and go out whenever the weather was suitable. It is interesting to note the architectural accuracy of the photographs. We know that if the shape of a building is to be accurately shown, the camera has to be kept absolutely level. Keith knew clearly how to solve the distortion of vertical convergence and therefore went to considerable lengths to ensure that it played no part in his picture-making. In many cases he appears to have used tall tripods, or high viewpoints, to ensure that the building is of a recognisable shape. To him control was the essence of success yet for many in the art world he seemed to be offering clear proof that photography was not an art. Many painters claimed that, as photography was solely dependent on light, the photographer need only be an unskilled intermediary. Photographers often retorted that painting was likewise dependent solely on pigments and brushes. Many considered that, if photography was to be regarded as an art form, its role must be that of an imitator, producing photographically what had hitherto been produced by the artist's brush. To Keith and others, the dual role of photography – as record but also as creative image – seems to be quite clear. The problems of equating and uniting the two offered a set of challenges which he willingly accepted.

Keith's understanding of lighting and his ability to control its effects is faultless. In his photographs he reveals a sympathy with his subject matter which hitherto had never been demonstrated as effectively. Even Hill and Adamson had only rarely deviated from a particular quality of lighting, and they had been much more immediately concerned with the juxtaposition of figures and objects than with the quality of the light falling upon them. While for other photographers light merely made their photography possible, for Thomas Keith it was often the very reason for the photograph. Others merely lit their compositions, for Keith the character of the light itself became a vital part of the photographic composition, and was often its inspiration. His work is, at the same time, topographical and elemental. It conveys the atmosphere and the essence of the place without necessarily describing its physical attributes.

Keith's pictures of Rosslyn Chapel are not very descriptive but could become a simple geometric pattern. In his view of the south doorway, shown in strong lighting [fig.42], the stark outline of the doorway itself, opening into the blackness beyond and into the churchyard through the opposite door, is transformed into a wonderful piece of design. The segmental arch stands alone amidst blackness to concentrate and focus attention on its ornate stonework. This use of strong oblique lighting helped Keith to isolate his subject from its surroundings and thus to accentuate it. No other lighting conditions would have produced such an evocative statement on the beauty of the Chapel. No other contemporary process could have conveyed that feeling so completely. The other photographs form part of an extensive series of lighting variations on the architectural details of the south side, from which Keith doubtless learnt a great deal during his early experiments. Again, in these glimpses of the Chapel, the skilful use of light emphasises

43. John Forbes White, *South side of Rosslyn Chapel*. Waxed paper process, original print in the Edinburgh City Libraries.

and enhances the image; weight and tone are used to make statements that are both clear and decisive. Through his pictures, Rosslyn Chapel could be seen as never before.

Another person who was to demonstrate an extraordinary photographic interest in Rosslyn was Thomas Keith's brother-in-law John Forbes White (1831-1904).[62] Keith communicated much of his own enthusiasm and expertise to White. It therefore seems desirable to give some account of his contemporary work: Keith's earliest dated photographs are of 1854, White's of 1855; both men worked by the waxed paper negative process which, at the time, was giving way to the collodion on glass method invented by Frederick Scott Archer (1813-1857).[63]

A particularly fine print of Rosslyn Chapel is in the Central Library in Edinburgh [fig.43]. It is the extraordinary resemblance of this photograph of Rosslyn Chapel to the photographs of the same subject in the Keith collection that suggests a probable, perhaps even a certain connection between the two men. According to his daughter, White became acquainted with Keith during his university days.[64] There was initially something of a teacher/pupil relationship between the two brothers-in-law, with Keith, the elder, acting as the instructor and initiator. White however was soon as good as his master, as is clear from his early negatives dated to 1855. His picture of the south doorway of the chapel is very similar to the one taken by Keith. Both images are constructed with a singularly hard light, exploiting the contrast of the light and dark sides of the arch against the slope of the shadow and changing the shape of the carved segmental arch with light on the top and with dark on the lower part – making a Gothic geometry of the picture to match and emphasise the stone reality. It is worth noting, however, that White's image is cropped on the top and the bottom and so it appears less composed. Excursions were probably made together, with the two enthusiasts operating in the field with very similar, if not identical equipment, producing negatives up to 12in x 10in in size. The paper negative preparation was laborious; exposure in the camera – supported on a heavy and rigid stand – took from two to four minutes in favourable light; the development of the individual negative took up to an hour, and printing off could take the best part of the day if the weather was dull.

Taking pictures of the south side of the Chapel, Keith and White progressed greatly in using the process as a means of creating atmosphere rather than merely of varying appearances. The buttresses appear under strong sun, teaching the photographers much about the quality of the medium with which they were working. Architectural features are clearly defined, always within carefully considered compositions, where the special and tonal relationships are totally controlled. As their photography was confined to what little spare time they had, their ideal conditions were initially enforced rather than created. It is, however, certain that they learned fully to understand and exploit these conditions, turning practical necessity into a particular aesthetic which became an integral part of their vision. Very early in their short involvement with photography the two men had learned that lighting, used carelessly, can detract and confuse: used skilfully, it can raise even an apparently mundane subject to the highest levels of beauty.

Another important figure of the nineteenth-century history of photography who was enchanted by the ancient and decorative character of Rosslyn was the Englishman, Roger Fenton (1819-1869).[65] Fenton's studies of architecture were almost certainly influenced by his attitude to architecture and the arts in general, and perhaps most of all by his experience in Paris in the 1840s. While in France he would have been aware of the work of Eugène Viollett-le-Duc (1814-1879) and the *Commission des Monuments Historiques* in France, and the publications of John Ruskin in England, of the revival of

44. Roger Fenton, *South side with porch at Rosslyn Chapel*. Albumen print, signed and dated 1856. Private Collection.

interest in both late medieval architecture and the preservation of ancient monuments. In Paris, in October 1851, Fenton visited the headquarters of the *Société Héliographique*, where he met the French photographer Gustave Le Gray (1820-1882) who produced several waxed-paper negatives taken by himself for the *Commission des Monuments Historiques*. The recognition in France of the value of preserving historic buildings and of the role that photography could play in this, had led the French government to commission photographers to document important regional sites. Fenton must have been all too aware of the contrast between this and practices in Britain, where the documentation, preservation and conservation of ancient monuments remained a predominately antiquarian and amateur pursuit, and where it was left to amateur societies, such as the Royal Photographic Society or the Architectural Photographic Association, founded in the 1850s, to promote the potential of photography for this kind of historical documentation.

On his first trip to Scotland in 1856, Fenton visited and photographed Rosslyn Chapel between the two phases of the restoration. There are only two surviving images of Fenton's precious photo-reportage, and both represent the Chapel's south porch

46

45. Roger Fenton, *South porch of Rosslyn Chapel*. Salted paper print, signed and dated 1856. Victoria & Albert Museum, London.

[fig.44 and 45]. One of them, where the use of the figure to emphasise scale is perfect both in positioning and effect, is superb. The artistic merit of the picture depends on, and is enhanced by, its sheer technical excellence.[66]

The phrases 'the camera never lies!' and 'photography, the instructor of the architect'[67] express clearly the favourite prejudices of those in the architectural field who sought to replace the hand-drawn image with the much more powerful and more convincing photographic report. In Scotland this interest in the possibility of a 'perfect' record of the conditions of a building aroused enthusiasm in David Bryce, appointed in 1860 as 'architect of the restoration at Rosslyn'. The art historian Joe Rock in his study of the Scottish Victorian photographer Thomas Vernon Begbie notes that: 'there is a large group of negatives of Rosslyn Chapel, obviously taken over a period of time and recording the building before and during its restoration in 1860-61, under the guidance of David Bryce'.[68] The architect probably asked Begbie to record different parts of Chapel with more than forty exposures. According to *The Builder*, almost all the carving was re-tooled and sharpened.[69] Begbie's photographs of the interior and of the details may have been of use in determining what, if any, damage had occurred.

46. Thomas Vernon Begbie, *South Aisle looking east with open door* (1860-61).
Contemporary print from original (stereoscopic pair, right hand image) glass negative,
City Art Centre, Edinburgh.

47. Thomas Vernon Begbie, *View of the Choir looking east* (1860-61). Contemporary print from original
(stereoscopic pair) glass negative, City Art Centre, Edinburgh.

48. Thomas Vernon Begbie, *View of the south aisle looking west with a figure in one of the two exposures* (1860-61). Contemporary print from original (stereoscopic pair) glass negative, City Art Centre, Edinburgh.

As reported above, it is interesting to note that in some of these negatives a row of holes, all at the same height, appears in the piers – Neg.125, 177, and 428 [fig.46, 47 and 48]. These photographs, taken before the holes were filled during the restoration, provide new evidence – not previously noted in the architectural history of the Chapel – for the existence of some form of screen between the nave and the aisles. This hypothesis will confirm a stronger similarity between Rosslyn Chapel and Glasgow Cathedral where a wooden screening existed to separate the central choir from the ambulatory. The fact that Rosslyn Chapel was divided in two different parts, a central choir for the main functions of worship and an ambulatory leading to the Lady Chapel or the Crypt, makes much more sense as a late gothic plan than the open plan which appears today. In this sense Begbie's work becomes an extraordinary *reportage* that clarifies in a scientific way the condition of the Chapel before the restoration, and architectural evidence within the building itself.

The large number of negatives by Begbie of Rosslyn Chapel, could also suggests that he may have had a concession to sell photographs of the building.[70] The negatives were produced using Archer's wet collodion process, but not before Begbie had tried albumen (egg white), which was introduced in 1848 as support for the silver iodide emulsion.[71] From the evidence of his notes on the edges of some negatives, we know that Begbie used dextrine, a solution made from boiled starch. What the photographer did not perhaps realise is that dextrine is also a polariser and this may explain the extreme contrast of some of his negatives.[72]

Begbie also photographed Rosslyn Chapel with a stereoscopic camera. The stereoscope was the most significant form of visual imagery in the nineteenth century.[73] The

49 and 50. Thomas Vernon Begbie, *View of the south side of the Chapel with one figure beside the entrance,* 1860-61 (top). *View of the south side of the Chapel with one figure beside the entrance and another figure beside the north door,* 1860-61 (bottom). Contemporary prints from original (stereoscopic pair) glass negatives, City Art Centre, Edinburgh.

stereoscopic or 3-D pictures at first were produced using the daguerrotype process and were expensive to make. The advent of paper prints and glass negatives brought the price down considerably and made these ingenious little toys available to a much wider public. Two photographs taken by two lenses, the same distance apart as the human eyes, when viewed together in a special viewer gave the effect of three dimensions. Almost every middle-class Victorian household had a stereo viewer of one sort or another by the end of the 1850s. Stereo cards with paper prints were the commonest. However, glass stereo slides, to be viewed by either reflected or transmitted light, and transparent paper views were also available. Stereo 'diorama' views were a novelty of the late 1850s which achieved considerable popularity. These made use of the fact that the thin paper could transmit light. By reflected light the viewer was shown a daylight view of the place or building. As light was allowed through the paper from behind, the daylight faded, to be replaced by a moon and a dark heavy sky. The advantage of the stereo camera was that its small size and small lens allowed much shorter exposure times, thereby permitting more pictures to be taken in a working day. Moreover since the exposure times themselves were greatly reduced, truly instantaneous pictures were possible for the first time.

One of Begbie's stereophotographs taken in the south aisle of the Chapel [fig.48] shows two different instantaneous exposures: one with no human scale, a clear architectural scene, and another one in which a 'rough' figure appears illuminated by a strong beam of light, creating a suggestive *contrejour* effect at the edge of the open door and the rest of the aisle. These are not to be considered photographic failures but intended precisely by the photographer testing the depth of field with his own camera. On the other hand we know the various experimental materials Begbie used to create mellow and partially unfocused images of the Chapel. These 'polarised interpretations' of the south side of the Chapel are made to give a new visual effect producing little impression of depth: through a stereoscope viewer the observer will not appreciate the 'realism' of the three-dimensional solidity of the facade, but he will be catapulted into new visual phenomena in which the perception of space is perceived by impressions of light and shade. In these two images [fig.49 and 50] the pronounced stereoscopic effect depends on the presence of figures located in the middle ground. Here, to organise the image as a sequence of receding planes, Begbie places the figures between the two doors on opposite sides of the Chapel and repeats the experiment in a second exposure, where only one figure is used and the second door is closed. There are some similarities between Begbie's use of the stereoscope and classical stage design, which synthesises flat and real extensive space into an illusory scene. As with theatrical space, where the movement of actors on a stage generally rationalises the relationship between the points represented in the scene, Begbie makes use of 'moving' figures to create a deeper perspective.

As well as his experimental images of the exterior, Begbie generated some fine images of the Chapel's interior. One of the problems posed by any exposure in this spacious but dark interior was the need to balance the light coming in through the windows to avoid losing too much of the highlight detail. Optical deficiencies in the lenses become readily apparent where low light levels caused photographers to use wide apertures. In fact, in the stereo view of the nave the architectural detail around the upper window is washed out, like a halo, and this effect was produced by internal reflections within the lens. The device of containing this binocular perspective within two circular frames contrives to create a very stimulating visual effect.

Most of the famous photographers of the 1860s and 1870s dabbled with stereo images, since the demand for these views was so great that they were guaranteed to sell whatever they produced. No matter how banal the subject, if it was in 3-D someone would buy it and marvel at the reality they could see through the twin lenses of the viewer. One of the great figures of commercial stereoscopic photography in Scotland was George Washington Wilson (1823-1893) the Aberdeen photographer.[74] Wilson was particularly concerned to avoid what has been called 'the toy effect', and used longer-focused lenses to achieve 'a much more natural and life-sized effect'.[75] Much technical information comes from Wilson's own writings in *The British Journal of Photography* where he explains his working methods.[76] On stereophotography he writes: 'I am never satisfied unless I can get objects comprehended, even in a stereoscopic-sized plate, to *compose* in such a manner that the eye, in looking at it, shall be led insensibly round the picture, and at last find rest upon the most interesting spot, without having any desire to know what the neighbouring scenery looks like'.[77]

Wilson's contribution to the photographic representation of Rosslyn Chapel is enormous. He started taking photographs of the Chapel in 1859, and from 1861 to 1863 he added to his collection a substantial number of exterior and interior views. It is easy to follow the order in which every single shot was taken, thanks to the numbering impressed on each glass plate that appears with the location of the view. We know that all Wilson's early negatives were taken by the moist collodion process, and developed with protosulphate of iron.[78] We can also say that one of his first attempts to photograph Rosslyn Chapel was with a stereoscopic camera. An important description of his stereoscopic *South Door of Rosslyn Chapel*, compared with a picture taken by 'Mr Archibald Burns of Edinburgh,'[79] appears in *The British Journal of Photography* of the time:

> Mr. Wilson's copy of this subject is taken upon a larger scale than that of Mr. Burns, and consequently less of it is included. The upper windows which form so remarkable a feature in Mr. Burns's, are wanting in Mr. Wilson's copy, but this absence is fully compensated by the increased beauty of the effect of the open doorway, in the embrasure of which a lady is standing, as if about to enter. At the opposite side of the building another door is open, at which there is a gentleman looking in, while still further off is a third open door, through which is seen a row of garden railings, and a portion of the hedge. Of the two windows visible, many of the squares of glass are wanting,[80] and the larger scale upon which it is taken permits of a better examination of the beautiful carved-work with which the structure is adorned. Both of these specimens are in their way masterpieces of art, and we should not like to part with either of them… We think it but right to mention that though Mr. Burns's representation of Roslin Chapel is remarkably graphic and effective, the delicacy and softness of Mr. Wilson's rendering, together with the introduction of the figures, causes his specimen of this subject to be more of a finished picture.[81]

The article continues with a description of another stereoscope view of the *Interior of Rosslyn Chapel*, where the author describes Wilson's photograph as 'one of those beautiful illustrations that the archaeologist will delight in'.

> The massive pillars… seem but barely able to support the capitals and heavy architraves literally loaded with ornamentation of the most florid character. A gleam of sunshine falling on a huge square block of stone glorifies it; and the general harmony of light and shade, combined with breadth and detail, unite to constitute this a perfect picture which the eye never wearies of gazing on, and which, while we gaze, communicates a sensation of satisfaction and repose that is truly soothing.[82]

We know how a 'gleam of sunshine' in Rosslyn had earlier evoked an artistic response on the part of Joseph Michael Gandy and William Delacour. The kind of diffused shade they managed to reproduce in their works was exactly what many 'pictorial' photographers wanted to capture as well. They were inspired by such artistic compositions in painting. One is an image of the south aisle looking east [fig.46] by Begbie. He shows a row of columns on the left leading to the Apprentice Pillar and the entrance to the crypt. The photographer was deeply impressed by the achievement of the original builders, and in this image he tries to convey that the arrangement of the colonnade is as perfect as its design is artistic. Apart from being successful technically,

51. William Dyce, *Rosslyn Chapel, view of the south aisle looking towards east*. Oil on canvas signed and dated 1830. Private Collection.

this image closely resembles a painting of 1830 by William Dyce (1806-1864) which shows the same view through the south aisle with the door open, through which an intense 'gleam of sunshine' enters the Chapel [fig.51]. According to Marcia Pointon this 'painting is in no sense an architectural study and the chief interest lies in the play of sunlight which floods through the loosely-swinging door, illuminating the sandy interior but failing to touch the mossy dampness of the corners or illuminate the Bible and the rosary which lie abandoned in the foreground'.[83] Also, if there is 'an air of questioning, of a narrative incomplete'[84] that pervades Dyce's painting, Begbie, in a different medium, employs an identical depth of perspective to convey scale, with columns retreating into the centre of the image to add drama to the visual impact of the battle between light and shade.

As the concept of the artist-photographer became more common, and as more artists turned to photography, photography was still judged against painting. Photographs were reckoned to be inferior or better than engraved views of nature or of works of art.[85] In

Scotland this debate about 'Art and Photography' brought to the attention of the public the 'pictorial' photographer William Donaldson Clark (1816-1873), who, in his article 'Photography as a Fine Art', declared that 'there certainly is such a thing as *photographic art*'.[86] Clark was very close to artistic circles, where he was a friend of such painters and photographers as Samuel Bough (1822-1878) and David Octavius Hill. His closest artist friend was the landscape painter Horatio McCulloch (1805-1867), with whom he went on several painting and sketch expeditions. Clark's pictorial compositions of his architectural subjects are the result of this collaboration with an artist. He considered that in these 'subjects the photographer, has to a limited extent, the power of giving expression by developing his plate to a certain point, and bringing out some parts more than others, as well as by skilful printing; but this power is within very narrow bounds indeed'.[87] For him a photograph, however beautiful in detail is, in point of feeling and expression, greatly below the works of a great artist. His view of the *South doorway of Rosslyn Chapel* [fig.52] can be seen as a distinct form of 'Fine Art'. Unlike

52. William Donaldson Clark, *South porch at Rosslyn Chapel*. Albumen print, 1860. Scottish National Portrait Gallery, Edinburgh.

53. Sir David Young Cameron, *South porch of the Chapel*. Etching, 1899. Private collection.

several contemporary photographers, he was able to catch, in a slightly oblique view of the porch, a combination of force and delicacy. This was determined by the fusion of the strong architectural photographic reality of the exterior and the interior darkness sublimated with a patch of light on the moulded base of a pier.

While the status of photography and its claim to be regarded as an art was very much the subject of debate, Clark's way of seeing the Chapel was emulated by artists of the time. In fact the *South Porch of Rosslyn Chapel* [fig.55] by the Victorian painter Josiah Wood Whymper (1813-1903) clearly resembles Clark's point of view in his porch picture and the interior effect of light where the pillar appears from the darkness. It is interesting to note that in this case, the photographic image formed the basis of a work of art. Fifty years later David Young Cameron (1865-1945), while etching the Chapel, made use of the same image as Whymper.[88] He reproduced, in his own style, many details photographed by Clark. In his *Roslin* [fig.53] the narrow portal allows the eye to enter and pierce the dark interior before reaching a portion of the window and the base of the pier slightly touched by a beam of light. With this interplay of dark and light Clark and Cameron, respectively as a photographer and artist, bring to their images the very tensions of the architecture they describe. Cameron was fascinated by Rosslyn's architecture, and his different states of the etchings of the south porch reveal a sure grasp of the complex design [fig.54].

54. Sir David Young Cameron, *South porch of the Chapel with figure*. Etching, 1899.
Hunterian Art Gallery, Glasgow.

Clark's eye for striking and 'pictorial' compositions was perfectly matched by his competence as a technician. He may well have received advice on improving the photographic process from his brother Thomas Clark, who was professor of Chemistry at Aberdeen. Despite the long exposure time required, he chose to use mainly the collodion-albumen process, which meant that plates could be prepared in advance, avoiding the necessity of setting up a tent for preparing and developing negatives immediately. The use of the wet collodion plate led to a great expansion in the number of professional photographers. The ability to produce high-quality prints quickly and efficiently led to the introduction of print shops, and prints of local views were soon to be found in the general stores of most villages. The family scrapbook, instead of just including sketches, now contained photographic prints of holiday locations.[89] The Victorian scrapbook became more and more popular in the 1850s and 60s, so the number of photographers producing material for it grew.

The popularity of Rosslyn Chapel was reflected in the work of these tourist photographic card producers. James Valentine (1815-1880), for example, built up an enormous postcard industry in Dundee, depicting most popular tourist attractions of the day and demonstrating the enormous potential for commercial exploitation of the

55. Josiah Wood Whymper, *The South Porch, Rosslyn Chapel*. Watercolour, 1858. Ruskin Foundation, Ruskin Library, University of Lancaster.

56. Alexander Adam Inglis, *View of the Chapel from north west*, c.1880. Contemporary photograph from original albumen print, Edinburgh R.C.A.H.M.S.

57. Samuel Gosnell Green, *View of the Apprentice Pillar*. Woodcut from *Scottish Pictures drawn with pen and pencil*, 1883.

Victorian public's voracious appetite for real and vicarious travel. His complete set of twenty cards of the Chapel describes the building's features and the legends associated with it. One in particular, representing the restored chancel [fig.58], has been marked with a black arrow on the albumen print to indicate the position of the legendary Apprentice Pillar, to help the viewer identify the 'principal character' amid this feast of intricate decoration and elaborate Victorian church furniture.

The numerous photographs that appeared during this period prove that there was hardly a picturesque scene or view of the Chapel that had not been photographed. In

58. James Valentine, *Rosslyn Chapel postcard marking the Apprentice Pillar with arrows.*
Albumen print glued on paper, c.1870. Private collection.

the 1880s, the only photographer who distinguished himself for the originality with which he portrayed the Chapel was Alexander Adam Inglis (*fl*.1881-1914). Inglis's wide-angle photographs could be seen as images of the absence, the equivalent of a still life, where the building stands majestic as a cathedral [fig.56].

The wood-cut process, taken from photographs and published in guides and tourist books as a cheaper form of main illustration, provides the final stage in the history of the representation of the Chapel. During the late nineteenth century the use of photography in printed books underwent radical changes. At first, skilled wood-engravers would simply copy photographs onto woodblocks in the same way as they had traditionally copied artists' drawings, and these blocks could then be used to print the image onto the page at the same time as the text was printed. The basic method remained popular for high-circulation periodicals for the remainder of the century, although a number of technological improvements were made. The most important of these involved the transfer of images directly onto woodblocks by photographic means, the block then being cut or engraved by hand by a skilled engraver. The block was later duplicated on a copper plate in order to permit large print-runs to be obtained from it.[90]

In 1883 the Rev. Samuel Green published *Scottish Pictures drawn with pen and pencil*, in which many of the illustrations were made directly from well known photographs.[91] The Rosslyn image, for example, representing an interior view of the Lady Chapel from the south aisle [fig.57] may have drawn inspiration from the photograph by William Donaldson Clark exhibited at the Photographic Society of Scotland in 1858-1859, *Roslin Chapel – Interior* [fig.100]. At first glance the two images may show differing compositions; however, a closer perusal reveals many similarities. The main one is in the placement of the column in the left hand corner, foreshortened in Clark's photograph and then shown with its base in the woodcut. The two columns in the Lady Chapel are also presented from the same viewpoint. The final result could be considered almost akin to theatrical stage scenery, although used for commercial purposes in a 'pictorial' guide of Scotland.

59. Anonymous, *Interior view of the Choir with furniture*. Detail of a woodcut from George Eyre-Todd, *Scotland Picturesque and Traditional*, London 1895.

Any number of such engravings can be found in other late-Victorian and Edwardian guides. Guides that might properly be called 'grotesque' rather than the more common epithet of 'picturesque'! One in particular is in *Scotland Picturesque and Traditional* by George Eyre-Todd [fig.59], where the merging of a picture of the nave by Wilson and a Valentine's detailed postcard showing the church furniture [fig.58], becomes in the hands of the wood engraver a very unusual representation.[92] What makes the image absurd is the introduction of some visitors, drawn to a false perspective scale. The woman on her knees praying in the front of the altar, for example, is half the size of the lectern, while a second lectern, which appears in the photographs, has never been completely reproduced in the engraved image, showing the top of this piece of furniture floating on air in the nave.

Fortunately 'the camera never lies'! and with all these photographic 'verities' we may witness a frozen instant in time, though it is one that is mediated both through the eye and the tastes of the photographer and the medium he uses. 'The moments are the photographers'; they have chosen them, captured them, and isolated them from time before and time to come. What is to be shown is delimited by the photographers.[93] As Nikolaus Pevsner notes:

> The power of the photographer to strengthen or destroy the original is at any rate undeniable. In a building the choice of the views, then of the angles, then of the light, simply makes the building. It can let the nave of the church appear tall and narrow or broad and squat — almost regardless of its real proportions. And, what is more, it can bring out a detail so forcefully that it carries more conviction on the plate than in the original. The possibility of 'isolating details from surroundings'… is the photographer's greatest privilege.[94]

We, as viewers, are invited to share Rosslyn Chapel's fragments of eternity as recorded through their techniques.

3

FROM ANTIQUARIAN TO PICTURESQUE PERSPECTIVES

...the whole place is highly picturesque, and had fate made me a painter only, you would have seen many fine views of this delightful and intriguing dell.

Letter from J.M.Gandy to J.Britton, 17 December 1806.

3.1. The Gothistic Eye

ANTIQUARIANISM, which had it roots in Renaissance thought, was a popular intellectual and cultural pursuit throughout the eighteenth and nineteenth centuries. The antiquarian work of collecting, compiling and presenting material which explored the past was seminal to the formation of social and national identities. The veneration we now feel for medieval architecture was restricted in the seventeenth and early eighteenth centuries to very few among the intelligentsia, whose chief regard was for Roman and later Greek architecture. Since the Gothic style was classified as monstrous and barbarous, the architecture of the Middle Ages had for a long time been ignored or misunderstood. This lack of respect for medieval buildings and their subsequent neglect led to a situation in which many interesting and valuable buildings were ruined. Only a few antiquaries and topographers cared about Gothic structures, such as Sir William Dugdale, William Stuckeley in the 1740s and Horace Walpole, Francis Grose, John Carter and Richard Gough in the later eighteenth century. In fact it is thanks to them that Gothic architecture had not only received appreciative attention from many, but had become the fashion, especially among romantic travellers. The cultural historian Michael Sadleir captures perfectly the revived antiquarian approach to ruined national antiquities, with the following words:

> To the Gothistic eye, however, a ruin was itself a thing of loveliness – and for interesting reasons. A mouldering building is a parable of the victory of nature over man's handiwork. The grass growing rankly in a once stately courtyard, the ivy creeping over the broken tracery of a once sumptuous window, the glimpse of sky through the fallen roof of a once proud banqueting hall – sights such as these moved to melancholy pleasure minds which dwelt gladly on the impermanence of human life and effort, which sought on every hand symbols of a pantheist philosophy.[1]

Inevitably, antiquarianism and antiquarians had an impact on both the 'reading' and reality of Rosslyn Chapel. In this period the growth of travel provided archaeologically-minded visitors with an opportunity to experience the 'truth' of ancient sites and to

61

test any abstract theories they may have held about the past against the evidence of medieval architecture itself. Thus what Sadleir describes as 'the Gothistic eye' came to be refined by a knowledge of what was actually there, while at the same time the desire to provide a building with an imaginative (or imagined) life led to a romantic sympathy best exemplified in the poetry and novels of Sir Walter Scott, who frequently uses the fabric of a medieval building as the starting point for a creative image of the past. Here fiction and fact can be combined in a intoxicating mixture which has proved particularly powerful in the case of Rosslyn Chapel and Scott's stirring tale of his imaginary last minstrel.

We must begin however with the moderate measured interest of an earlier Age of Reason. Among the early eighteenth-century antiquaries in Scotland, a man who surely encapsulates these 'Gothistic' sentiments is Sir John Clerk of Penicuik (1676-1755). Despite the fact that he is remembered for his classical antiquarian taste, initiated in Rome during a Grand Tour, on his return to Scotland 'he transferred the enthusiasm for antiquities gained abroad to the domestic scene'.[2] Clerk, who 'assumed something of the role of a Scottish Lord Burlington,'[3] was well acquainted with the strikingly romantic fragments of the ancient buildings at Rosslyn, since both the Castle and Chapel were very close to his own estate at Penicuik. Attracted by the rich complexity of the architecture of Rosslyn Chapel, he made notes on the sequence of rectangular carved stones set immediately beneath the parapet of the north wall. With the close

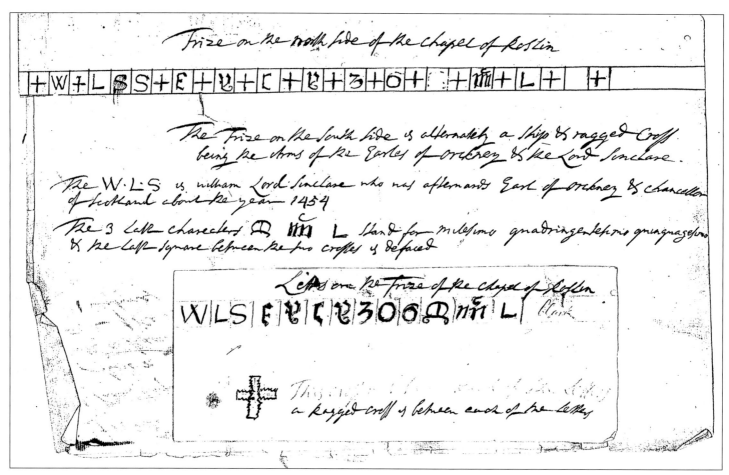

60. Sir John Clerk of Penicuik, *Sketch of frieze on north side of Rosslyn Chapel*, c.1738. From Clerk Muniments at the National Archives of Scotland [GD 18/5111].

focus of an antiquarian he recorded the 'frieze' which displayed letters and Roman numerals interspersed with shields bearing the engrailed cross, the heraldic symbol of the Sinclair Family.

In 1735 the estate of Rosslyn devolved to General James Sinclair, who descended from the Dysart branch of the Sinclair family.[4] Clerk and the General were soon to become collaborators, and it was to him that Clerk forwarded his sketch [fig.60], in which he had annotated the following lines:

> The Frize [sic] on the South Side is alternately a Ship & ragged Cross being the Arms of the Earlses [sic] of Orkney & the Lord Sinclare.
>
> The W-L-S is William Lord Sinclare who was afterwards Earl of Orkney and Chancellor of Scotland about the year 1454.
>
> The 3 Latter characters M CCCC L stand for millesimo quadrogentesimo quinqagesimo & the last square between the two crosses is defaced.[5]

The interpretation of the inscription by the Victorian scholar Andrew Kerr is very similar to that suggested by Clerk. He reads it as 'W L S F Y C Y Z O G M iii 1 L', which he expanded to 'William Lord Sinclair Fundit Yis College Ye Zeir of God MCCCCL [1450]'.[6]

We might think of this annotation by Clerk as typical of someone who was deeply interested in recording the inscriptions of the past. However Sir John's concern went far beyond the simple interpretation of its characters, since it was he who first pioneered the conservation of the Chapel, which in the 1730s was in a ruinous condition. Medieval buildings were, he said, the honour and pride of any country, and thus should be preserved.[7] Some eight letters, sent from General Sinclair to Clerk between 1738 and late 1740s, provide a record of the first practical attempt to conserve Rosslyn Chapel and to protect the Castle from falling into decay.[8] It is important to note that the correspondence is not dated by year, and it is not possible therefore to establish a secure chronology for the events they describe. Nevertheless a study of the letters reveals a range of attitudes to the antiquarian approach and also records the transformation of many of the architectural features of the buildings at Rosslyn. While both men were evidently concerned to preserve the Chapel as a notable antiquity, they took an uncompromising and highly practical view of its conservation and in this Sir John was perhaps more enthusiastic than the General, who had to foot the bill. Together they planned a new roof over the aisles and east end of the Chapel; glazed all the windows; demolished a dangerous portion of the tower at the Castle; and made plans for a new house to be designed by the architect William Adam.[9] Sir John seemed anxious to encourage the General to complete the repair works and to start the new building enterprise at once. An undated letter from the General to Clerk gives important information of the progress of this work and the men whom Clerk had recommended should be employed at Rosslyn: Patrick Lindsay (d.1753)[10] and John Baxter the Elder (d.1753).

> I am greatly obliged to You for Your favour, that inclosed [sic] the inscription on the Front of the Chappel [sic], I have put it in to Provost Lindsays [sic] hands as You directed, and he was in hopes that he will get it unriddled for us. I am very glade [sic] that Mr Baxter has gone to

work with the Chappel [sic], because it would give me the outmost pain
if any dissaster [sic] happened to it in my hands, notwithstanding of its
having been most ridiculous in me, ever to have intangled [sic] my self
with it. Had the wholl [sic] gone to George Lockhart[11] as was intended
when I allowed my self to be drawn in, it would not have given me much
trouble to have heard that the highest stone of it was the lowest, but as
matter now stands, the sooner its [sic] repaired the better. My rage for
building is not so strong as to give me the least itch towards making a
New House, and for what I at present think if ever I do erect a new
House, it shall not be at Rosslin.[12]

Clearly Sinclair, who lived in London, would have no new Scottish residence, even
though it were to be designed by such a well-known architect as 'Mr Adams'. William
Adam's involvement in a Rosslyn project may however explain the choice of John
Baxter the elder for the restoration of the Chapel. Baxter, an Edinburgh master mason
of considerable repute, in fact not only enjoyed the patronage of Clerk, but between
the 1730s and 1740s was employed to build a number of country houses in Scotland
which were designed by Adam. It seems that John Clerk had organised a collaborative
effort on the part of Adam and Baxter for the care of the Chapel, the demolition of a
portion of the 'Forecastle' and the re-use of the stones for a planned new building. In
a second letter to Sir John, the General explained how Baxter would try to compute
the expenditure required for clearing the area in the front of the Castle, and calculate
the costs of the mason work that would be wanted to make the house 'up to his
plan'. Subsequently the General insisted in finding out what sort of windows would
be most proper for the Chapel. What emerges from these two letters is the fact that
the General was concerned about saving the Chapel, while Clerk was keen to promote
the building of a new mansion house in the Rosslyn area as well. Another letter ends
with strong words in which the General, based in London, states clearly that he is not
interested in building on a property which he might well sell. The 'Romantik' glen was
not a sufficient reason to settle down in Scotland. It seems Sinclair is only interested
in the preservation of the Chapel, which had been in the ownership of his family since
its foundation in 1446 and which he wanted to reopen as a place of worship for future
generations.

I am honoured with Your's, and am most sensible of the frindly [sic] and
nighbourly [sic] concern You have shown in my little affairs at Rosslin.
Provost Lindsey is in hopes of geting [sic] the inscription You sent him
made intelligibell [sic], and has also undertaken to get us information
about the best and cheapest way of Glazing Church Windows. Since my
Brother seems to relish the Reparation of the Chappel [sic] better than
he did, I intreate [sic] that while he is in the taste of the thing, that
the work may be done well and substantialy [sic] let the cost come out
as it will. As that part of the House that You call the Forecastle will
undoubtedly tumble soone [sic] down of it self, wer[e] it not better that
it wer[e] taken downe [sic], by which the matterials [sic] may be layed
by in some order and preserved, for what ever use we may afftterwards
[sic] find for them. If you think that the timber, Sclates [sic], and Stones
are worth the saving, You had best give directions to Mr Baxter to take

them downe [sic], but in this do as You will. I can not reconsile [sic] my self to the thoughts of Building a new house, because it may be expected that I should make a good one, and that cannot be done without laying out more money then I probably can afford, wher[e]as if I repair the old one, there will be fully as much House as I shall ever want, and by that I shall tye [sic] my self up from falling into extravanganceys [sic], which it's but too likely a New Seat and new Plan would draw me into. Besides all this, I conceve [sic] that the only beauty of that place is the Romantik wildness of the River, the rockey banks, and the fall of watter [sic] or the Linn, and these views can not be all had but in the present situation. If there can be a right access made into the old Castle, and that part of it repaired and made lodgeable, in or near to that Plan sent me by Mʳ Baxter, I shall be willing to lay out on the doing it 500, or 600, pounds, but if it should require more, I am determined never to think of living there, and consequently to sell it again though at considerable loss, reserving however the property of the Chappell for my Brother,[13] and that I hope will excuse me to the world for my folly of ever having meddled with it.[14]

From a financial point of view, Clerk's assistance with the Rosslyn project seems to have been well organised. Sir John acted as intermediary between the owner of the estate and the workmen employed. He even suggested that the General should get his brother 'to lay out £25 yearly for repairing the Chappell'.[15] The only difficulty was the fact that Sinclair had no control over the quality of the work done and had to rely completely on Clerk's decisions. In relation to the demolition of the 'Forecastle', he postponed any decision until he was there himself: 'As I hope to have the pleasure of seeing You soone [sic], I shall not now trouble You with any thing relating to the pulling down the walls of the old Castle, but leave the disscussion [sic] of that point till I can have the happiness of considering of it with You on the spott [sic]'.[16]

Unfortunately, this kind of on-the-spot inspection did not take place in time to save many features of the Chapel now lost. As already mentioned, the exterior of the Chapel continued to be visually unchanged until the beginning of the eighteenth century, when its condition became alarming. Baxter provided a new roof over the aisles and the whole of the eastern part of the church, besides reinforcing its walls. It was he who was responsible for changing the appearance of the building and who drastically altered it – despite the General's wishes – by removing the tracery of the great East window. He added a pitched roof in slate, no doubt intended to keep the vaulting perfectly dry, but so high that it covered more then half of the clerestory windows on the north and south walls, as can be seen in Delacour's survey of 1761 [fig.27-28]. These windows were shortened at the bottom, and the space filled up with bricks and mortar.[17] What is quite surprising is that the General was in fact greatly concerned about the result of the works, as a letter written on 3 March makes clear:

Since You was so kind as take the trouble to direct the repairing of the Chappell, I have all alonge [sic], left that to You, to do in it as You had in mind, and indeed every thing about it has been done to my satisfaction [sic], but the high raised rooff [sic] that Mʳ Baxter put up to darken the great Window on the East end, and of which I complained to you in such maner [sic], that I was in hopes to have found that Eye sore removed,[18] and that part of the rooff [sic] made flatter and slated over before the severity of the Winter came on; but M[r] Baxter being so little at home, has perhaps made it escape Your memory. There was one other thing that I wished to have had done for me, and if my memory do's [sic] not missgive [sic] me, You said You would take the trouble of ordering it and that was to cause some Workman measure the Windows that You thought nessesary [sic] to give light, to know what quantity Yoales [sic] of Glass would be wanted to Glasse [sic] these windows, that I might with the assistance of Peter [sic] Lindsay while here, make provision for it.[19]

These matters were to end controversially. From this point onwards, relations between Clerk and the General seem to have been strained. The architect that Clerk had suggested apparently lost interest in the job and the General had to take things into his own hands, ordering the boundary wall to be increased in height and employing workmen himself.[20] His last letter to Clerk reads as follows:

I am favoured with Your letter giving me an account of Your having been at my old Kirk, and of the missmanadgment [sic] You saw there, by the various and different work Men of all sorts that had been employed. I do assure You that I am most sensible of the missmanadgment that must arise from that way of doing, which partly proceed'd [sic] from nessessety [sic], and by no means a choise [sic] of mine. When first I was prevailed on to undertake that piece of old Family nonsense of repairing the Chappell, I put it entirely into the hands of M[r] Baxter, who even before he was called off to Lord Garlies [sic] work was very negligent about it, and caryed [sic] on things very slowly, but affter [sic] he went to Galloway there was a tottall [sic] stop I belive [sic] for a Year. People then upbraiding me for having things half done, there was one other man imployed [sic] and I belived [sic] by Your recomendation [sic], he piddled on about it for some months, and could not be brought to help and highten the Walls of the Kirk Yard, which was absolutly [sic] necessary for the preservation of the Windows after I had been at the expense of Glasing [sic] them, this Fellow I say neglecting to do it, and seeing some of the Windows nea[r]ly broken, I did my self order a Mason somewhere from about Dalkeith to do this work, and he is the only Workman, first and last, that I employed my self in this ridiculous work, however now that it is done, the Work Men must be payed, imploy [sic] them who will, and orders shall be given about it. I thank You for the trouble that You have taken in seeing the work meassured [sic], and wish that You may also have put a price on it.[21]

While the General's sense of frustration and even disappointment about the 'piece of old Family nonsense of repairing the Chapel' is clear, this was not the opinion of contemporary antiquarians, who thought that Rosslyn, with its new high pitched roof, looked more 'Gothistic' than before, and fully approved the work. On his northern tour of Scotland in 1758 Sir William Burrell noted in his diary on 17 October: 'Roslin Chapel, entire, the property of General Sinclair, who keeps it glazed and in the best repair, a proceeding which will always do him honour and procure him esteem in the opinion of every good man and admirer of antiquity'.[22] Similar appreciation appeared in *An Account of the Chapel of Roslin* published in 1761, where the author, under the pseudonym of Philoskensis, writes: 'Of late years this chapel was in great danger of becoming quite ruinous through the injuries of weather: but to the great honour of the late General St. Clair, then proprietor, be it remarked, that he happily prevented that, by putting new flag-stones on the roof, and new wooden casements with glass into all the windows. He likewise laid the floor of the chapel with new flag-stones, and rebuilt the high wall round the caemeterie; so that one may venture to say, these repairs have cost a very considerable sum'.[23]

From the later eighteenth century a noticeable shift of attitudes to the Chapel occurs. Now antiquarians *appreciate* the 'Gothistic' qualities of the place more than the practical concerns of Sir John Clerk and the General. The key recorder in this regard must be Richard Gough (1735-1809), whose enthusiasm for Rosslyn almost knew no bounds. It was Gough who revealed the identity of Philoskensis as the Episcopalian Bishop of Caithness, Dr Robert Forbes (1708-1775), a man 'whose modesty deprives the world of his observations'.[24] Forbes republished his *Account* in 1774 and dedicated it to William Sinclair of Rosslyn. In 1778 James Murray, the Edinburgh printer based in Parliament Square, published another edition of the same account. Murray's reprint did not acknowledge the author and changed the dedication to one 'inscribed to the Ancient Fraternity and Free accepted Masons'. It may be that the author and the printer of the 1778 edition were both Freemasons. Indeed, William Sinclair became the first Grand Master Mason of the Grand Lodge of Scotland in 1736, with the reprint coincidentally appearing in the year of his death. The *Account* itself provides a description mainly of the interior of the Chapel as it was in the middle of the eighteenth century. It mentions much of what is now questioned as accepted fact; for instance the legend of the 'Apprentice Pillar'. It also reveals that our understanding of the symbolism within the Chapel has advanced considerably as, for example, there is no mention of the 'Green Man' and its pagan and Celtic origins, the numerous examples of which are simply referred to as 'grotesque' or 'antique' heads and foliage. The *Account* demonstrates also that there appear to have been changes, not only in interpretation, but also in the physical fabric of the Chapel. It confirms the fact that the Chapel was never completed, as the author explains that the foundations extending from the unfinished west wall had been uncovered during ploughing.

It is interesting to note that Forbes recorded an architectural feature of the Chapel which was never discussed again in later descriptive accounts. He explains how: 'The middle pillar on the fore part of the altar, has a capital cut into flowers *de-luce* in the first kind of basso-relievo, as some parts of the sculpture are quite free of the pillar, and the light passes through the openings'.[25] As has been pointed out earlier, the light effects in the east end of the Chapel attracted Gandy and Daguerre, and captured the attention of Walter Scott when he described, in poetic language, the 'building seen on fire'. Many other phantasmagorical legends were related to the Sinclair family, but none of them referred to this artefact. Forbes, in his 'Gothistic', almost organic, description, reveals the seed which would have inspired writers, poets and painters. A capital's carving which filters the light and radiates it in the mode of a flower must have been a powerful emotional addition to their legends.

The illustrator of the *Account of the Chapel of Roslin* was the Edinburgh engraver Andrew Bell (1726-1809), who was associated with William Smellie (1740-1795) in the 1771 publication of the *Encyclopaedia Britannica*. Bell learned the art of engraving from Richard Cooper (c.1730–1764) to whom he was apprenticed. His work consisted mainly of book illustrations. Bell's engraving facing the frontispiece of the *Account*, described as *An inside Perspective View of the Chapel of Roslin*, is one of the earliest perspective views of the interior of the Chapel. A similar perspective view made by William Delacour, or by one of his pupils, and dated the same year, suggests, since Bell's engraving was issued in 1761, that the drawing was strongly influenced by this image [fig.24]. Bell's view of the Chapel is a geometrically accurate perspective construction of the building in the style favoured by architectural treatises of the period. The method of showing on a plane surface the representations of the vault and the flooring suggests the use of a perspectival grid as an aid to the composition. This calculated application of the principles of perspective projection using shadows and reflections gives the impression of the Chapel appearing higher than in reality. The Chapel is also shown in another plate drawn by Bell, 'View of Rosslyn Castle from the South', in Forbes's account.

The *Account of the Chapel of Roslin* of 1761 with its two engravings by Bell became a collectable item for many Scottish and English antiquarians. Its diagrammatic engraved plate representing the section through the central nave and the aisles added to its appeal. The antiquarian print collector was a significant figure in Britain in the late eighteenth and early nineteenth centuries, existing as both a cultural historian and connoisseur and contributing to a rich museum heritage through the legacy of some extraordinary print and drawing collections. One of the most important British antiquarian print collectors was Richard Gough, who traversed nearly the whole of Scotland in 1771, on a 'topographical tour', making copious notes. Known for his researches into late-mediaeval buildings, Gough was captivated by Rosslyn Chapel, and therefore he not only recorded the building personally but compiled a catalogue of printed images of it. Most of the drawings produced while he was at Rosslyn represent architectural details such as pinnacles, pedestals and window foliations. Gough also recorded the new window shutters and the protective iron bars, seen both from inside and outside the building. In his rough sketches of the windows there certainly is a tendency towards a chronological ordering which depended on an accurate observation of form and structure in window-head and tracery. Gough may have known John Aubrey's unpublished *Chronologia Architectonica* of the 1670s in which it was stated that 'the windows the most remarqueable, hence one may give a guess about what Time the Building was'.[26] Aubrey (1626-1697) was a pioneer in devising an architectural taxonomy in parallel with those of the natural sciences, by a close observation of detailed examples dated from documentary sources. Gough made use of Aubrey's scheme to classify and understand the underlying geometry of every single architectural feature at Rosslyn. This is evident from the large quantity of drawings made, almost forty, for the most part numbered in sequence. His response is thus not primarily aesthetic, it is antiquarian.

Gough shared his knowledge and interest in Rosslyn with the Scottish antiquarian George Paton (1721-1807), with whom he corresponded between 1770 and 1774.[27] They met in Scotland both in Paton's home near the Edinburgh Custom House, and at a rendezvous in a coffee house on the Royal Mile, where they talked about the contents of their respective print cabinets with their reference books before them. Over the years, their opinions were gradually transformed, inspired by new encounters with impressions, or engraving texts. It was in this private world of antiquarianism that Gough's collection of numerous drawings and engravings of Rosslyn Chapel, today preserved at the Bodliean Library in Oxford, was first developed. Paton's library and his antiquarian and topographical knowledge were placed freely at the service of the English antiquary.[28] Gough, in the preface to his second edition of the *British Topography*, refers to the valuable assistance he had obtained from his indefatigable Scottish friend.[29] In one of his first letters to Gough, Paton wrote: 'I had almost forgot to acquaint you that there are several views & c. of *Roslin* in "Father Hay's collection 2 or 3 Vol. folio M.SS." which he presented to the Faculty of Advocates many years ago, which escaped my Memory when you was in that Library, some weeks hence when our Parliamentary Calls for Accounts are over I shall spend an Afternoon there & make out a List of these Views…'[30] This list of visual records of the Chapel was later published by Gough and then reprinted in 1835 by James Maidment in his introductory notice to the *Genealogie of the Saintclaires of Rosslyn*.

A marked feature of the correspondence between Gough and Paton is the discussion of authorship and the methods by which print images were produced, and the effect this had on their subsequent artistic musings. In relation to the Chapel's diagrammatic section and interior view made by Bell, Paton informed Gough that he owned the original drawing from which the engraving was obtained. According to Gough: 'Andrew Bell's design of the inside of the Chapel in Mr. Paton's custody, is better than his etching that accompanies Mr. Forbes's description of it'.[31] The English antiquarian acquired many copies of Forbes's description of the Chapel until Paton revealed in a letter the impossibility of getting any more of them:

> I am sorry I cannot serve you at present with any more of the Account of Roslin as the whole of that Years Edinb.[r] Magazine was condemned for waste paper, but y.[e] Printer sensible of his foolish Mistake proposed reprinting on his own Risque not only that but all the Accounts of Parishes &.[a] that he can meet with whi[ch] have already been printed, which design I shall push him on to execute & then will have an opportunity of supplying your Calls.
>
> You may be assured every thing new that is published in the line of Views, Etchings, plans [sic], &.[a] shall be purchased & sent you.[32]

By the end of the eighteenth century the interest of individual antiquaries had become more specialised. Like Gough, Lieutenant George Henry Hutton (d.1827) had as his hobby an intense interest in Scottish archaeology. His ambition was to produce a complete listing of the medieval churches in Scotland with special attention given to their physical aspects. He visited many sites of ecclesiastical buildings, sketching and measuring and, when he was away on military duties, a series of Scottish correspondents wrote and drew on his behalf. The work itself was never completed, but there remain over two hundred drawings, which were probably envisaged as compiling a 'Monasticon Scotiae'.[33] As we can imagine, the Collegiate Church at Roslin was on Hutton's 'Gothistic' map. The only drawings made by him of the Chapel were two pencil sketches: the first representing the West end and the second a carefully delineated detail of Sir William Sinclair's tombstone.[34] He also added to the visual records several notes taken from Gough's publication and other sources. Hutton's intention to rely not only on physical remains but also on documentary sources reflects another facet of the antiquarian tradition.[35]

61. Astle Thomas, *Seal of Sir William St Clair, sixth Baron of Rosslyn, in a charter of confirmation from Alexander III*. Engraving from *An Account of the Seals of the Kings, Royal Boroughs, and Magnates of Scotland*, 1792.

What attracted the antiquary was not only the individual character of an object, but the qualities in a monument which brought the past into the present. The past of Rosslyn Chapel, which as we have seen was to make such a vivid impression on Gandy's imagination, appeared as no well-defined period in his architectural composition *The Tomb of Merlin* [fig.6]. With its varied and sometimes extravagant style, and the subtle interplay between light and emotion, Gandy's work demonstrates the archaeological sensitivity of him and his contemporaries. His analytical method was, however, that of the antiquary. In a letter to John Britton, Gandy reported his discovery, in Astle Thomas (1735-1803), *An Account of the Seals of the Kings, Royal Boroughs, and Magnates of Scotland* (1792), of the seal of Sir William Sinclair, sixth Baron of Rosslyn, on a charter of confirmation from Alexander III [fig.61].[36] He noted that the form of Sir William Sinclair's name was very similar to that spelt out on shields along the north cornice of the Chapel, and described how Slezer's view of it was 'the most correct', but 'defective in placing and proportion of some of the ornament, which should conform to the height of the masonry from bed to bed'.[37]

In Scotland during the first half of the nineteenth century the antiquarian discourse became a literary genre in its own right, of which the masterpiece was penned by one of the greatest writers of the time, Sir Walter Scott. The relationship between Scott and antiquarianism is a key one. It is important to bear in mind the influence of the various illustrated editions of the Waverley novels, where actual historical characters and locations were integrated with imaginary ones. Though Scott was to satirise the national passion for the past in *The Antiquary*, whose principal figure is drawn as a composite from a number of antiquaries he personally knew well, in time he was to become that figure himself; as the house he created at Abbotsford shows only too clearly.

Following his personal taste for the past, Scott designed his house to incorporate many features taken from the most interesting buildings in Scotland. The architect responsible for the plan was William Atkinson (c.1773-1839), although Sir Walter himself and his friends, Daniel Terry (c.1780-1829), Edward Blore (1781-1879), and

James Skene of Rubislaw (1775-1864), intervened with their own suggestions. The wonderful ornamentation of the interior of Rosslyn, in particular the pendant bosses in the Lady Chapel, were to be copied and reproduced in the library ceiling to enhance the antiquarian atmosphere. Scott had casts made from the celebrated south aisle carving of the Angel reputed to be holding the heart of King Robert the Bruce. It is said that after the death of Bruce, Sir William Sinclair was chosen along with other Scottish noblemen to carry Bruce's heart to Jerusalem and deposit it in the Church of the Holy Sepulchre. They never reached their destination; during a fierce battle the Moors killed the Scottish knights. The survivors took their dead – and Bruce's heart – for burial back in Scotland. Scott was fascinated by the courage of these Scottish knights. He built and adorned Abbotsford as carefully as he collected books and antiquities – not for show, but because they afforded him rational and permanent enjoyment.

Robert Pearse Gillies (1788-1858), a special friend and protégé of Scott, certainly entered into the antiquarian spirit when he described in a letter 'the satisfaction of visiting Roslin Castle and Chapel' with his 'friend Mr Pinkerton, the well known antiquary'.[38] He explains how 'Nothing can be considered more beautiful than the scenery or more venerable than the ruins'.[39]

Scott once said: 'A chronicle of Roslin …a minute record of the lives of its various inhabitants, how they fought and caroused, loved and hated, worked and played, would be worth more than all the mere romances that ever were penned, as a fund of amusement and instruction. But we have only vague outlines; imagination must do the rest'.[40] It might almost appear that Gillies, whose attitude went far beyond the purely antiquarian aspect, took this statement literally when recounting what was later defined as the 'Roslin Raid' in his *Memoirs of a Literary Veteran*. Here his personal and imaginative legend related to the Chapel:

> …for, having this much in common with the author of 'Waverley', that I
> was fond of antiquities, I proposed a secret excursion to Roslin Chapel at
> the dead night; that we should enter it by the window of the sacristy on
> the east, provided with a dark lantern, and all necessary implements, and
> should dig up and carry away at least one of the twenty coats of armour
> which are said to be mouldering under the cold stones of the chapel.[41]

The sacrilegious plan was later abandoned, but the idea caught the imagination of his antiquarian friend John Jamieson (1759-1839), who wrote a ballad entitled the 'Raid of Roslin'.[42] Knowing, as he did, that the threatened raid had not taken place, the ballad's author nevertheless chose to imagine the event, and with liveliness and humour versified a series of incidents from the birth of the plot to its close – 'the said close being effected by means of an evil tongue that blabbed, and a party of dragoons from Piershill barracks, who were sent to protect the chapel, and capture the marauders'.[43] Gillies thought that the ballad afforded 'a notable instance of good nature, vivacity and bonhommie, in an antiquary so old and study-worn'.[44]

From fanciful recreations to accurate reconstructions, the Castle and Chapel together became an important 'archaeological site', rich with literary parallels as well as appealing to elevated antiquarian tastes.

> I wish we knew more that we are ever likely to do of the powerful
> family that once owned this castle and chapel… Doubtless there were

beauteous damsels, as well as belted knights, that now 'sleep the sleep that knows no waking' under these cold stones; anxious, of course, were the days and hours which they spent within these castle walls; intricate and hazardous the adventures in which they were engaged.[45]

These words by Scott herald the end of that brilliant alliance of the artist, the poet and the antiquarian, a relationship which was soon to be outmoded and would be lost well before the end of the century. In retrospect the writer and his followers created an outstandingly rich and stirring synthesis of Scottish national history, so strong that even today we are still unable to visualise Rosslyn Chapel in any other terms.

3.2. A Highly Picturesque Place

Joseph Michael Gandy, during his visit at Rosslyn in 1806, in addition to survey drawings of the Chapel, produced a few sketches of the scenery surrounding the building. He explained in a letter to John Britton how 'the whole place is highly picturesque,' and described his fascination wth the location and a certain regret at not being able to record the beauty of Rosslyn's scenery as a landscape painter would have: 'had fate made me a painter only, you would have seen many fine views of this delightful and intriguing dell.'[46] These sentiments found expression in a selection of drawings in his sketchbook which show a wide open space mostly taken up by a piece of waste ground, overgrown by bushes, so that the walls of the nearby ruined Castle and the Chapel's pinnacles are seen somewhere far off; in another sketch the river Esk looks like a narrow ribbon, while the Chapel can barely be seen at the far end of the composition. Why did the draughtsman need this area of waste ground? All his life Gandy had indefatigably studied ancient architecture, provided a setting for Soane's contemporary projects, and had depicted buildings as though they had risen as part of their natural surroundings. In this regard, he was strongly influenced by Giambattista Piranesi (1720-1778), who had shown the remains of Roman buildings in all their greatness and all the beauty of their ruined condition, thereby emphasising the architectural powers of nature. With just such a piety about nature's creative power, Gandy contemplated Rosslyn's ancient trees spreading their branches across the rushing stream, the steep and overhanging cliffs covered with hazels, the waterfall that plunges into a dark den, and many other picturesque elements, as a 'sentimental journey' that, in the second half of the eighteenth century, had become an inevitable part of a man's artistic education and his way of life. 'Picturesque journeys', or series of sketches made on the spot at places visited, were of this variety.

It was the Rev. William Gilpin (1724-1804) who more than any other focused the attention of the British reading public on the Picturesque, with his books of 'picturesque tours', published from 1782.[47] Gilpin defined the term 'picturesque' as 'expressive of that peculiar kind of beauty, which is agreeable in a picture,'[48] and this he found to be uneven and irregular, having contrasts of light and shade.[49] This definition did not satisfy the two aesthetic theorists Richard Payne Knight (1751-1824) and Sir Uvedale Price (1747-1829), who examined the word etymologically and found 'picturesque' to mean *after the manner of painters*, from the Italian idiom *pittoresco*.[50] According to the art historian Christopher Hussey, author of a detailed analysis of it, the Picturesque arose from the effect of the Italian seventeenth-century landscape painting, especially the work of Claude Lorraine (1600-1682) and Salvator Rosa (1615-1673), upon British taste in the eighteenth century. He writes: 'This habit of viewing and criticising nature as it were an infinite series of more or less well composed subjects for painting had been gaining in popularity all through the eighteenth century... The picturesque view of nature was then the new, the only, way of deriving aesthetic satisfaction from landscape.'[51] The Picturesque as a prelude to Romanticism was a mode of vision.

In eighteenth-century Scotland the Picturesque developed largely in emulation of the work of Alexander Nasmyth (1758-1840) who admired Claude's paintings during his visit to Florence, Bologna, Padua and Rome, and produced what must surely be the most influential landscape paintings in the history of Scottish art. His paintings were not straightforward depictions of Scotland, but views of an ideal and perfect land blessed with all the characteristic features of Italy that enchant the northerner's eye: intensely blue skies, warm and brilliant light, fertile fields and meadows, luxuriant woods, streams of crystal water, noble and ancient buildings. These ingredients are harmoniously grouped and dispersed across a canvas depicting *Rosslyn Chapel and Castle* (1789) where the scene is bathed in the glow of evening sunshine [fig.62]. The view of this open landscape is constructed with a broad and generous sense of space, and designed around the siting of the two historical buildings. This is a picture which celebrates the grandeur of Rosslyn's picturesque beauty where man has a presence but does not dominate. In the mind of the picturesque painter it is no longer the Chapel, but the nearby Castle which becomes the dominant feature of the scene, while the

62. Alexander Nasmyth, *Rosslyn Chapel and Castle*. Oil on canvas, c.1789. Private collection.

romantic landscape, which links the two monuments together, becomes the focus of interest for the next generation of artists at Rosslyn.

At some stage between 1785 and 1792 Nasmyth opened a landscape school at his house at 47 York Place in Edinburgh. He insisted upon drawing *en plein air* as a basic skill and took his pupils on sketching trips.[52] His aim was to teach from nature rather than coping from great masters or antique casts. Rosslyn Chapel and Castle, just seven miles form the centre of Edinburgh, became a favourite haunt for his pupils to practice sketching; they included Hugh William Williams (1773-1829) and the Rev. John Thomson of Duddingston (1778-1840). With the spirit of an antiquarian Nasmyth taught them how the history of Rosslyn was part of the anatomy of the landscape itself. According to Joe Rock: 'If Williams was Alexander Nasmyth's pupil in 1790, he very soon began to overtake him in originality of view. Even allowing for the difference in age – Williams was Naysmith's junior by fifteen years – they obviously inspired and influenced each other, to the extent that it is often difficult to know who was imitating whom.'[53] A comparison between their respective views of Rosslyn Castle and Chapel [fig.62 and 63] shows how the points of view and the atmosphere surrounding the buildings are very similar, while the two different ways of framing the Chapel are

63. Hugh William Williams, *Rosslyn Castle from North [Chapel in the background]*. Watercolour, 1805. Private Collection.

clearly influenced by the variety of picturesque interpretations of the place. However the main difference between the pictures can primarily be attributed to the use of different media: Nasmyth's painting is an oil on canvas and Williams's picture is a watercolour.[54]

As evidence of Nasmyth's historic appreciation of Scottish scenery and architecture, his engineer son James, remembering the atmosphere of his childhood home, recalled in *An Autobiography* his father's attitude towards the preservation of historical seats.

> In those early days of art-knowledge, there scarcely existed any artistic feeling for the landscape beauty of nature. There was an utter want of appreciation of the dignified beauty of the old castles and mansions... His fine sketches served to open the eyes of their possessors to the priceless treasures they were about to destroy.[55]

During the years in which Nasmyth was aiming to document these 'priceless treasures' and transcribe them in pictorial images, information about the historical past of Rosslyn – and in general of all Scotland – became much more accessible with the publication of two important books: Thomas Pennant's two *Tours in Scotland* published in 1771 and 1774, and Francis Grose's *Antiquities of Scotland* in 1789 and 1791.

Francis Grose (1731-1791) was in Scotland during the summers of 1788, 1789 and 1790, recording the castles and religious buildings of the country. He relied on a group of fellow antiquaries who shared their knowledge and their drawings.[56] His view of Rosslyn Chapel, according to Britton, was 'very slight and trivial.'[57] In the National Gallery of Scotland there is a view of Rosslyn Chapel, recently attributed to Patrick Gibson (1782-1829), that corresponds very closely to the view published by Grose in 1789. The architecture appears to depend on Grose's view, while the foreground foliage is added by the draughtsman. It is however far larger than the drawings Grose normally made, which were related to the size of intended engravings.[58] for his part, Pennant did not publish any view of the Chapel, and confined himself to writing a detailed account which stressed the connections between the building and Scottish Freemasonry.[59] The publications of these two antiquarian topographers were closely bound up with the concept of picturesque landscape and stimulated an interest in Scottish history that was only to be satisfied by the writings of Sir Walter Scott.

Scott's *The Lay of the Last Minstrel* (1805) brought the beauties of Rosslyn Glen to the attention of a wider public than would otherwise ever have heard of them, but the Esk valley was a noted beauty spot many years before Scott lived there, and he was far from the first poet to celebrate its charm.[60] Suffice to say that in September 1787 the poet Robert Burns (1759-1796), after a night's carousing in Edinburgh in the company of the painter Alexander Nasmyth, walked out to Rosslyn and had breakfast at the old inn by the gate to the Chapel. A later report recounted that: 'An old woman takes care of it, and shews each crypt and buttress with the greatest possible minuteness to those who are led by curiosity to gaze on the beauties that mark this Pile.'[61] Burns's thanks to the legendary landlady, Annie Wilson, are recorded in the poem beginning 'My blessing on y.ᶜ, honest wife!'[62]

While tourism scarcely touched Scotland before the 1750s, by the turn of the century hardly a tourist to Edinburgh failed to visit 'the stately chapel' over which the author of *The modern universal British traveller* gushed with praise: 'When we view the whole of this structure, it convinces us of the propriety of what Mr. Walpole has advanced, namely, that gothic architecture was brought to the greatest perfection in the fifteenth century.'[63]

People took to travelling as a tolerably comfortable leisure activity. 'Where once they had travelled only when necessary, now they began to *tour*.'[64] The search for 'simplicity and wildness, and all circumstances of remote time and place'[65] marked Dr Samuel Johnson (1709-1784) and James Boswell's (1740-1795) visit to the Chapel during their famous expedition to Scotland in the autumn of 1773. Both men left the quiet and elegant pleasures of London literary life in order to undertake an arduous journey on horseback in a country quite foreign to Dr Johnson, which he sometimes professed to dislike. Boswell's diary entry for 20 November 1773 records that they both 'surveyed Roslin-castle, the romantick scene around it, and the beautiful Gothick chapel, and dined and drank tea at the inn.'[66]

Joseph Farington (1747-1821), another well-known English visitor to Rosslyn, recorded a 'very picturesque matter about the place.' In the account of his arrival at Rosslyn in the autumn 1801, which seems to have been a long and wet trip, he describes the Chapel as 'remarkable for being a most curious specimen of high finished Architecture. It may be classed with the Gothic but every part seems to be a specimen of the fruitful fancy of the Architect, who appears to have adopted no pattern that was invented by another but to have laboured to produce unceasing variety as far as his limits would allow.'[67] Upon completing a pencil drawing of the scenery, he recorded in his diary that 'Rosslin is a place that has been allowed to run to weed, and its principal beauties are in consequence so difficult to be seen that it is probable few go there who have a full idea of it.'[68]

Despite Farington's negative view of the amenities of Rosslyn, improvements in local transport were soon made which provided a regular coach service from Edinburgh's city centre, contributing greatly to the rediscovery of the Chapel and encouraging interested parties from all parts of the country to visit the building. Amongst these William Wordsworth (1770-1850) and his sister, Dorothy (1771-1855) were noted visitors in 1803.

On 4 May 1805, Dorothy Wordsworth wrote to Lady Beaumont about her Scottish tour that, 'When we were in Scotland we spent several days in company with Mr Scott – we were at his house, he limped by our side through the groves of Roslin… and pointed out every famous hill, and told some tale of every old Hall we passed by.'[69] The Wordsworths were particularly attracted to the Chapel, now in a fairly advanced state of decay and appearing at least partially returned to nature; in other words, it had become a ruin that was part architecture, part nature. Besides finding that condition more picturesque, they also observed that the creeping vegetation over the sculpted decoration brought the stones to life. Certainly it is in Dorothy's detailed *Journals* that a modern reader will find one of the most stirring descriptions of the Chapel ever written on a picturesque tour:

> The architecture within is exquisitely beautiful. The stone both of the roof and walls is sculptured with leaves and flowers, so delicately wrought that I could have admired them for hours, and the whole of their groundwork is stained by time with softest colours; some of those leaves and flowers were tinged perfectly green, and at one part the effect was most exquisite: three or four leaves of a small fern, resembling that

which we call adder's tongue, grew round a cluster of them at the top of a pillar, and the natural product and the artificial were so intermingled that at first it was not easy to distinguish the living plant from the other, they being of an equally determined green, though the fern was of a deeper shade.[70]

This description does not have the character of a purely private diary. It was not jotted down, from day to day, but written at leisure after her return, while the events recorded were still vivid in her memory, and when she could see the whole tour in something like its artistic perspective.[71]

Two years later a more aristocratic woman and amateur artist, Elisabeth Leveson Gower (1766-1839), Duchess of Sutherland, was to contribute her own graphic descriptions of the Chapel. In 1805 she made some sketches of the Chapel [fig.64

64 and 65. Elisabeth Leveson Gower, *Interior view of the Lady Chapel* (left). *South side view of the Chapel* (right). Engravings from *Views in the Orkney and on the north Eastern Coast of Scotland Taken in 1805 and Etched in 1807.*

66. John Sutcliffe, *View of the South aisle towards the Apprentice Pillar*. Tinted lithograph, c.1850. Private collection.

and 65] which were later printed as etchings in a limited edition, with several other scenes in Scotland.[72] The Duchess excelled especially in watercolour landscapes and loved to depict the picturesque scenery of her native country. Concerning this Britton wrote: 'the example is truly honourable to the good taste and liberal character of the accomplished amateur, and it is hoped will excite emulation among the higher classes of the fair sex.'[73]

An unbound copy of a lithograph 'drawn from nature and on stone by John Sutcliffe' appeared in the 1850s and curiously represents a view of the south aisle towards the Apprentice Pillar [fig.66]. The children playing with two dogs and the two ladies give a human touch to the scene, but are on a different scale to the architectural features. The insertion of a lady sketching the Apprentice Pillar is certainly a tribute to the Duchess of Sutherland and her Rosslyn etchings.

Subsequent representations of the Chapel and its surroundings in the early nineteenth century – for the most part published – served the purpose of enhancing its status as a monument and promoting its historic significance. Both the views as well as the written comments, whether aesthetic, historic or of a topographical nature, provided not only an analysis of the geographical environment but also an attempt to aggrandise the architectural reality. As Rosslyn was seen as a great moment in the history of

67. Edward Blore, *Interior of Rosslyn Chapel*. Engraving by H. Le Keux from Sir Walter Scott, *Provincial Antiquities and Picturesque Scenery of Scotland with Descriptive Illustrations*, 1826.

Scottish architecture, so its elements were enlarged and the scale of the building enhanced (typically by the introduction of tiny figures) to make its physical size equate to its cultural standing. Examples of this type of visual deception appear in the work of Henry Sargant Storer (d.1837) and his brother James (1781-1852),[74] George Cuitt Junior (1743-1818)[75] and Thomas Mann Baynes (1794-1854).[76] Their views reflect a contemporary judgement of the architectural and landscape quality of the place, acceptable both to scholars and for the general public. What is most important in all these representations is the search for a new quality in the image.

The imitation of nature was still a valid concept, but at the beginning of the nineteenth century a new fascination for artifice was born, which is seen in the work of the Minister of Duddingston Church, the Rev. John Thomson (1778-1840). An amateur, though one of the most original painters of his time in Scotland, Thomson studied briefly with Alexander Nasmyth while a student at Edinburgh University, and was friendly with Sir Henry Raeburn (1756-1823), whose landscape backgrounds were the inspiration for the characteristic freedom of Thomson's paintings. He was also a life-long friend of Walter Scott, for whom, as for Thomson, landscape was a subject rich in historical associations. In his paintings Thomson was able to depict the originality of the Scottish character, but without renouncing the use of ingredients that are typical of the Sublime and the Picturesque. According to the art historian Renzo Dubbini: 'He knew how to combine different meanings and themes and keep them in balance, a talent that may have appealed to Scott as an ability to reflect on analogy and on how languages are modified.'[77] The oil-painting *Rosslyn Chapel and Castle* gives a further original contribution to the historic meaning of the place. In this painting the Castle is in a higher position in the valley and appears at the same height as the Chapel. This modification and falsification of the nature of the place is a clear reference to Walter Scott's theory of analogy between the arts. Thomson's contribution to painting here is rather an addition to the repertoire of sporting scenes in landscape than the introduction of a new point of view.

In 1818 Thomson came in contact with Joseph Mallord William Turner (1775-1851) and the draughtsman-architect Edward Blore (1787-1879), after a proposal had been made

68. William Raymond Smith after Joseph Mallord William Turner, *View of Rosslyn Castle and Chapel*. Engraving from Sir Walter Scott, *Provincial Antiquities and Picturesque Scenery of Scotland with Descriptive Illustrations*, 1826.

69. Edward Blore, *View of Rosslyn Chapel*. Engraving by G.B. Cook from Sir Walter Scott, *Provincial Antiquities and Picturesque Scenery of Scotland with Descriptive Illustrations*, 1826.

in that year, to publish a large work to be called *The Provincial Antiquities and Picturesque Scenery of Scotland*, illustrating the chief picturesque features of the country: its castles, its churches, abbeys, woods and hills. Leading artists of the day were to be employed to provide the plates, while Scott undertook to write the descriptive letterpress.[78] For this work, Turner provided a much more accurate version of the scene than Thomson's oil-painting as, in the plate representing Rosslyn Castle, the Chapel emerges through the foliage from a distance and is in a higher position than the Castle [fig.68].[79]

Blore had met Scott in 1816 when the poet was anxious to find an architect who could interpret his own ideas for the architectural drawings in the *Provincial Antiquities*. Blore's friendship with Scott resulted in his employment as 'manager' of the work; owing to financial difficulties and Scott's failing health, only two volumes were issued. He drew three illustrations of Rosslyn Chapel: the external view [fig.69] corresponds to Grose's engraving, whereas the views of the interior are drawn in a way that alters the height of the central nave, thus making the Chapel look like a Scottish Fonthill Abbey [fig.67]. This lack of proportion is actually caused by the presence of a few visitors, who were drawn to a small scale.[80] This play on lighting and perspective, which can also be noticed in Daguerre's Diorama painting of a few years earlier, creates an extraordinary illusive effect.

Between the 1820s and the 1830s picturesque tours to Scotland were no longer the preserve of wealthy aristocrats, of Scottish artists exploring their home landscape, and of visiting English painters plotting their own itinerary of picturesque places: many educated middle-class families, such as John Ruskin and his parents, started making picturesque tours regularly. He knew Rosslyn Chapel from childhood and revisited it throughout his life as a continuous source of inspiration. Fired by his visit in 1838, Ruskin in his autobiographical *Praeterita* (1885) entitled one of the chapters 'Roslyn Chapel' and made two extraordinary drawings of the interior of the Chapel from different viewpoints [fig.70 and 71].

70. John Ruskin, *Rosslyn Chapel Interior*. Pencil on paper, 1838. Ruskin Foundation, Ruskin Library, University of Lancaster.

71. John Ruskin, *The Apprentice Pillar*. Pencil drawing dated 1838 appeared as Plate X in "Praeterita" – *The Works of John Ruskin*, vol. XXXV, George Allen, London 1908.

The same year the Liverpool landscape and topographical painter William Gawin Herdman (1805-1822) gave particular attention to light and shade in his watercolour devoted to the *Interior of Rosslyn Chapel showing the Apprentice Pillar* [fig.72] which was exhibited at the Liverpool Academy in 1838. He also wrote essays and pamphlets on a wide variety of subjects, including curvilinear perspective, which he adopted for a very curious outlined 'Perspective Design' of the Chapel [fig.73]. According to the author the greater 'truthfulness' of this image, which first appeared in *The Art Journal* for 1st November 1849 and later reissued as a plate in his *Treatise on the Curvilinear Perspective*

72. William Gawin Herdman, *Interior view of the Chapel showing the Apprentice Pillar.*
Watercolour, 1838, Walker Art Gallery, Liverpool.

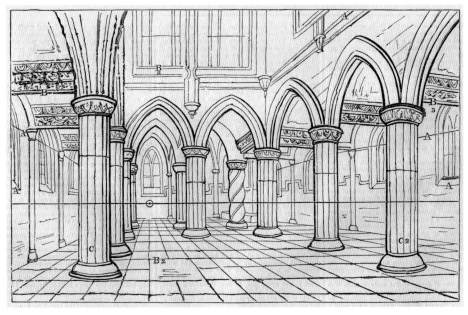

73. William Gawin Herdman, *Outline perspective drawing of the interior view of the Chapel showing the Apprentice Pillar.* Drawing published in *The Art Journal*, 1 November 1848.

of Nature (1853), had reached a synthesis of perspective and 'natural vision' that, in his view, had never been accomplished in previous theories.

Not surprisingly, given this context, apart from Ruskin's affection for the building and Herdman's optical theories about its architectural representation, tourists required new and up-to-date guidebooks of Scotland, but they also devoured Scottish prose and poetry, pictures and illustrations. Very soon there was a massive upsurge in books on Scotland, fuelled partly by the boom in travel and partly by revolutionary developments in the techniques of book production. The views in the *Provincial Antiquities* were engraved on copper plates which produce only a few hundred impressions before their finely incised lines become coarse and indistinct. From 1822, however, engraving on copper was largely replaced by engraving on a much harder material, steel. This can be used to print many thousands of impressions of engravings with the most minutely differentiated gradations of tone; indeed, without the use of steel plates, the complex light effects which enchant the viewer's eye in Thomas Higham's (1796-1844) line engraving of the Chapel would have been impossible for a long and profitable print-run [fig.74].[81] The same period also saw the invention of a totally different process, lithography, which produces illustration of a very distinct atmosphere and subtlety, evoking the softness of a pencil drawing. Lithography, as its name implies, involves drawing on stone rather than metal, and a chemical process rather than one of incised lines. Artists rapidly adopted lithography for the reproduction of paintings (earlier, engravings had been used for this) and for the creation of original works. Rosslyn Chapel became one of the first architectural subjects on which the possibilities of the new technique were tested in Scotland.

74. Thomas Higham, after George Cattermole, *Rosslyn Chapel*. Engraving from Leitch Ritchie, *Scott and Scotland*, Edinburgh 1835.

75 and 76. Samuel Dukinfield Swarbreck, *Rosslyn Chapel: Interior* (left), *Rosslyn Chapel – The East Aisle, or Lady Chapel* (right). Tinted lithographs from *Sketches in Scotland, drawn from nature and stone*, 1837.

As a result of these new markets and new printing techniques, pictures of Rosslyn Chapel started to appear in many different types of books. The shift to the picturesque coincided with a new phase of antiquarian research and with the publication of such works as *Sketches in Scotland Drawn from Nature and on Stone* (1837) by Samuel Dukinfield Swarbreck (fl.1830-1865) and *Scotland Illustrated in a Series of Views* (1838) by Thomas Allom (1804-1872), William Henry Bartlett (1809-1854) and Horatio McCulloch (1805-1867).[82]

In the three views of Rosslyn Chapel included in Swarbreck's collection, the influence of Edward Blore was dominant. In other cases it is possible to recognise the influence of other famous painters of panoramic views, such as Turner and Thomson, or a graphic quality inspired by the drawings of well-known architects made in preparation for the restoration of important monuments. The picturesque was employed to arrange, present and reconstruct the image of significant buildings of the national heritage. Engraving served the purpose of achieving descriptive precision, while the newly devised technique, lithography, proved to be more suitable for expressing the emotional character of a view. The immediate entrance to the Chapel is through a narrow pointed archway, which in the frontispiece sketch from the collection is hidden from view. The second and third views are interiors, showing a carpenter, during a moment of rest, admiring the magnificent structure surrounding him and a mason working on the flooring with a trowel, who is illuminated by a light beam that makes the whole scene amazingly visionary. In *Rosslyn Chapel – Interior* [fig.75] a drooping flag near the first of the small pillars seen in the sketch, indicates the spot where the ancient Lords of Rosslyn rest. The Apprentice Pillar forms a striking feature in this view. The reader is informed that the holes seen in some of the pillars are said to have been made by Cromwell's soldiers, when turning this sacred edifice into a stable and barrack-room; while the dark pillar was blackened from the fires then kindled against it. In the view *Rosslyn Chapel – The East Aisle, or Lady Chapel* [fig.76] the Apprentice Pillar is again introduced, and forms a striking contrast to the plainer style of two other pillars. In the text which accompanies the plate Swarbreck explains how the second Earl of Rosslyn, Sir James St Clair Erskine (1805-1837), is interred under the furthest slab seen in the sketch; and immediately under the beautiful pendant boss, called Star of Bethlehem, above the nearer slab, lie the remains of his Countess.

Set amidst dramatic scenery, the unfinished late-medieval masterpiece of Rosslyn Chapel awoke genuinely romantic feelings. It had a religious, historical and mystical appeal for any visitor. However, it cannot be denied that the picturesque appeal was by far its most attractive feature. Parallel and simultaneous with the development of the picturesque ideal, grew up the spirit of conservation. The introduction of masons into Swarbreck's views presages the restoration of the Chapel. Soon, as a consequence of the repairs to be carried out at the Chapel, it would lose the charm it had as a ruin. Stripped of its awkward roof and wooden shutters, the slow process of repairs lent to the image of the Chapel a hint of artificiality, which would begin a new chapter in its history far removed from the one intimately linked with the development of Scottish narrative prose, poetry and painting.

4

VICTORIAN RESTORATIONS AND CONTROVERSIES

...so unique a gem should be preserved to the country.
Queen Victoria at Rosslyn Chapel, 14 September 1842.

4.1. The Unmaking of Pictorial Beauty

In the early and middle Victorian periods Rosslyn Chapel was to be extensively restored under the care of James Alexander Sinclair Erskine (1802-1866), the third Earl of Rosslyn. His work precipitated extensive debate, not only on the level of intervention that was appropriate to such a historic structure but also on the ideas and ideals of contemporary conservation. Lord Rosslyn inherited the title in 1837, and in that year immediately turned his attention to the poor state of repair of the Chapel, to which his father had previously done little more than the minimum to keep the structure standing. Two architects were to be involved in this work: the exterior, which received Lord Rosslyn's immediate attention, was repaired by William Burn (1789-1870) between

77. David Octavius Hill and Robert Adamson, *The Architect William Burn at Rosslyn Chapel*. Calotype, c.1843-1848. Scottish National Portrait Gallery, Edinburgh.

89

78. David Octavius Hill and Robert Adamson, *David Roberts*. Calotype, c.1845.
Scottish National Portrait Gallery, Edinburgh.

1837 and the mid 1840s, while the thorough restoration of the interior was consigned to Burn's one time partner David Bryce (1803-1876) from 1861.

One of the most important issues in the history of Rosslyn's restoration was whether the romantic lichen- and moss-covered chapel should be restored to its condition prior to its decay or whether it should be preserved in its ruinous state. Many early nineteenth-century visitors had admired the carvings and the walls which were 'beautifully tinted with all the variegated blotches an incrusted vegetation can bestow'.[1] Time and the luxuriant growth of vegetation had lent the Chapel a new beauty, so that when the idea for the restoration was first mooted in 1837 two factions had already formed: wild nature lovers and building lovers. This is how a correspondent to *The Scotsman* described the nature of the conflict. He wrote that in the case of two such antagonistic points of view, it should be recalled that the preservation of the pictorial effect had always been a leading principle both in designing and in the execution of buildings.[2]

The restoration of Rosslyn Chapel started in the spring of 1837. On this occasion Samuel Dukinfield Swarbreck published his album of lithographs entitled *Sketches in Scotland* which bears a dedication to the Lord Rosslyn and carries a view of the south door of the Chapel on its title page. In his notes Swarbreck explains how 'the exterior of the chapel is undergoing a very extensive repair by its owner, the Earl of Rosslyn, under the eminent direction of William Burn, Architect, and in strict unison with the original architecture; thus securing to after ages these rich remains of Gothic art'.[3] All the requirements for the conservation work were clearly set out by Lord Rosslyn in a letter addressed to Burn in which the architect was 'requested to cause immediate examination of the state of the Chapel of Roslin, and send a report upon the same'.[4] According to his letter the Earl planned to remove the high sloping roof added by John Baxter the elder in the 1730s and replace it by a new lower one over the aisles, 'thereby discovering the whole of the windows and rendering the appearance of the roof more in conformity with the original plan'.[5] The old slate roof was removed, but it was a long time before the glazing was completed and the standing structure made watertight. The reason for this delay is not clear, though the Chapel may have been left open on purpose to let plenty of air into the building to allow the stones to dry out.

While Lord Rosslyn and Burn no doubt believed that they acted in a responsible way in these works of restoration, a major Scottish artist who at that time was undoubtedly a force to be reckoned with, was horrified by what he found while making a series of oil studies of the Chapel. This was David Roberts (1796-1864).

Roberts [fig.79], who regarded himself very much as 'a true Scot', was a man of considerable character, charm and generosity, as well as an artist of surprising

79. David Roberts, *The Entrance to the Crypt*. Oil on panel, 1843. Victoria and Albert Museum, London.

80. David Roberts, *Rosslyn Chapel from north-east*. Watercolour, c.1840. Private Collection.

81. David Roberts, *The south porch of Rosslyn Chapel*.
Watercolour, c.1842. Private Collection.

82. David Roberts, *The south porch of Rosslyn Chapel*. Oil
on canvas, 1845. Blackburn Museum and Art Gallery.

originality. He had known Rosslyn Chapel from his childhood and revisited it as a constant source of inspiration throughout his life. The Scottish bible in stone – as the Chapel is sometimes termed[6] – with all its fascinating sculpted decorations, became Roberts's gateway to the Near East. Throughout his extensive artistic travels, even when faced with wonderful and unequalled architectural remains abroad, he would paint the beauties of Egypt, Syria and the Holy Land, as he had done in Scotland, 'on the spot *à la Roslin*'.[7] His renowned love for the Chapel is manifest not only in the quantity of paintings he made of the building itself [fig.79-84], but also in many of the letters which he wrote from Rosslyn to his daughter, Christine Bicknell (1821-1872). One of them in particular captures the artist's impressions within the Chapel where, according to Roberts's own words, 'there is a combination of light & shade I have never met with in any subject, colour and richness of detail peculiar to itself'.[8]

Roberts's response to the 'beautiful little chapel' was truly romantic. He could not approve any change to the site, scenery or architecture of the place, and believed that these should either be left untouched or, if work were really required it should be carried out with a careful gentle hand. These feelings set his pen in motion with an intensity indicative of a ruling passion, so that soon after the restoration works had begun he wrote pungently sarcastic letters to all his friends.

In 1842, to mark Roberts's eastern journey and safe return to Britain, the Royal Scottish Academy gave a Public Dinner at which the famous and historically minded Lord Henry Cockburn (1779-1854) presided. It would seem that Roberts used the occasion to raise his concerns about the work that was being carried out at Rosslyn, for a few weeks after meeting him Lord Cockburn records that he received the following letter:

> Previously to the recent alteration, the lateral aisles were covered with a temporary and slated wooden roof, which, from its slanting position, covered in a great portion of the windows that light the upper part of the chapel, and served to exclude not only a great current of air, but, together with the then built up state of the great east window, tended in a great measure, by the exclusion of the wind, to the preservation of the interior, by fostering as well as sheltering that green mossy vegetation which had nearly overgrown every part of it; whilst, at the same time, the exclusion of the light itself spread that 'dim religious light', which, even at mid-day, impressed upon the mind those feelings of awe and solemnity so befitting and becoming the long forsaken sanctuary.[9]

According to Roberts the removal of the roof above the aisles, together with the opening of the great east window, destroyed the solemnity of the place. At the same time, the bigger window openings increased the flow of air and was drying up and destroying the vegetation which, to an artistic mind, 'tended so much towards the preservation of the building'.[10] He insisted that 'the *restoration*, as it is called, of the east window, *is not a restoration*, but a monstrous blunder', and ends the letter pessimistically with the emphatic assertion that Rosslyn Chapel might be known to posterity only by 'the skeleton of its ruin'.[11]

The following reply from Lord Cockburn speaks for itself: 'My Dear Roberts, ...I was at Roslin last week, and thoroughly agree with you about the state and prospects of the chapel. I have sent your letter, as I did your former one, to Lord Roslin's [sic]

93

agent. He had told me before I last heard from you that his lordship intended to glaze the windows, chiefly in consequence of your opinion'.[12] Caught in the cross-fire of these conservation issues Lord Cockburn reminded Roberts that Lord Rosslyn and his father had spent a large sum on the restoration and were therefore 'entitled to great consideration and tenderness'.[13] Although Lord Cockburn had an undeniable standing as a champion of preservation in the Scottish capital, it would appear that the nature of the restoration at Rosslyn did not concern him much. He probably thought that Burn was conscientious and would be sensitive to the delicacy of his situation.

The restoration of Rosslyn Chapel at this particular time occurred when attitudes to conservation and to architectural practices were coming under ever increasing scrutiny. While Burn may have believed in good modern workmanship, such as he had employed in the ashlar refacing of St Giles Cathedral in Edinburgh between 1829 and 1833, antiquarian and picturesque considerations led others to see the quest for solidity as a goal more likely to damage the building than to secure its continued quality. For them a poor restoration could have been more disastrous than the ravages of the centuries, and new work might destroy the integrity of the monument. They questioned whether Burn was aware of the fact that a restoration could transform an old building into a new one, and destroy its historic interest. Through careful restoration Burn felt he could give back the monument the richness and splendour it had lost and conserve for posterity the unity of the appearance and the interest of the details of the Chapel.[14] Roberts was not of the same opinion. Perhaps his hostility to Burn's method is best illustrated by his comment, after a detailed inspection of the restoration works, when he remarks: 'we will see what will be the next *dodge* of the modern beautifier of Roslin Chapel – From his having been out there the Sunday Morning before I went, I think he must have *smelt a rat*'.[15] Roberts, by that time, was planning to attack Burn in a series of critical letters which were to be published in the local papers. The campaign involved the close friend of his youth, David Ramsay Hay (1798-1866), with whom he was trying to pull influential strings to have the east window closed up again, the remaining windows put in a proper state and to save the picturesque beauty of the interior.[16] He made no secret of his intentions in Edinburgh, planning that public opinion could be guided in the debate through more correspondents than himself.

The public controversy started with what Roberts described as the 'Herioter's letter', in which his friend James Ballantine (1808-1877) under the pseudonym of 'an Old Herioter' described his return to Edinburgh where, to his great surprise, he found a total wreck and ruin of 'those touching memorials of a bygone age... which hoary veterans had pointed out' as the scenes of the most remarkable events in Scotland's history.[17] The letter appeared in *The Scotsman* for Wednesday, 8 November 1843, under the title 'Antiquities in and around Edinburgh'. The real object of the letter is not immediately apparent. Ballantine began with a number of nostalgic memories, building up to an emotional crescendo in defence of Rosslyn, where, as a boy, he had frequently been on his holidays, and expressing his desire to moderate the flood of light which now destroyed the atmosphere and all the associations of the place. Ballantine wrote in explosive terms of alteration, tasteless innovations, damage, destruction, dilapidation and restoration, which all, in the end, meant different degrees of negative or destructive activity in the Chapel. As a disciple of Roberts, Ballantine criticised the 'excess of light, which oppressed the eye' and complained of the 'monstrous aperture' which 'stood yawning and gaping', and through which came rushing 'the cold east wind, sweeping down fragments of the venerable structure'.[18]

83. David Roberts, *The Apprentice Pillar*. Watercolour, 1830. Victoria and Albert Museum, London.

The 'Herioter's letter' was admired by Roberts for the delicacy with which attention was gradually drawn to the subject, without making a direct onslaught from the start. Ballantine's main aim was to defend an icon of Scotland's architectural heritage for future generations, and he ended with the following words:

> I sincerely trust that this notice will meet the eye of those concerned, and that the noble Earl of Rosslyn will without delay cause a survey to be made of this beautiful chapel. If it be allowed to remain much longer in its present state, it will get rapidly more and more dilapidated... Scotland will lose what has always been considered one of the most remarkable proofs of the princely wealth of her ancient nobles – artists and lovers of art will regret the loss of sculpture and tracery which cannot be replaced.[19]

Ballantine was of the Romantic school, and seems to have believed that the mosses and lichens that covered the interior of the Chapel were essential to its conservation. The winds blowing into the building caused the plants to dry out. When they died and fell to the ground, pieces of sculpture came with them. He therefore wanted the building to be closed up and the old roof by John Baxter to be replaced.

Surprisingly, the effect of this letter was not what was expected. It seems generally to have passed without notice, causing in Roberts enormous disillusion and anger. Only a moderate letter under the pseudonym of Civis, published two weeks after the 'Herioter's letter', followed in *The Scotsman*.[20] Full of indignation at the lack of public interest, Roberts wrote a livid letter to Hay: '...let them be for ever fallen, and never mention the name of Scott again, the sacralege [sic] comitted [sic] upon that chapel under the name of restoration is enough to rouse him from his grave...'.[21]

At this point Roberts decided to head up the preservation battle himself, and it necessarily became a more personal matter. Since Lord Cockburn had already been involved in the controversy, he considered it fair to make the text of his original letters to the judge known to the wider public. These letters, identified as correspondence sent to a 'learned and eminent personage in Scotland', were published in *The Scotsman* for Wednesday, 6 December 1843.[22] A few days before, Roberts had written to Hay: 'if interested [?] they do not rouse our countryman to take some steps to avert its destruction then, in the devils [sic] name, let it tumble, with this proviso, – that when it does fall – the conceited author of the mischief be – the only one under it –'.[23]

Spirited exchanges continued with Hay, who found it doubtful that Burn's plan could ever be carried out, while Roberts continued to admire 'the green tinge of age', which in his view gave Rosslyn a great picturesque charm.[24] The picturesque features had a specific meaning that appealed to a nostalgic sensibility prevalent at that time. It was John Ruskin who later on revolutionised ways of seeing, insisting upon fidelity to Nature above all other considerations. Ruskin was both an admirer and a critic of Roberts's work. The fact that the Scottish artist took up the position of an anti-restorer, as an admirer of the green overgrown state of the Chapel, while at the same time representing the building as completely dry and tidy, did not make any sense to Ruskin (compare fig.91 and 84). He complained that in particular one of the interiors of Rosslyn Chapel [fig.79] 'instead of showing the exquisite crumbling and lichenous texture of the Roslin stone, was polished to as vapid as smoothness as ever French historical picture'.[25] Yet he stated: 'it is bitterly to be regretted that the accuracy

84. David Roberts, *Interior of Rosslyn Chapel, looking south-east.* Watercolour, 1828. Private Collection.

and elegance of his work should not be aided by that genuineness of hue and effect which can only be given by uncompromising effort to paint, not a fine picture, but an impressive and known *verity*'.[26]

In addition to the restoration controversy, another reason there was no love lost between Roberts and Burn was certainly the fact that the artist took exception to the architect's support for the illustrations in *The Baronial and Ecclesiastical Antiquities of Scotland* by the English architectural illustrator Robert William Billings (1813-1874). Published between 1845 and 1852, it became the most beautiful book ever produced on Scottish architecture, and involved the preparation of more than two hundred drawings for engraving. Billings travelled frequently to Scotland, sketching on the spot and sending the result to his engravers in London. He chose the best engravers available, including John Le Keux (1783-1846), to accurately translate his sketches into steel engravings. The investment required for a long-term project such as this was shared between Billings, Burn and the publishers, William Blackwood and Sons. While his works were criticised for failing to provide plans of the buildings described, Billings's acute observation and ability to capture visually the character of a building encouraged an appreciation of the buildings he chose to include. He devoted no less than nine plates to Rosslyn Chapel, in which much of the enduring appeal stems from their meticulous composition. Each plate is a model of clarity, as he skilfully encompassed the aesthetic and the informative within the restrictions of a single engraved image [fig.87, 89, 90, 93]. Billings was also particularly sensitive to the value of the architectural details of the Chapel and spoke of this himself in 1852 when he lectured to the Architectural Institute of Scotland about the 'Economy of Scottish Architecture'.

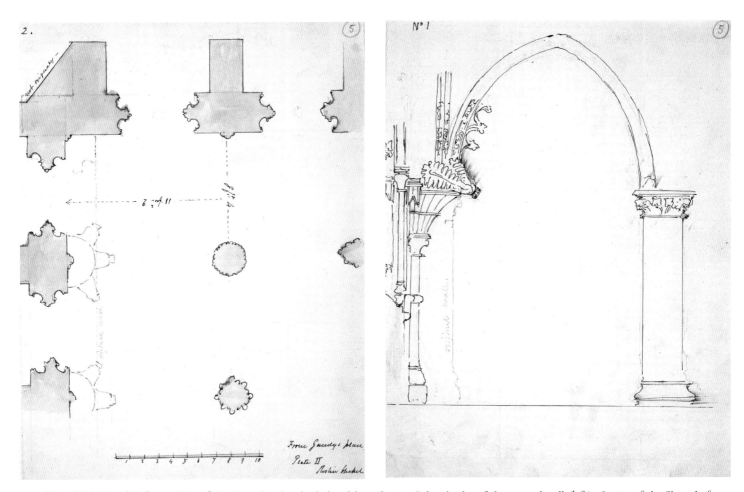

85 and 86. David Roberts, *Plan of the Chancel with red ink dotted lines showing Roberts's idea of the east-end wall* (left). *Section of the Chancel of the Chapel* (right). Pen drawings, 1846. From the album *Documents,* Private Collection.

The Scottish have always been taken for an economical nation, but they sometimes carried this feeling of economy into most extravagant architectural faults. In general, however, they carried their decoration only so far as it was absolutely necessary. Take one of the pinnacles of Roslin Chapel, for instance. There are three sides in sight, and these, as you know, are richly carved. The crockets are beautifully finished, and not only that, but the face of the pinnacle itself is a perfect network of elaborate detail. Go to the back (the fourth side), and you will find that, where you cannot see it, it is as plain as possible... Economy was the order of the day wherever nothing could be seen. They carried their decoration only so far as it seemed absolutely necessary, but not one jot further.[27]

Billings was deeply committed to promoting an appreciation of the architecture of the Gothic period, a theme in his various volumes which became a vital source for architects working in the local Gothic Revival manner or in the Scottish Baronial style. 'Who is Mr Billings?', Roberts wrote to Hay, after saying that 'The work you allude as forthcoming on the monastic remains of Scotland I will be glad to see – but wish it had fallen to better hands, than the restorer or renovator of St Giles's Cathedral and Roslin Chapel'.[28] Roberts would unquestionably have made a more artistic job than

Billings, but it would have been impossible to fit such a project into his programme of wandering in Europe and in the Near East. Nevertheless he never relinquished his original intention of doing a distinct and personal work on Scotland.[29] During the summer of 1846 Roberts entered into an arrangement with James Duffield Harding (1797-1863), William Leighton Leitch (1804-1883) and many other artists to execute forty drawings for a work called *Scotland Delineated*. To enable him to complete this, Roberts travelled to Scotland during September and October, visiting Edinburgh and Rosslyn, and making sketches and copious descriptive notes of all the chief monastic and baronial remains he then saw. Although charming, this work was not a success, coming rather late in a series of similar books; it was also too expensive. The frontispiece of the text, drawn by Roberts himself, represents the south entrance to Rosslyn Chapel and a group of people in Highland costume [fig.88].[30]

87. Robert William Billings, *Rosslyn Chapel. The North Aisle*. Engraving from *The Baronial and Ecclesiastical Antiquities of Scotland*, 1845.

Confirmation of one of the reasons for publishing the book comes from another letter by Roberts to Hay in which he states: 'The work on Scotland has fairly started, I have done eight drawings, Melrose, Porch of Roslin Chapel Tittle [sic] page, the Castle from Greyfriars, High Church of Glasgow, Roslin Chapel Exterior, Linlithgow, Falkland Palace & St Andrews – and if The Great Burn, do not look sharp – he may burn his fingers, in authorship – if he may not have done it as an architect – I hope in the descriptive part of Roslin Chapel to have an opportunity – of pointing out *his* improvements...'.[31] And in connection with Burn's restoration of the east window tracery, he continued: 'Pray could you not get one of your clever lads to take the measurements of the East Window – and draw it to a scale – I am rather anxious to ascertain whither [sic] or not the double arch of the division actually terminates *below* the spring of the external arch. – as such is my impression – Pray think of this – there are nothing like facts'. A few lines later he says: '...so [we] will leave him that obscurity to which in after times his works will conjure him'.[32]

There is no doubting the validity of Roberts's judgement on this issue of discontinuity in the appearance of the east window tracery. It certainly shows the artist's great interest in formal coherence and architectural accuracy. However, we should recognise that

88. Tom Picken after David Roberts, *South porch of Rosslyn Chapel as a frontispiece of 'Scotland Delineated'*. Tinted lithograph, 1847.

89. Robert William Billings, *Rosslyn Chapel. Head of one of the East Windows*. Engraving from *The Baronial and Ecclesiastical Antiquities of Scotland*, 1845.

in bringing his particular sensibility to the building and seeking to preserve transient pictorial effects, he was promoting a methodology that would certainly be unacceptable to modern restorers. He had brought the feelings implicit in any close contact with a work of art, in this case a Scottish architectural icon, into creative collision with all, or at any rate most, of the practical considerations of his age. As Ballantine was stirred to write in the closing lines of Roberts's biography: 'It is always curious and often instructive, to note the little incidents in early life that often influence a man's career... Roslin Chapel had a large share in making him an architectural painter.'[33] With hindsight, we may also add that it was the perseverance of the Earl of Rosslyn and Burn in the face of Roberts's criticism which should be lauded today, for without it Rosslyn Chapel might well have become another ruin in the British landscape.

4.2. Britton's RIBA Lecture

IN January 1846 John Britton gave a lecture at the RIBA 'on the design, construction and architectural characteristics of the fragment of the Collegiate Church at Roslyn'. Most of the events relating to the debate that grew up as a consequence of Britton's RIBA lecture can be followed in the summary published in *The Builder* and some detailed notes made by Samuel Joseph Nicholl (1826-1905), who attended the lecture as a young member of the Institute. The author of the article in *The Builder* sums up Britton's talk on the Chapel with a long quotation from Father Hay's manuscript,[34] whereas Nicholl gives a more interesting account of the paper, recording briefly the debate that it aroused. 'Roslyn Chapel is a fragment of a building that may be called unique' he writes, 'and if it had been found on the banks of the Nile, every detail would have been delineated, and [a] most exaggerated account of its beauties published'.[35]

According to the magazine, after tracing the history of the building, Britton described its several parts, and pointed out apparent peculiarities, such as the singular character of the details, the varieties of the arches and the crypt-like chamber connected with the east end. Nicholl notes comparisons with King's College Chapel in Cambridge and Henry the Seventh's Chapel at Westminster,[36] and includes a curious sketch of a stone beam at Bristol Cathedral thought to be similar to one at Rosslyn. From the sketch it is not possible to see what point Britton was making, the only peculiarity of the drawing apparently an iron support added later, probably during a phase of restoration. There is no description of 'a number of excellent drawings' shown to the audience, but we may suppose that Britton made good use of Gandy's published plates, probably making large hand-painted diagrams for the occasion.[37]

It is rare in architectural history to have two completely different versions of the same event with a chance to compare them. When this happens it is hard to discern where the truth lies. In this case, one account reports what seems to have been a heated discussion, and the other a mild and well-mannered public event. The warmth of the debate is apparent from Nicholl's ingenuous notes in which Professor Thomas Leverton Donaldson (1795-1885) remarked that 'in England we do not find any example of the middle age showing such bad detail as at Roslin'.[38] For the author of the article in *The Builder* Donaldson was merely 'anxious to hear the style of the building accounted for'! Though according to the article he spoke also of the 'great want of purity' at Rosslyn, observing that 'in England, there was no Gothic building whereof the details were impure'.[39] Now that Rosslyn was removed from an approving nationalistic context its architectural detail was subject to critical review. Many had spoken of its richness yet, according to Donaldson, in reality the sculpture of the stonework is vigorous rather than fine and is not as accurately cut as one might expect. Donaldson, we should note, was not alone in expressing this unorthodox opinion of the quality of the Chapel: a little later the famous French architect Eugène Viollett-le-Duc would describe the Apprentice Pillar as a bunch of sausages.[40]

For Robert William Billings, who participated in the debate, the general style of the building was the same as other buildings in Scotland, showing a mixture of styles but vulgarised by bad workmanship; however, much of the design itself remained beautiful.

90. Robert William Billings, *The Eastern Aisle – Rosslyn Chapel*. Engraving from *The Baronial and Ecclesiastical Antiquities of Scotland*, 1845.

He also drew the attention of the audience to the fact that a series of figures, similar to the 'Dance of Death'[41], had been recently discovered on the arch rising from the north-eastern corner of the Chapel, and crossing diagonally over the northern-most bay of the Lady Chapel. William Burn, the architect for the restoration of the Chapel, also spoke at the meeting. While working at the building he had had the opportunity to investigate the Chapel, and caused an 'excavation, three feet wide, to be made from one end of the chapel to the other in the centre', in the crypt and in each aisle. All had been dug down to the foundation; but 'nothing was found'.[42] By excavating Burn believed he had disproved the traditional story, given currency by Sir Walter Scott, that ten barons of the family were buried in the Chapel or the crypt.

The Near East comparison – 'if Rosslyn Chapel been found on the bank of the Nile' – probably caught the attention of another person invited to the lecture, but who since he was not a member of the Institute had chosen to sit at the back. Burn can hardly have expected to see him there, since we are talking about his major antagonist, David Roberts.[43] One peculiarity of Roberts, which gained him popularity in early Victorian Scotland, was his polemical opposition to anything Burn did to threaten the Chapel. Consequently the Rosslyn RIBA lecture became the theatre for a vehement dispute between the artist and the architect. The debate is detailed in Roberts's personal letters to his Scottish friend Hay and the contents of the recently discovered album 'Documents Relating to Roslin Chapel'. The latter completes the picture of what really happened, since it contains the correspondence between Roberts and Britton, emphasising the artist's response to the Chapel itself and his disagreement with Burn's procedures. The following month Roberts was writing to Hay his impressions of the meeting:

> I rec.[d] an invitation from Little Briton to attend a Lecture he was to deliver upon Roslin Chapel, which took place as you are aware at the Architects Institute Grosvenor S.[q] I of course accepted of it – although personally known almost to every member and ended on the most friendly terms with all the leading members – I was rather surprized to find your friend B. take his place beside the President – and seemed really to be a person of great consequence I mean in laying down the laws, upon certain disputed points in a very decided and authoritive [sic] manner – and such was the weight they seemed to carry with them that no one was bold enough to dispute them...
>
> When asked by some of the members whither [sic] he could throw any light upon the peculiar style as varying from that of all others, he seemed a *little abroad* – but at last venturing to give an opinion on the apprentices pillar – that the history given by The Old Woman who used to describe it was the correct one – Viz. that the apprentice really was the most talented of the two the master being as he supposed a *paukey* (these are his own words) man – and ergo ignorant, (I by no means see that should follow – [sic] took advantage of the superior Talent of his pupil – But upon a question being put to him whither [sic] he could consider that the Master Mason, who designed Roslin Chapel – he very wisely in my opinion declined answering and sat down – I daresay he now thinks it would have been as well had he continued to sit, or at least held his tongue – for afterwards the lecturer had occasion to draw the attention of the members to a sugestion [sic] thrown out by me, – That upon a close examination of the East end or *Chancel* – I found the whole had been removed outwards to give room for the service of the Various Chapels – This seemed to take him so much by surprise – Whither [sic] from the novelty of the thing or at my presumption – that he at once contradicted – and affirmed that the present appearance is a part and whole of the original design.[44]

Roberts was the first person to comment on the great peculiarity of the internal east wall of the chapel where the springers for the ribs of the vaulting are set not in the side of the wall but on a system of corbels projecting far from it. He contended that the east end wall had been pulled down after the vaulting was finished, and rebuilt three feet further back, and the top of the wall-shafts corbelled out as they now are to meet the groin ribs. He also endeavoured to prove his thesis from the fact that the buttresses at the north and south-east angles of the east front had been connected with those of the north and south fronts by a splay in the wall which was in itself most unusual.[45] For Burn, who was caught on the hop by this suggestion, the aisle at the east end, which is considerably wider than the side aisle, was part of the original design and was never intended to have been the same width. He considered that the altars were probably in the same style as the Chapel and that the crucial measurement between the pillars and the altars was equal to the width of the aisles. Roberts did not accept Burn's hypothesis, as he believed that the evidence of the structure proved that the Lady Chapel had undergone a radical transformation since it was first built. He was given no proper response to this idea and, dumbfounded 'by the abuse of Sir Walter'[46] and the boldness of Burn's assertions, left the meeting in disgust.

The location of the eastern buttresses and the bay spacing at the east end is a real oddity of the plan of the Chapel [fig.85]. Normally the eastern, or corner, buttress of each aisle would align with the end of the east wall. At Roslin the buttress is set further into the building, to the extent that its eastern corner aligns on the plan with the inside rather than the outside of the east wall. One would also expect that the angle between the eastern buttress and the adjoining buttress in the east wall would be a simple right angle. Instead the discrepancy in alignment is masked by a broad diagonal section of masonry between the side and end buttresses. Why was this irregular arrangement adopted? The eastern bay is longer than the others, and if the buttresses had been normally positioned this would have shown up clearly on the external elevation. The arrangement adopted masks this discrepancy and gives the illusion that externally the eastern bay is actually the same width as the rest.

Juggling with the plan is also apparent on the interior. The aisle windows in the eastern bay are centred between the buttresses, which means that on the internal elevation they are set considerably to one side (the west) of the actual bay centre [fig.86]. The ribbed vaults of the eastern chapels are aligned with the window arches. In fact on the north side the window is west of centre, so that the ridge ribs are set at an angle to meet the window head. In effect the vaults are planned to fit square bays, rather than the physical space they cover, which is oblong. To accommodate the square-planned vaults the eastern vault springer responds are massively corbelled out, and this has been turned into a decorative feature by the introduction of large diagonal pendants. Was this the intended design, or is it, as Roberts believed, an expedient caused by juggling with the bay spacings? The lower vault springers, below the pendants, seem conventional enough. In fact they seem hardly adequate to support the cantilevered structure above. The arrangement of the pendants and their jointing is careless, badly designed and clumsily executed. This suggests expediency, rather than careful planning; though the effect is breathtaking since it gives the impression that the eastern ribs of the vaults are hanging unsupported in space.

It is Roberts's great quality that, through a careful examination of the structure of the building, he was in a position to put forward a new interpretation of the Chapel's evolution which cannot be discounted and may well be correct. He wrote about it to John Britton, stating his reasons for reaching the conclusion that he had, and accompanied his letter with a section and ground plan in which he highlighted with a red ink line the original wall of the east end [fig.85, 86]. These drawings – all preserved in the album 'Documents Relating to Roslin Chapel' – were also sent to Burn, 'affording him the opportunity of retracting what he said'.[47]

In the face of this evidence Britton felt it was necessary to send a separate communication to the members of the Institute.

In the paper I read at the Architectural Institute, it appears from Mr. Roberts's remarks, that I was not sufficiently explanatory about the *extraordinary construction* of the eastern wall, and the alterations effected by rebuilding it after it had been once raised. I certainly did not make any comments or criticism on Mr Roberts's ingenious and original theory; but intimated that I agreed with him in believing the wall does not occupy the site as at first planned and intended by the architect. It occurred to me on a cursory consideration of the subject, that the whole plan had been marked out on the ground, from the '*draughts drawn on eastland boards*', which were '*carved by the carpenters*' as described in Father Hay's MSS., and that when the masons had carried up the walls and the pillars of the whole building to a certain height, and had also *prepared* much of the superstructure, particularly those remarkable stone beams, or lintels which extend over the aisles, and their connecting vaultings, the architect discovered that the space at the east end, between the easternmost pillars

91. John Adam Houston, *Sir Walter Scott in Rosslyn Chapel*. Watercolour, 1854. Private collection.

and the wall, was not wide enough for the religious services at the four altars, placed under so many windows in that wall. This I believe is Mr. Roberts's opinion, and I do not feel inclined to doubt, much less to dispute it. But as the subject is very curious, and perhaps unparalleled in architectural construction, I would recommend a careful examination of the eastern wall in conjunction with those on the north and south sides, and particularly the positions and formation of the angular buttresses. Further, let the ground be excavated and explored, to ascertain if there be any remains of foundation between the present eastern wall and the three pillars.[48]

The debate was about to enter a second phase when Roberts addressed a later meeting of RIBA members in defence of the romantic stories told about the building in *The Lay of the Last Minstrel*. Britton had criticised Scott's poem, saying that there were ten mistakes made in reference to Rosslyn. According to Roberts:

> The Lecturer… concluded by stating that however poetical the legend might be – the whole tradition was a tissue of *falsehoods* – endeed [sic] – that in about twenty lines were contained as many falsehoods – in which he was followed by our distinguished Architect who instead of… throwing some light – on the singular construction… quaint ornaments and grotesque sculpture – told us that he had dug a Trench up the centre and latteral [sic] Asles [sic] of the Chapel – and having only found *one* vault with a wooden coffin, he could perfectly confirm all that Mr Briton [sic] had said – and that the whole thing was a *falsehood*.[49]

92. J.A.Bell and Joseph Clayton Bentley, *Interior view of the Chapel with Sir Walter Scott.* Engraving, c.1840. From the album *Documents*, Private Collection.

107

93. Robert William Billings, *The south side of Rosslyn Chapel*. Engraving from *The Baronial and Ecclesiastical Antiquities of Scotland*, 1845.

Roberts knew that this story originated in Father Hay's account, which, as well as referring to the Sinclair Barons buried in their armour, entered into minute detail on the appearance of the last baron buried in his armour when his grave or vault was opened up.[50]

> Now the opinion of most I have spoken to on the subject competent to judge is that the crypt or small Chapel was devoted to that purpose and that they were placed in stone coffins, which we know was the case at Holyrood and like those also, at the breaking out of the reformation these would be amongst the first to be ransacked and pillaged – The supernatural light – I consider may be also equaly [sic] and simply explained – on the Burrial [sic] of one of so great a family – the religious display and pump would be magnificent the Chapel will be lighted up for the funeral mass – and the removal of the body to its final resting place would be by torch light – the remembrance of this – as contrasted with the sad reverse of this once proud family – would attatch [sic] to the whole thing a supernatural origin – hence the tradition.[51]

The principal point at dispute was, whether or not the 'ten barons' in their mail were ever buried in the Chapel. The discussion become rather too drawn out, until a member of the Institute 'humorously terminated' it by quoting the following words: 'The Knights are dead; their swords are rust, Their spirits with the Lord, I trust'.[52]

Britton's reaction to Roberts's defence of Scott, may be gathered from a letter dated 3 February 1846, which he sent to the RIBA, which was also published in *The Builder*.

> I learn that Mr. Roberts brought before the members of the Architects'
> Institute some remarks on the paper I read there on the 12th of the

94. George Washington Wilson, *View of the south side*. Albumen print, c.1870. Private Collection.

last month. As I was not present at the meeting, and my statement or judgement is impeached, I beg you will do me the justice to give insertion to the following brief remarks in self-justification. On quoting the following lines from Sir Walter Scott's 'Lay of the Last Minstrel', I said there were almost as many errors, or mis-statements, as lines; at the same time passed a high eulogium on the commanding talents of that accomplished author. Before reading the stanzas I observed, 'This building, as well as most of the old edifices of the country, has some marvellous story, or silly romance, or incredible legend connected with it. Such matters may serve as themes to embellish or diversify the stanzas of a poem, the pages of a novel, or the annals of a fabulous chronicle, but are unworthy of notice, by the architectural antiquary, or philosophical historian.[53]

At this point of the letter Britton presents a version of Sir Walter Scott's famous lines with the ten mistakes printed in italic type:

> Seemed all on fire, that *chapel* proud,
> Where Roslin's chiefs *uncoffin'd* lie;
> Each baron for a sable shroud,
> Sheathed in his *iron* panoply.
> Seem'd all on fire within, around
> Deep *sacristy* and altar's pale;
> Shone *every pillar foliage* bound,
> And *glimmered* all the dead men's *mail*;
> Blazed *battlement*, and *pinnet* high,
> Blazed every rose-carved buttress fair;
> So still they blaze, when fate is nigh
> The lordly line of high St Clair.[54]

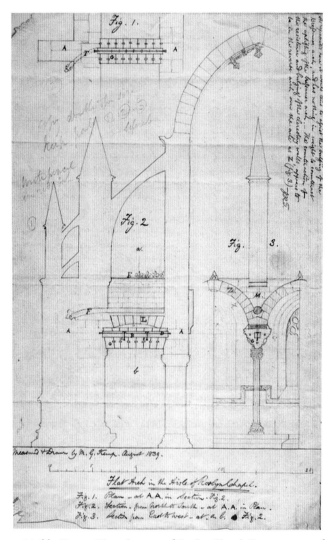

95. George Meikle Kemp, *Three diagrams of Rosslyn Chapel*. Pen over pencil on paper, 1839. From the album *Documents*, Private Collection.

Britton points out that the lines are quoted not to afford any architectural or historical information, but to show the general 'fictions and fallacies of poetry'. He explains the errors as follows:

> Although there are not quite so many errors or mis-statements as lines, the number of words in italics shew that they are very nearly so. The building is not a *chapel*; it was erected and founded as a collegiate *church*, and had it been completed, would have been a large and splendid edifice. The best authorities that I have consulted do not say any thing of *uncoffin'd* chiefs in *iron* panoply; nor is it likely that such ever could be allowed. Putrified dead bodies would have excluded living ones from the church. There is no appearance of *sacristy*. Instead of *every pillar foliage bound*, there is only one thus adorned; and this has given origin to a puerile story, which the old female cicerone of the building may repeat and believe, though none but an old woman will give two moments' credence to. I believe there are not any *battlements* to the building, and I do not know that the world *pinnet* is either architectural or archaeological.[55]

110

96. Thomas Kemp, *View from the crypt of the Chapel*. Pencil sketch, c.1850. Writers Museum, Edinburgh.

While Roberts and Britton seemed to have come to a degree of agreement following this controversy. Burn remained obdurate. In the last letter to Hay on this subject the artist writes that he has no intention to be a bore:

> ...with some curse about the Great Burn – I have heard nothing farther of him, nor yet do I know whether he has ever again shown face in the Institute, Briton [sic] like a true briton has recanted and with drawn his asertions [sic], respecting the Great Sir Walter – him and I are friends once more –
>
> The other remains dogged and too proud I suppose to admit he was wrong – there let him rest.[56]

To return to the recently discovered album 'Documents Relating to Roslin Chapel', it is important to note the care Britton gave to the preparation of his lecture which the papers reveal. As an author Britton made meticulous notes about the building which he had been studying for a number of years and used to the full his Scottish contacts in procuring up-to-date information about it. He asked the young architect of the Scott monument, George Meikle Kemp (1794-1844), to visit Rosslyn to inspect the flat arches over the side aisles in order to produce a drawing representing the section of the building and showing its method of construction [fig.95]. Kemp's section was later to be reproduced as a diagram for the lecture.[57] As well as Gandy, Roberts, Kemp, and James Fergusson (1808-1886), Britton's intricate network of contacts also included Edinburgh librarians like David Laing (1793-1878), Keeper of the Signet Library, and David Irving (1778-1860), Keeper of the Advocates Library, both of whom contributed scientifically to the historical analysis which he later presented. Even the eminent Sir Walter Scott, who became one of Britton's correspondents during the publication of the *Architectural Antiquities*, copied personally two different versions of the Mason's Charter of 1630 from Father Hay's manuscripts. Although Scott had died in 1832, Britton did not forget to mention and acknowledge the Scottish poet fourteen years later when writing: 'Roslin Chapel is one of the singularities of Christian Architecture, and to Sir Walter I am indebted for the communication of some curious documents illustrative of its origin and history'.[58]

The section which Kemp prepared for Britton in 1839 adds a further twist to a complicated story. The English architectural writer, quite rightly, was anxious to understand the principles construction on which the architecture of the Chapel was based, and turned to Kemp as a Scotsman knowledgeable about the local late-medieval styles for his assistance. The album 'Documents' contains the drawing which Kemp sent, a cross-section of one aisle and half nave; but sadly for Britton no reference was made to the east-west section that Roberts was to find so intriguing. Moreover this survey made by Kemp is very similar to a section made by the English architect Edward Cresy which was engraved and published in the late 1830s.[59]

The contribution of Edward Cresy (1792-1858) is interesting, since his engraving of Rosslyn appears not in an antiquarian or strictly architectural publication, but in a work of engineering entitled *Practical Treatise on Bridge Building and on the Equilibrium of Vaults and Arches* (1839). In his work on bridges, one plate with three sectional

97. Edward Cresy, *Three different sections of Rosslyn Chapel*. Engraving from *Treatise on Bridge Building and on the Equilibrium of Vaults and Arches*, 1839.

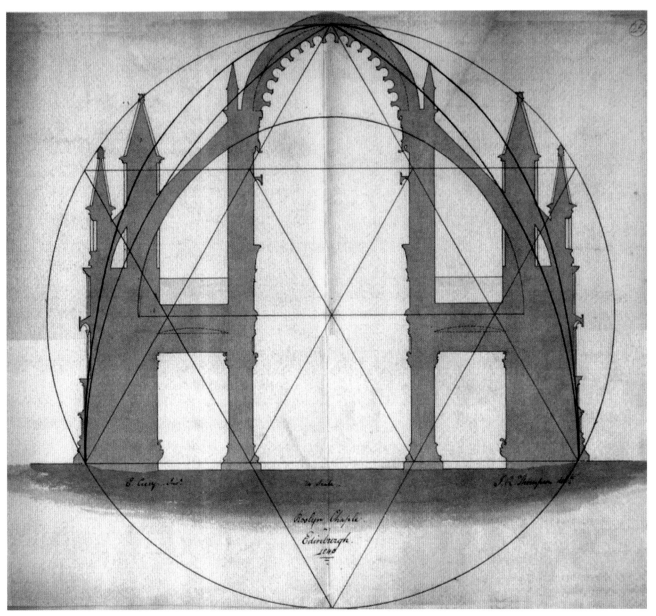

98. John Thompson, *Section through the nave with geometrical figure based upon a circle*. Pen and wash drawing, 1840. From the album *Documents*, Private Collection.

engravings of Rosslyn Chapel [fig.97] is included to show the principles by which medieval architects achieved balance and stability in their masses. To effect this, Cresy maintained, a perfect knowledge of geometry was required.[60] At Rosslyn this was clearly demonstrated in the circumstance that, as the arch became flatter and the force of its expansion necessarily greater, the walls and buttresses were proportionally increased in size.

According to Cresy the structural design of Rosslyn Chapel is extremely simple. The eastern chapels show that the masons were quite capable of building ribbed vaults; however the main vaulting scheme reverted to using barrel vaults, which were a common feature of late medieval Scottish architecture. At Rosslyn the high barrel vault is combined with a full Gothic buttressing system with double banks of pinnacles and flying buttresses. Cresy accurately measured all these elements, to enable the practical architect to deduce from them the principles of their construction.

As to the subsequent history of the album 'Documents Relating to Roslin Chapel', it would appear that Andrew Kerr (d.1887), the architect of the 1880s extension to the west front of the Chapel, had access to it when compiling the long and stimulating study of Rosslyn which he published in the *Proceedings of the Society of Antiquaries of Scotland* in 1877. Kerr quotes directly from Britton's correspondence and also makes use of Edward Cresy's studies completed in 1839 and John R. Thompson's[61] geometrical analysis of the building signed and dated 1840, which are all bound in the volume. Thompson clearly referred to Cresy while making his own drawing of the Chapel.[62] He was especially interested in the hypothesis advanced by Cresy on proportion in Gothic architecture, and the inherent understanding of geometry possessed by medieval architects. In reference to these ideas he superimposed on Cresy's section a geometrical pattern of a six-pointed star relating to the proportions of the Chapel [fig.98]. Kerr, having seen this study, without acknowledging the author, developed the same concept for plate XII in his essay on Rosslyn, and explained that 'a geometrical figure based upon a circle, the diameter equal to the width of the building, applies to the section, defining not only the proportion, but the construction of the edifice'.[63]

Britton's meticulous collection of papers in the album of 'Documents' illustrates, in an unusually dramatic manner, not only new and unknown aspects in the evolution of the visual history of the Chapel, but also a remarkable instance of the intriguing process by which many architects of the nineteenth-century added their contribution to the modern understanding of the building. As Britton was moved to write, 'instead of the vast architectural planet, the cathedral' we should confine ourselves 'to one of its satellites, the Chapel of Roslyn'.[64]

In the words of Britton, Roberts and Cresy we can read a modern sense of historical consciousness. With their insights they provided a new approach founded on respect for the past – no longer on purely aesthetic responses – but based on the building's significance as a monument in the development of the nation's architecture.

4.3. The 'Antique replicas' controversy.

In 1860 responsibility for the works of restoration at Rosslyn passed to David Bryce, one-time chief clerk and later the partner of William Burn from 1841 to 1850. Bryce had a lively appreciation of the 'sculpturesque' character of many old Scottish buildings, and his concern at Rosslyn was to consolidate the decorative detail with which the building was loaded. Operations were begun initially for the purpose of enclosing the family graves and executing some necessary repairs on the east end of the Chapel. At that time there was no intention that the building should be used again as a place of worship. That idea seems to have originated with a family of Episcopalians who lived in the vicinity and felt it was inconvenient to go to Edinburgh every Sunday. In looking for a new church the Episcopalians seem also to have promoted the notion of cleaning the walls and the carving.[65]

The full scale of the work undertaken by Bryce is difficult to tell with certainty. Four letters written by the architect to Lord Rosslyn survive, giving information on

99. Thomas Heaphy, *Interior view from the north aisle looking towards the south aisle*. Watercolour, c.1825. Private collection.

115

100. William Donaldson Clark, *The Apprentice Pillar from the south aisle*. Albumen print, 1860. Scottish National Portrait Gallery, Edinburgh.

what repairs were in hand between 1859 and 1861. And there is visual proof that alterations were carried out in the collection of drawings and photographs dating from before and after the restoration. As had happened with Britton, Burn and David Roberts, the employment in the restoration of the interior of a practically minded professional like Bryce was to provoke a storm of protest, against both the extent of what was done and indeed the whole idea of restoration. In letters to the national press the leave-well-alone zealots had usually the upper hand – their fulminations provided entertaining column inches for the editor – yet it must be said that however quick Bryce's critics were to expose any weakness in his methods, they display a remarkable reluctance to identify the exact location of his supposed irresponsible actions.

A letter to the Earl, dated 16 March 1859, introduces us immediately to the detail and practical nature of Bryce's concerns:

> I had altered the cope stone of the altars, making the one a plain moulding and the other a splay, leaving one as originally intended that your Lordship might see the effect in the different ways; and having turned up different authorities on the subject, ~~that~~ I find that it is not inconsistent to have an ornamental cope, but will attend to your Lordships [sic] wish to have Ropes – the running ornament would in my opinion look better. I entirely approve of the Monumental Brasses in the floor.
>
> There has been a small altar at the window over the stair down, finishing at the top in a level with the window sill – this I propose to restore, and also to put a landing place over the stair, sufficiently broad to admit of a person standing in the front of the altar – this can be done and

leave ample head room for the stair. And there can be little doubt that such a landing has existed – It is however not necessary that this should be done at present unless wished by your Lordship – With regard to the Burial Vault, I intend to cover over the grave in the centre compartment, about 5.3 below the level of the pavement, and then to form a catacomb on each side of the space, this would give space for three burials in that compartment as shown, but if two are only required a little less width would be sufficient – I aprehend [sic] that the graves in the centre will be deep enough to admit of this, without being disturbed, [sic]

My idea of the Railing was to make it portable extending between the pillars but not touching them, inserted into iron or Brass sockets sunk into the stone work – not to be higher than 3.6 above the floor and to be very light, and it should return along the old seat which forms the parapet wall of the stair down, placed close to the outside so that a person could not walk between the Railing and Stair.[66]

From this extract it is clear that Bryce tried not to do any work that he considered might diminish the overall integrity of the Chapel's original plan. He was careful to consider historical precedents when designing the space for the altar, and he was also convinced that there was once a landing place at the stair and so was happy to place a new one there. The altar and stair he refers to were those at the east end, next to the entrance to the Crypt. It is evident from comparing the photographs of William Donaldson Clark and George Washington Wilson that there was indeed some work carried out in this part of the building. Clark's photograph of the east end taken in the 1850s [fig.100], shows crumbling stonework at the head of the stair; whereas Wilson's

101. George Washington Wilson, *Interior of the Chapel, the Apprentice Pillar*. Albumen print (from a stereoscopic pair), c.1880. Private collection.

102. Henry Le Keux after Edward Blore, Interior view from the east end. Engraving from Sir Walter Scott, *Provincial Antiquities and Picturesque Scenery of Scotland with Descriptive Illustrations*, 1826.

photograph [fig.101], taken after the completion of the restoration, demonstrates how the stone was built up and replaced. The two photographs of the east end reveal many other differences in the Chapel's fabric. In Wilson's photograph there is a railing between the Apprentice Pillar and its neighbour, while there is no sign of this fixture in the earlier photograph by Clark. It is probable therefore that the rail is the one referred to in Bryce's letter. In Wilson's photograph the rail does not touch the central pier: instead it stands between the piers, exactly as Bryce intended. Repair work is also apparent in the piers themselves: that in the foreground of Clark's photograph has a hole three-quarters of the way up, but by the time of Wilson's visit the hole had been filled in. Various other differences may be noted: the glazing seems to have been replaced; the sculptural carvings appear more precise in the later record; and the base of the Apprentice Pillar has been replaced.[67]

103. Thomas Vernon Begbie, *View of the Lady Chapel looking south*, c.1860. Contemporary photograph (from a stereoscopic pair) from original glass plate negative, City of Edinburgh Art Centre.

While study of the visual records can be useful in clarifying the changes that were made at Rosslyn, it can also be misleading. A good example of this is provided by the drawings and photographs of the Mason's Pillar in the south-east corner of the Lady Chapel. Three visual records of the Pillar show it with a plain shaft: Blore's view of 1826 [fig.102], Swarbreck's lithograph dated 1837 [fig.76] and Begbie's 1860 photograph [fig.103]. In contrast to these is Wilson's photograph of the Mason's Pillar taken in the 1880s, where the internal faces on the shaft of the pillar – two on each side – are clearly carved [fig.104]. From this one could deduce that Bryce decided to alter the appearance of the Mason's Pillar with little regard for its original design, since his rather free-wheeling approach to the fabric of the Chapel is exactly what is constantly opposed by the architect's critics. However, in a letter dated 4 June 1861 Bryce writes to the Earl explaining his recent observation:

...I am not sure that your Lordship is aware that the Pillar in the opposite side and corresponding with the Apprentices Pillar has at one time been ornamented not in a spiral form but with upright ornament and at some previous repair the ornament has been partly cut out and new stone without carving introduced, the other stones where entire being plastered over.[68]

This could be seen as evidence of two things: firstly that Bryce, by carving the Mason's Pillar, was restoring it to its original design, and secondly, that either Burn had covered over the original carving, or more probably that there had been some earlier repairs carried out at the Chapel which are undocumented.

There is little further evidence of what exactly was done by Bryce at Rosslyn Chapel. Early photographs of the Chapel do indicate, however, that a primary focus of Bryce's restoration must have been the carvings, as they are visibly more defined in

104. George Washington Wilson, *View of the three piers in the Lady Chapel.* Albumen print, c.1870. Private Collection.

120

later photographs, and it was here that Bryce's methods and approach to architectural conservation met criticism head-on.

In the modern world it is often hard to credit the extent to which Victorian people would engage in local causes or the intensity with which the expression of different views was made. Rosslyn in 1860 to 1861 became a *cause célèbre* of national significance. If we want to catch the flavour of the debate caused by this second phase of restoration, it is papers such as *The Scotsman, The Times, The Builder,* and *The Building News*, which – because they report the opinions of anonymous writers, men who hid their identities under pseudonyms – best convey the intensity of feeling of that time.[69]

The debate, as is so often the case in conservation matters, centred on the issue of what was necessary and whether the restorers had attempted to do too much. Lord Rosslyn, his architect and builders were practically minded men who focused their attention on real problems and, no doubt, were anxious to do a good job. Their critics were people of sensibility who have the distinct impression that things are going awry and that it is time to call a halt to proceedings which they feel to be unnecessary and which they do not totally understand.

One of the most heated and provocative letters of the controversy appeared in *The Scotsman* on 7 May 1861. The author of this, under the pseudonym of Randolph, gives an emotional account of the 'deplorable Moodification [sic]' at the Chapel. According to Randolph the restored Apprentice Pillar which Bryce had had re-tooled appeared diminished in diameter by 'this decortication', while its delicate and wonderful tints were completely gone, leaving the pillar 'scraped, peeled, flayed, standing raw, naked and ashamed... a lamentable result of the *nimia diligentia*, which works such havoc in our world.'[70] This scraping was to be carried out on each of the other piers in what was defined by Randolph as 'a process as difficult and as ruinous to all beauty and life as would be the barking of a noble oak.'

The accusatory tone of the letter to *The Scotsman* becomes stronger when Randolph refers to the responsibility of Lord Rosslyn, who though 'noble in his tastes as well as in presence and in name,' was not sufficiently aware of the fact that the Chapel was a 'priceless record of the past,' and a 'unique relic of the genius of its time and of its art.' Lord Rosslyn, he argues, has to be convinced that in this case 'restoration is not preservation, but destruction.'

> Suppose you have a dear old lady, beautiful in youth, beautiful still – not in defiance of old age, but because of it. There she sits, graceful, becoming, with the harmony of the time and goodness, and, it may be, the touch of sorrow overcome, all about her; with the pathetic beauty and delightfulness of repose and peace, in manner, in voice, in thought and feeling, in dress, in posture – subdued to settled quiet, waiting till her time comes, 'in the world, not of it.' Fancy your going in some morning and finding her 'restored', sitting bolt upright in a cloud of crinoline; her once silvery hair, which lay like a gentle moonlit cloud on her forehead, 'restored' by being removed, and somebody else's staring black tresses instead; her cheek blooming *ab extra*, her cheeks plumped out *ab intra*, and all the other horrors of artificial rejuvenescence – imagine your anger, and humiliation, and distress. Such is pretty much what is being done to that dear old Ladye Chapel of ours.

An interesting reply to this letter was published two days after. The sender, a man who signes himself as Shandwick, explains that if the Apprentice Pillar has been scraped and peeled, it will be also quickly restored, and that nothing can be said to prevent Lord Rosslyn carrying out, in their 'full integrity', the restorations he had ordered. Moreover, although the building was mutilated by the iconoclasts of the Reformation period and latterly by curiosity-hunting tourists chipping off portions of the ornaments to enrich their collections, it appeared to him to be in an excellent state of repair. He writes:

> On reading 'Randolph's' epistle, I have no doubt prudent people will deeply regret that he had not chanced to see operations in the Chapel until they had been finished. I would not like to quote the old Scotch proverb to 'Randolph'; but I would simply put to him the question – If the old lady to whom he refers were to be peeled of her old dress, would he not prefer to have her redressed, than to have her set in her old chair in a state of nakedness?[71]

It may be of interest here to quote the sarcastic reaction to this letter from another anti-restorer:

> Your correspondent, Shandwick, seems highly delighted with the operations, and hopes that they will be carried out to their 'full integrity'. I am surprised that he does not propose to paper and paint the old lady of Roslin, now that she has been deprived of nature's dress, and doomed to sit in naked stone, as she will be sure to catch cold.[72]

One of the most remarkable images representing the actual state of the Chapel, immediately before the restorations by Bryce were begun, is a watercolour by John Adam Houston (1813-1884), who romantically inserted Sir Walter Scott seated near the Apprentice Pillar in the Lady Chapel completely covered by lichens and mosses [fig.91].[73] Though to a modern eye the wet stone and damp-infested structure is appalling, it is just this decayed state of the building which an anonymous artist celebrated in a letter to *The Scotsman* in 1861. He is scandalised by the fact that the main characteristics of the place – 'the features which render it in the eyes of my profession such an object of interest, of study, and of affection'[74] – were to be forever lost. It was, he thought, 'one of the very few ecclesiastical remains in this country to which, with reference to the interior of the building, the term *picturesque* could be applied.'[75] The gulf which separated this picturesque appreciation from the aims of the practical restorer is delightfully set forth in a later passage from this letter. Not only was Rosslyn 'a most perfect specimen of art,' but nature, as it were, 'taking up the work where man had left it, after it had ceased to serve the religious purposes for which it was founded,' had 'put forth to it her own wondrous hand, bestowing on it a grace beyond the reach of art, winning it back to herself; not destructively, ruthlessly, or contemptuously, but gently and kindly, adorning it with lichens and mosses and delicate ferns, making it all the year round a *place of summer greenerie*.'[76]

Bryce's restoration rapidly changed this *picturesque* character of the interior. With the cleaning and rechiselling of the piers, the architectural lines were made hard and regular, while the green colouring was destroyed to bring to the surface a bright yellow sandstone, as *The Scotsman*'s first correspondent wrote 'a mechanical look was creeping over it.'[77] In another letter published a few days later, a curious visitor to the Chapel gives a more detailed account of the procedures adopted. He is greatly opposed to the use of new sandstone on the exterior that will never harmonise with the old – 'tinting may hide the evil for a little, but it will soon be thrown out by the weather' – and he is scandalised by the thoroughness of the reworking Bryce proposed: 'The cherubs are to be provided with new noses, and the seven deadly sins are to be chiselled and purified by ruthless muriatic acid.'[78]

> Quaint things they must have been originally, but look at them now, without one particle of originality, expression, or grotesqueness, and it is well known that these are the great features of the carvings in Roslin Chapel. Compare the faces of the old figures with those of the new. The first are as full of quaintness and expression as the others are devoid of them. There is one bracket in particular that I should like to call attention to. All that remains of the original was a pair of wings reversed, and the end of a rope. Now, that puzzled the modern sculptor not a little. Well, what has he made of it? Why he has simply turned an ordinary individual upside down, with something like a night-shirt on, a flat expressionless face, his hands stretched out betwixt his toes, and the rope passing very gently and gracefully round them.[79]

Notwithstanding these public attacks, Lord Rosslyn's intentions were fully carried out. The idea was to go on with the restoration of the carvings and rechiselling of any of the pillars except the three eastmost, on one of which the surface was completely redressed. To furnish the chancel, new stone altars with the Sinclair cross carved on them were built; however these were judged to be 'clumsy structures, very like small kitchen dressers.'[80] The broken pieces of architecture near the entrance to the crypt, as recorded in Thomas Kemp's sketches [fig.96], were mended with solid masonry, creating a stone bench attached to the Apprentice Pillar.[81] The placing of an iron railing around the Lady Chapel was probably no doubt dictated by concern purely to prevent the public constantly walking over Lady Rosslyn's grave. The mason hewing a new step at the south door is clearly recorded by the *provocateur* 'Hair Pencil', who states that the time-worn entrance 'over which no one ever stept without turning round to gaze upon and admire it; the joy of every artist, the most perfect thing of its kind in Britain, is to have a new step, yes, a span new step, sharp, and square, to keep the water out.'[82] The result of this intervention can easily be identified by a comparison of photographs of the porch in the 1850s with what can be seen today [fig.15 and 42]. These demonstrate the difference between the old worn sandstone and the sharply moulded work replaced by Bryce's sculptors. It is interesting to note that, after the removal of the eighteenth-century roof to the Chapel in the 1840s, followed by the insertion of mullions and tracery in the east end window looking into the nave, the glazing was not completed until Bryce's intervention, or if it was, it was not waterproof.[83] A confirmation is given by 'Hair Pencil' in his 'winter-report', where we understand that the rain water had been filtering through the building for more than twenty years. The fact that the Chapel was exposed to the effects of the external atmosphere is confirmed by the early photographs taken by David Octavius Hill. In his calotypes dated to the mid 1840s, the higher level windows are unglazed. The glazing, in fact, appears to be *in situ* only five years later in Thomas Keith's sun-pictures and in Roger Fenton's extraordinary albumen prints [fig.44].

According to one correspondent in *The Scotsman* in June 1861, the idea that the Chapel had been standing for years without either door or windows, and going to ruin in consequence of the exposure to damp and other effects of the weather, was not at all true. This writer explained how it had for many years had both, with the exception of the clerestory windows, which for a long time had no glazing, but even these were protected from the effects of the weather by the sloping roof then covering the north aisle, which rose considerably above the level of the windows, and so covered them that visitors often mistook them for the arcade of a gallery [fig.99]. Indeed an old custodian, called John Oughton, took especial care to insist upon this use in his guide to the building, with the further addition, that it was a gallery for singing boys and girls. He also focused the attention of Victorian readers on the matter of the ventilation of the Chapel with the following remarks:

> The present doors and windows have been in their place for nearly twenty years, at which time both exterior and interior underwent a thorough repair in all that was necessary for its preservation and stability, under the judicious guidance of Mr Burn, architect, who had the extraneous roof over the north aisle removed and new windows fixed in the north clerestory and other parts of the building, but unfortunately these were made fixtures, which has proved a complete hindrance to airing the Chapel; and hence a great deal of that dampness existing at present arises from the stagnation of the air within, and not from external causes, as has been supposed, and could be very easily obviated by having a portion of the windows made to open; when the free circulation of air would very soon clean the walls of all extraneous matter without the aid of either scrubbing-brush or chisel, now so ruthlessly applied.[84]

Inevitably the flood of letters to *The Scotsman* increased the number of visitors who wanted to see all that was left of the beauties of the Chapel before they were 'scraped into nothingness', as most of the correspondents asserted. One of them, however, another unnamed writer who was keen on classical references, 'went out to mourn, like another Caius Marius, amid the ruins,'[85] but returned 'a convertite' and convinced that what was there done was necessary work performed by faithful and loving hands.[86] This writer has left a very interesting description of the restoration team:

> From the suddenness and loudness of the outcry as to destruction, I expected to see in the Chapel a score or two workmen scrubbing, chiselling, pumice-stoning, &c.; but I found only a slow and gentle work of restoration, which has been going on quietly, and more or less continuously, for a number of years, in the same quiet and careful style. Two workmen only are employed.[87]

Their names were Lawrence Baxter and J. Lawrence Tweedie,[88] both captured by an anonymous photographer during the restoration work in the Lady Chapel [fig.105]. According to the 'convertite' correspondent, they washed away with care the lime

105. Photographer unknown, *Sculptor Lawrence Baxter and J. Lawrence Tweedie in the Lady Chapel during the 1860s restoration work*. Contemporary photograph from original albumen print, RCAHMS.

and whitewash that deeply encrusted many parts of the structure. At the same time every bit of original carving was minutely examined; and where it was in tolerable preservation it was left untouched; where the stone was rotten, a mould was carefully taken of it in stucco; and a fresh stone, selected from the original quarry, of precisely the same shade, was carved to the model and substituted. The decayed stone was then cut out and the new one slipped into its place.

In June 1861 a long article entitled 'The Restorations at Roslin' appeared in *The Scotsman*, and a few days later was republished in *The Times*. It contained a good deal of correspondence between the Secretary of The Architectural Institute of Scotland and the Earl of Rosslyn. Members of the Institute had asked the secretary to write to Lord Rosslyn to protest against the work of restoration. One of the resolutions announced in the secretary's letters was to the effect that 'nothing in the shape of restoration, except what is expressly called for to prevent the building falling into decay, can be acceptable to those interested its preservation'[89] and another states:

> That they consider the cutting away of the brackets under the niches
> in the piers of the east wall, with those in the jambs of the windows

125

adjoining, and the substituting of copies in their place; the re-carving of the string course under the windows, with portions of the carving on the Prentice Pillar, the renewing of... the east wall, and the rebuilding and finishing of the altars as new executed, with the scraping and cleaning of the east range of pillars, as not only unnecessary but highly mischievous in principle, tending to throw doubts on the authenticity of the whole of that portion of the Chapel and thereby entirely destroying its value architecturally and pictorially.[90]

As a consequence of these views, the Institute suggested that Lord Rosslyn should desist from carrying on with any further restoration. Lord Rosslyn's reply given below was, in effect a refusal to comply with the request of the Institute. He wrote:

> I regret to find that the Fellows of the Architectural Institute have adopted views entirely at variance with those which I entertain on this subject, and on which I have acted. I must premise that I have neither made nor intended to make any alterations on the original 'structure', and that no sculptured stone has been or will be removed, except to be replaced with an exact *fac simile* from what I believe to have been the original quarry. I cannot admit that an anxiety to preserve pictorial effect is a valid reason against the restoration of architectural ornament to its original purity and design, nor against the removal of dirt and incrustations which conceal the sculpture or obliterate the beauty of the original workmanship. It has cost no little anxious labour, and no slight artistic skill to trace out and restore in their perfect entirety the original forms of many of the architectural ornaments, of which the Fellows of the Architectural Institute consider the restoration to have been 'unnecessary and mischievous'. Had these restorations not been made, the lapse of a few years would have made their decay so complete that it would have been impossible to trace out the original design, and a knowledge of the details of the ornamentation of the Chapel could only have been acquired by posterity by a reference to drawings of doubtful accuracy, or to the meagre accounts of it which have from time to time been published. I apprehend that the question at issue between myself and the Fellows of the Architectural Institute is – Shall Roslin Chapel be a ruin, or shall it be preserved as a sacred edifice from the natural decay of ages?[91]

Lord Rosslyn knew that the criticism had to be stopped, and in order to take the wind out of the sails of his opponents, he concluded his letter robustly: 'I consider myself as a trustee for my family and posterity, and as such I should not be justified in allowing this chapel, with all its beautiful architectural and decorative ornaments, to become a ruin either internally or externally.'[92]

With this powerful statement Lord Rosslyn revealed himself as a strong supporter of careful restoration. His opposition to the views of the Fellows of the Architectural Institute of Scotland was clear, and his views on the methodology of *fac simile* replacement was to provoke long and heated debate.

As we can imagine, the first reader to react against 'the old made young' was Randolph: 'If Lord Rosslyn was the happy master of the Venus of Melos which glorifies

106. James Valentine, *View of the lintels in the south aisle.* Albumen print glued on paper, c.1870. Private Collection.

that long gallery in the Louvre, would he set about restoring her arms? and where would he get their *fac similes* in our days?'[93] A supportive and intelligent reply to his questions appeared few days later:

> No one was ever so foolhardy as to suggest that the fine example of antique sculpture we have in the Venus of Melos should be provided with arms, and have the hair and drapery rechiselled by some second-rate sculptor, so that the statue might be complete, and the weather staining of the marble removed. Any one doing so would be held up to derision; neither would any one possessing a valuable specimen of a Titian or a Rubens ever think of placing it in the hands of a restorer with directions to clean away not only its leathery coatings of varnish, but all those mystic glazings of the artist which constituted the charm and beauty of the work, that they might see the colours in all their rawness and crudity. So do we now ask that Roslin Chapel should not be interfered with further than is absolutely unavoidable. Give us what is left of it entire and genuine.[94]

A reply to Lord Rosslyn from someone calling himself 'An Old Chip' was published 22 June 1861. This correspondent claimed to be well informed with regard to the work on the Chapel and to be in a position to refute 'his Lordship' point by point:

127

…with all the care that was taken then to not injure the original character of the building, there was work done to a certain extent unnecessary . . . All arguments, therefore, in defence of the 'restorations' now going on, based on the assumption that the place was going to ruin in consequence of exposure to damp, fall to the ground, and are valueless, as, with the exception of the broken portion of the shafts of two of the east pillars, there was nothing in the Chapel that could truly be said to require repair on the score of stability; and we can safely say that, in regard to decay, we do not know one whit of difference on any portion of the building for thirty years past.[95]

What this writer strongly believed was that most of the decay took place in the first century of the existence of the Chapel, and that the coating of moss formed upon the stone was a complete protection from atmospheric effects. In his opinion – not a particularly scientific one – it was only where it did not retain that coating that it was possible to find the disintegrating stone.

For although the stone is very soft when taken from the quarry, it becomes, as all other freestone does more or less, harder and more indurated by exposure to weather, to which nature adds by imperceptible degrees such a dense coating of moss, as ultimately forms a complete protection from the effects of the atmosphere, altogether different from anything having a tendency to waste the surface; and it is only where it does not retain that coating that you find the stone disintegrating and giving way, in which cases the stone appears in all its original raw and crude colour, in strong contrast with that around it.[96]

As to the propriety of the alterations in the cause of preservation, he quotes a letter from a gentleman – whose name is not given – with long experience of the nature of the stone and according to whom 'when the stone is of a deep purple it is apt to crumble into powder. As time and the exposure to the air causes the change in its appearance, the cause of the crumbling away also seems to be eradicated, and the stone becomes harder, or rather I should say, though the term may sound peculiar, *together*. Any re-exposure, therefore, of a new surface may be attended with some little risk, and I therefore should say *let well alone*. Nothing can be more beautiful than Roslin Chapel as it is.'[97]

Lord Rosslyn, in his reply to the Fellows of the Institute, disclaimed any intention to alter the original structure, but at the same time he virtually acknowledged what he had before denied when he farther stated and emphasised that no sculptured stone had or would be removed except to be replaced by a *fac simile*. He probably meant not the recreation of a lifeless copy, but the creation of a living work of art, based on a deep understanding and respect for the style and techniques of the medieval builders. He said however: 'I am doing what I conceive to be best calculated to preserve for posterity the full enjoyment of the contemplation of this unrivalled specimen of the architecture of the age to which it belongs… It is only by acting in the same way that we shall ever have an art of our own.'[98] By this he implied that any legitimate additions must be carried out in the spirit of the medieval craftsmen.

'Old Chip', however, did not give up entirely; and instead returned to the question as to how far such work was actually required for the preservation of the structure.

We are aware from an intimate knowledge of that particular part of the Chapel that most of the brackets and canopies that have been cut away were much broken, but not wasted; those brackets on the pillars between the windows in particular were as sharp and well defined in what remained of them as the day they were put up. Neither was there any difficulty in forming a conception of those parts that were wanting, sufficient being left to indicate what the original had been; the stone they were cut in was also of a fine quality, as is proved by all of the same colour throughout the chapel; it is the white, slightly tinged with red, and much superior in texture and enduring qualities to either the yellow or red, which are the colours that show most tendency to decay. It is said perfect *fac similes* of these have been substituted in place of the original, and we have no doubt such was the intention of his Lordship; but, as we also know practically, that while an experienced mason can give a *fac simile* of a moulding, and even to a certain extent of a piece of sculptured foliage, that it is preposterous to talk of him making a *fac simile* of the 'figure' by the eye alone, even although aided by plaster casts. If such was the case, what need would the sculptor have for all those costly and delicate appliances he uses to secure a faithful reproduction of his model? and [sic] are we to understand that the workman engaged in these 'restorations' was of such superior abilities that he could dispense with them? If so, his work would give evidence of it. Unfortunately we have not the originals to compare it with, but if any one will place himself in the centre of the chancel, and compare the new work with the angels and other figures over the caps of the pillars, he will find that while all of the latter have a distinct character and expression, those restored are entirely devoid of either – in fact, they are the merest inanities; and the stone they are cut in being of the yellow-coloured variety, is so soft and friable in its nature that any one conversant in these matters would with one glance feel satisfied of its unsuitability for the purpose, and that it was ill [sic] calculated for endurance.[99]

According to 'Old Chip', the Architectural Institute of Scotland did not insist on the preservation of the pictorial effect of the Chapel and gave Lord Rosslyn full credit for the restoration he had made; but they remonstrated when restorations took the form of cleaning away the time-staining accumulated in the course of centuries over moulded and carved work, and which neither concealed the character of the design nor obliterated the beauty of the workmanship, but enhanced the value of both by its softening influence. They certainly were opposed to the use of acids, the action of which tended to disintegrate the particles of the stone and hasten its decay; and they disproved of the re-chiselling which had diminished the size of the parts and destroyed the original proportions. In the end it was not only the loss of pictorial effect that they deplored, but the mischievous and dangerous principle involved which, if acted upon repeatedly, and continued through several generations, would ultimately leave nothing to clean, since the mouldings and enrichments would have totally disappeared, destroying the identity of the building.

Then again, it is quite clear that the questions at issue between his Lordship and the Institute, was not whether Roslin Chapel should be preserved against natural decay or remain a ruin, as they gave their unqualified approval to the necessary repairs. But what they objected to, and what every one objects to that has one spark of taste about him, is in the futile attempt to make Roslin Chapel look a new fabric, as has been doing of late; neither they nor we wish to see 'old friends with new faces' – it is not pleasant in any case, far less so in this; and when to aid in the attempt, they execute about one third of the cusped points on the arches with cement in place of stone (a fact by-the-by which his lordship keeps very carefully out of sight), it is simply ridiculous, and had his Lordship taken the trouble to have inquired into the matter he would have found there were many ways open to him for preserving the wasted stones without cutting them away.[100]

'Old Chip' suggested a close examination of the restoration work done by Sir George Gilbert Scott for Westminster Abbey,[101] where – according to his interpretation of Scott's renovations – instead of touching the stones with a chisel and mallet, they used a simple pair of bellows to remove the dirt, and did not even apply the preserving wash of silicate with a brush for fear of disturbing the particles of the stone, but had it applied with a syringe, and that the stone which formerly crumbled with the slightest touch became so hard it could not be abraded with a hard tool afterwards. In his words: 'a very different system surely from that pursued at Roslin, where the stone was scraped to the raw the one day, and then washed over with a dirty stain, procured by scraping off the green moss and diluting it in the water, the next.'[102]

As already stated, 'Old Chip's' views on restoration are clear, which is more than can be said of his prose. His long and detailed reply to Lord Rosslyn concludes the 'antique replicas' controversy. Here the last outcry *in extenso*:

> As his Lordship acknowledges himself acting as a trustee for his family and posterity, it might be worth his while, and perhaps repay his trouble, if he would take a careful look at what he has been expending his money upon, and without prejudice compare that portion with any similar portion of what remains untouched, which he may easily do by one glance from the chancel westwards. I will venture to say that if he does so in a fair and candid spirit he will be compelled to acknowledge that he has, with the single exception of where the repairs were actually necessary, been throwing his money to the dogs, and that much that is done would have been better left undone, and it may possibly occur to him that posterity will only associate his name with the destruction of much that was beautiful, and their enjoyment of what is left be marred [sic] by the knowledge that the ornamental portions of the Chapel have been so much tampered with; while the Fellows of the Architectural Institute will have the consolation to know that they have done their duty in trying to arrest this wholesale desecration.[103]

These arguments were no different from what David Roberts had said eighteen years previously in a way that was, however, less overstated and extreme. These words of 'Old Chip', 'Randolph', 'Hair Pencil' and many others, touch the core of all the subsequent objections to Burn and Bryce's restoration method: the old cannot be replaced by a copy, for with the destruction of a building a life is lost and the ousted spirit does not return to the copy – 'Man and womankind divides as usual on the motion, into ayes and noes. Those agreeing… that a primrose is more than yellow, that there is a sacredness in age, a beauty in natural decay, say to this motion, *No*. Those who agree with Lord Rosslyn… and think that the lost can be 'restored' and the old made young, and that a cast and a copy is as good as the first thoughts and first handiwork of genius, and that iron poured into a mould has not less meaning and virtue than when wrought by the cunning and the heart of a Hal o' the Wynd, &c. &c., say, boldly and authoritatively, *Aye*.'[104]

Today, at a distance of more than one hundred and forty years, the issues which are brought to prominence in this controversy still lie at the heart of conservation procedures. An architectural historian has to chose between the Chapel that is dry and structurally sound yet bearing all too clearly the evidence of later interventions, and one in which its decorative elements are decayed and crumbling. Modern practice would not approve of the use of muriatic acid to clear organic growth, since the acid itself attacks, in time, the cellular structure of the stones. By the same token, too much Victorian re-carving deadened the surface and diminished the authenticity of much sculptural relief; yet Rosslyn as it has come down to us today remains a speaking moment of the age that gave it birth, and without the confidence and self assurance of Burn and Bryce, it may be questioned whether this would otherwise have been the case.

5

CONCLUSIONS

The desire to break records at Rosslyn is supreme and
nowhere so uncontrolled.

> Ian C. Hannay, *Story of Scotland in Stone*, 1934.

5.1. The Visual Interpretation.

THE history of the restoration controversies at Rosslyn provides a good example of the
changes in nineteenth-century attitudes towards historic buildings. The structure of the
Chapel assumed both its external appearance and internal configuration as the result
of intense efforts by intelligent patrons and architects. As a consequence the structure
still can exercise its charm, expressing in an unforgettable way the pliability of later
Gothic forms. The Chapel, as it stands, proudly proclaims its status as a unique and
extraordinary building, above all in the Lady Chapel where the sculptural adornment

107. George Washington Wilson, *View of the Lady Chapel's ceiling*. Albumen print, c.1870. Private Collection.

108. Samuel Bough, *Midnight Mass at Rosslyn Chapel*. Watercolour over pencil,
heightened with white, 1862. Rosslyn Family Collection.

parades heraldic shields, huge projecting corbels formed by great pendants sloping
outwards from the east wall, and suspended pendants which adorn the keystones of
the quadripartite bays. The effort and expense devoted to such iconographical display
is without parallel in any other contemporary Scottish building.

It would be easy simply to ascribe the Chapel's fame and popularity to its richness
and visual impact. It cannot be denied that the prodigal elaboration of the carvings
is a very important factor, and there are many paintings, photographs and articles to
support this. However, there are other reasons for the Chapel's widespread appeal and
important position as a Scottish cultural icon.

Rosslyn Chapel attracts general and popular attention as a late medieval religious
edifice. In the eighteenth and nineteenth centuries it became a standard entry in the
antiquarian and archaeological accounts of Scotland and of Britain. It became so famous
that Billings, in his description of the Chapel, remarked: 'to describe minutely so
well known a building would be superfluous'.[1] The Chapel's late medieval origins
also appealed to the imagination, especially given the founding family's links to the
Knights Templar and Christian mystics engaged in their search for true knowledge and
enlightenment. The evocation of a noble, medieval Scotland appealed to the Romantic
notions of nineteenth-century writers: it was seen as an unfinished masterpiece by a
Knight of the Realm. Along with the actual history of the estate, the myths linked to
Rosslyn Chapel are equally captivating to any imaginative visitor: the macabre murder
of the apprentice who proved to be more skilled than the master mason; and the
legend, revived by Scott, that before the death of any member of the St Clair family
the Chapel seemed to be on fire. Its appeal is obviously far-reaching, is such that this
small exquisite building has become rooted in the cultural psyche of Scotland.

From the beginning of the twentieth century the artists who depicted the Chapel
started to experiment far more imaginatively with architectural ideas. Detailed plans
and elevations of how this 'pocket cathedral' might have looked, if ever completed,
were prepared by the Scottish architect and architectural historian Thomas Ross (1839-

109. Thomas Ross, *Aerial perspective view of Rosslyn Chapel from south-east as it might have been when completed*. Watercolour, 1914. National Library of Scotland, Edinburgh.

1930). He made a most charming perspective sketch of the finished nave and crossing with a fine centre tower and spire [fig.109]. In perfect keeping with the existing parts of the building, his Rosslyn Chapel in its supposed finished state became one of the major themes discussed in a paper read at Rosslyn in 1914.[2] In his paper Ross loses nothing in comparison with Sir Walter Scott when he uses terms like 'poem of stone', when he describes the vault of the chapel as 'powdered with stars' in a new *Paradise Lost*, or most of all when he concentrates himself on 'a fantastic fairy dream as no mortal ever dared to dream before'.[3]

The 'pocket proportions' of Rosslyn Chapel, its setting and its phantasmagorical light effects, as well as the eerie tales associated with it, have captured the imagination of poets, writers, amateurs and authoritative critics in the world of art and architecture. The analysis of the visual evidence amplifies our knowledge not only of the Chapel but also of the cultural tastes existing at different times and at different moments in English and Scottish society. Certainly the Chapel as seen and depicted by Captain John Slezer towards the end of the seventeenth century has a very different meaning from the building recorded by Joseph Michael Gandy in 1806 or the stereoscopic views of Thomas Vernon Begbie. Rich in artistic fantasy and legend, Rosslyn Chapel

110. Albany Ewbank, *Interior view from the Choir, looking east*. Etching, 1923. Private
collection.

was the perfect subject for exposure as a Diorama. In such a critical analysis of its history Rosslyn Chapel becomes a changing cultural icon for successive generations of architects, architectural critics and amateurs and a touchstone for essential value-judgements, made both in European and in national, Scottish terms.

It is also important to remember that certain images of Rosslyn have come to serve as more than architectural records. They have assumed iconic status, standing for something more significant than the marking of an individual interpretation. Suffice it to say that the fame of Rosslyn became crucial in the world of early photography, when the architectural nature of the building began to function as a type of merchandise. Like an 'industrial icon', images of the Chapel were often mass-produced and sold everywhere. There was an urge to create an accurate image which almost by accident has acquired today a quite different value as a unique historical document. Good examples are George Washington Wilson's photographs, in which the ceiling of the Lady Chapel is unveiled before the eyes, launching the viewer towards architectural settings far beyond ordinary horizons [fig.107]. The camera gave life to images that were totally transformed in their dimensions, their perspective, and above all in their luminosity. A new representation determined by a particular condition of perception can be seen in Roger Fenton's schematic view of the south porch [fig.45]. Here the gaze of the photographer, enhancing the powers of both vision and invention, was to become more penetrating and offered the mind of the 'artist' an opportunity to create a new universe. Few images in the history of photography have achieved this status.

David Roberts merits a special place in the history of representations of Rosslyn Chapel and its creation as a national Icon. The artist provided many dramatic, highly evocative views that convey his intimate knowledge of the Chapel, unadorned by meaningless or banal elements. In his works foregrounds are prominent, light effects permit a deep exploration of space, and perspectives become complex, revealing previously unknown aspects of the building. Rosslyn is depicted by Roberts from more then one side and both in internal and external views [fig.79, 81-84]. Such perspectives, in which the architectural features have often been devastated by time and events, are animated by figures who stand in contemplation of the structure, communicating its beauty and its fascination, conscious of their role as witnesses to a great historical patrimony. With this artistic premise in his mind, Roberts stands as forerunner of the anti-restoration movement, criticising the restoration architects for their destruction of the historical authenticity of the Chapel. He is the principal protagonist in the restoration controversy and his piercing eye and biting pen detect and denounce the futility of any attempt to restore such a unique creation. In this manner, Roberts brought Rosslyn with its context, atmosphere and history, to the forefront of Scottish national consciousness, not only for people interested in the qualities and values of great architecture, but also for the general public.

The evolution of the iconography of Rosslyn Chapel, as for any other building that has been prized for so long a time, serves to show not only how the notions of artistic representation have been transformed over more than a century, but also how the understanding of architecture itself has undergone, in successive periods, fundamental change. The image of a place belongs to a culture, and it impresses itself on the artistic memory of people. It is possible from these sources to acquire fully reliable and authentic testimony about it. Yet culture, as we know, creates and preserves several versions of the architectural image of the building at the same time, and these are not always compatible

111. *Giovanni Franchi's Cast of the Apprentice Pillar (1871) at the V & A.* Author's photograph.

one with the other. It is in their interaction that the authentic experience reveals itself. This work on Rosslyn it is not a dead sum of mechanically accumulated facts; it is a living unity. Every image influences all the preceding ones, changes their tone and value, opening new aspects in them, and finding, I trust, new echoes.

What then of the icon itself – the three dimensional reality of solid mass and ornate columns that stands even today in the heart of Midlothian? Every image, however brilliant and evocative, is no more than a two-dimensional record of a building whose actual reality and impact far exceeds any picture or photograph that can be made of it. In 1870 the authorities of South Kensington Museum took steps to secure a replica of part of the interior of the Chapel for inclusion in the North European Cast Court. Lord Rosslyn was approached and gave permission for workmen from the well-known firm of Giovanni Franchi to visit the Chapel in spring 1871.[4] In two weeks of work (stopping on Saturday and Sunday) they had taken sufficient casts for the Apprentice Pillar, together with the arches which butt up against the two windows and the vaults in the south-east corner of the Lady Chapel, to be reassembled at full size in London [fig.111]. This transposition of a portion of the building to the British metropolis must represent the true apotheosis of Rosslyn as an icon of national identity. It stands as testament to the labours of those artists, architects and historians who sought earnestly and enthusiastically to illustrate its quality and charm.

NOTES

1. ROSSLYN CHAPEL
1.1 History and Description

1. In preparing this work, it became apparent that during the eighteenth and nineteenth centuries there was little consistency in the spelling of the name Rosslyn, which has been retained by the Earl of Rosslyn. Artists, amongst whom David Roberts is a notable example, variously inscribed different works with different spellings, and these varied again in correspondence. In the following chapters, I have opted for consistency and used the ancient spelling of Rosslyn, except in quoted material or where the village of Roslin is being discussed.

2. For a full analysis of the collegiate churches of Scotland see Richard Fawcett, *The Architectural History of Scotland. Scottish Architecture from the Accession of the Stewarts to the Reformation 1371-1560*, Edinburgh 1994, chapter five entitled 'Rural and Academic Collegiate Churches'. See also George Hay, 'The Architecture of Scottish Collegiate Churches', in Geoffrey W. S. Barrow (ed.), *The Scottish Tradition: Essays in Honour of Ronald Gordon Cant*, Edinburgh 1974, pp.56-70.

3. Among these were the collegiate churches at Crichton, Biggar, Seton, Dunglass, Yester, Dalkeith, and Trinity Church in Edinburgh. For a detailed analysis of collegiate churches built to cruciform or 'T'-shaped plans, see Fawcett, op.cit., pp.166-181.

4. Another interpretation of the word Rosslyn is given by J. Brydone, in *Brydone's Guide to Roslin, Hawthornden &c., by the North British and Peebles Railways*, Edinburgh, 1858, p.16: 'The name was anciently Rosslyn, or Roslyn, and this orthography is still retained by the noble possessors of the property. It is said to signify a *rocky eminence* and a *waterfall* and the natural appearances of the locality favour this derivation. That proportion of the Esk, indeed, which runs over a rocky and sloping channel in the immediate vicinity is still designated *The Lynn*'.

5. A considerable historical literature exists for Rosslyn Castle and Chapel. Key works are: *Historical and Descriptive Account of Rosslyn Chapel and Castle with Engravings*, Edinburgh 1827; Thomas Smyth Muir, *Descriptive notices of some of the ancient parochial and collegiate churches of Scotland*, Edinburgh, 1848; Francis H. Groome, *Ordnance Gazetteer of Scotland: A Survey of Scottish Topography, Statistical, Biographical and Historical*, vol.VI, Edinburgh 1885; James Grant, *Old and New Edinburgh*, London 1882. Where not otherwise noted, information cited in the text is taken from these sources.

6. Richard Augustine Hay, *Genealogie of the Sainteclaires of Rosslyn, Including the chartulary of Rosslyn*, Edinburgh 1835, p.27. Hay's father died when he was about five years old, and his mother soon afterwards married James Sinclair of Rosslyn. The voluminous study made by Hay of the Sinclair family charters was completed in 1700, and part of it was published posthumously in 1835 by James Maidment. The edition was limited to a mere 12 (large) volumes. A smaller version was published simultaneously and limited to 108 copies, all of which are exceedingly rare. Hay's manuscripts – the principal source for the history of the Chapel – are kept in the National Library of Scotland (Adv. MS. 34.1.9.i). The charters and other formal documents related to the Rosslyn family are recopied in Adv. MS. 32.6.2., ff.3-82.

7. Barbara E. Crawford, 'Earl William Sinclair and the Building of Roslin Collegiate Church', in John Higgitt (ed.), *Medieval Art and Architecture in the diocese of St. Andrews*, [Tring] British Archaeological Association, 1994, pp.99-107.

8. *The Imperial Gazetteer of Scotland* (published in *c*.1860 without the name of any author or an exact date of publication) also states that Lord Sinclair 'built houses for the workmen to be employed in constructing the chapel, that he gave to each mason ten pounds a year, to each master-mason twenty pounds, to both an extent of land proportionate to the reward of the ability which they displayed, and to other artificers a commensurate extent of compensation and encouragement, and that, in consequence, he attracted all the best architects and sculptors from various parts of Scotland and of neighbouring kingdoms. He endowed it with various lands and revenues, and saw it rising in profuse magnificence of architecture; yet, after vast efforts and great expense, he left it unfinished'. See op.cit., p.664.

9. It was pointed out by Daniel Wilson in *The Archaeology and Prehistoric Annals of Scotland*, Edinburgh 1851, pp.629-30, that 'many of the most remarkable features of Roslin Chapel are derived from the prevailing models of the period (when it was erected), though carried to an exuberant excess. The circular doorway and segmental porch, the dark vaulted roof, and much of the window tracery are all common to the style. Even the singular arrangement of its retro-choir, with a clustered pillar terminating the vista of the central aisle, is nearly a repetition of that of the Cathedral of St. Mungo at Glasgow. Various portions of other edifices will also be found to furnish examples of arrangement and details corresponding with those of Roslin, as in the doorway of the south porch and other features of Linlithgow St. Michael's church, and also in some parts of the beautiful ruined church of St. Bridget, Douglas. It is altogether a mistake to regard the singularly interesting church at Roslin, which even the critic enjoys while he condemns, as an exotic produced by foreign skill. Its counterparts will be more easily found in Scotland than in any other part of Europe'.

10. According to Robert William Billings, in 'Rosslyn Chapel Description', *The Baronial and Ecclesiastical Antiquities of Scotland*, 4 vols., Edinburgh 1845-52, vol.IV, p.3: 'If all the niches which honeycomb the buttresses and pillars had each its statue, the building must have been singularly profuse in sculpture. Some of them are, however, so small and short, that it seems questionable if they can ever have been filled. Slezer's engraving of Rosslyn, more elaborate than most of his representations, depicts a multitude of images; but he is so absolutely deficient in his representation of existing details, that there is no trusting him for the non-existing. In the manuscript... of the zealous Father Hay... there is a minutely finished pen-and-ink view of the edifice as it was, or was supposed to be, before the iconoclasm. It is more minute than Slezer's, and still more abundant in statues; but it is not *so* minute and accurate as to make one believe that it represents statues that really existed. This sketch, by the way, shows the west end topped by a series of crow-steps – a statue on each step. In the same view, a circular window is represented as covering a part of the space at the east end, now covered by a modern restoration'.

11. In connection with the story, and perhaps even its recent origin, it is noteworthy that Slezer calls it 'Prince's pillar', as if named in honour of the founder of the Chapel. See John Slezer, *Theatrum Scotiae*, London 1693, p.63.

12. National Library of Scotland, Edinburgh, Adv.MS.20.3.8, ff.150r-154r, inscribed 'Charta Willielmi Sinclare de Roselin facta Ecclesia Collegiata quisdem, 1523'. This document is a late eighteenth century transcription in George Henry Hutton's hand of a charter from Hay's manuscripts.

13. See Robert Anderson, 'Notice of working drawings scratched on the walls of the crypt at Roslin Chapel', *Proceedings of the Society of Antiquaries of Scotland*, vol.X, 1872-4, pp.63-64.

14. Crawford, op.cit., p. 102.

15. Crawford argues that Lady Elisabeth's interest may be assumed from the quantity of heraldic evidence relating to her family present in the Chapel.

16. Hay, op.cit., p.107. Oliver is also quoted at p.33 of the same book, where no dates of birth and death are given.

17. *Ibid.*, pp.124-127.

18. In 1589 a Sinclair family member had one of his children baptised in the Chapel, to the fury of the protestant established church, as Rosslyn was not part of a parish; the minister who had officiated was made to beg forgiveness in public for his action. See W. McMillan, *The Worship*

of the Reformed Church of Scotland 1550-1638, London 1931, pp.254-255.

19. James Kirk (ed.), *The Records of the Synod of Lothian and Tweeddale, 1589-1596, 1640-1649*, Edinburgh 1977, p.31.

20. David Stevenson, *The Origins of Freemasonry: Scotland's Century 1590-1710*, Aberdeen 1998, p.55.

21. Letter from James Alexander Sinclair Erskine to William Burn dated 1836 (National Archives of Scotland, document GD 164/1013).

22. See Andrew Kerr, 'The Collegiate Church or Chapel of Rosslyn, its Builders, Architect, and Construction', *Proceedings of the Society of Antiquaries of Scotland*, vol.XII, 1878, pp.218-244. In the same volume of the *Proceedings* Kerr published another essay entitled 'Rosslyn Castle, its Buildings Past and Present', pp.412-424.

23. Lorimer's letter is addressed to George Prentice and dated 23 September 1913 (National Archives of Scotland, document GD 164/1022/2).

24. See Angelo Maggi and Helen Rosslyn, *Rosslyn, Country of Painter and Poet*, exhib. cat. National Gallery of Scotland April-July 2002, Edinburgh 2002, p.21.

25. For a valuable account of the founder's background see Barbara Crawford, 'William Sinclair, Earl of Orkney, and his family: a study in the politics of survival', in K.J. Stringer (ed.), *Essays on the Nobility of Medieval Scotland*, Edinburgh 1985, pp.234-53.

26. The romantic interpretations attaching to Rosslyn, particularly relating to the Holy Grail, the Knights Templar, and Masonic rites, have given rise to a large body of speculative literature. For this see: Andrew Sinclair, *The Sword and the Grail*, London 1994; Tim Wallace-Murphy, *The Templar Legacy and the Masonic Inheritance within Rosslyn Chapel*, Roslin 1995; Christopher Knight and Robert Lomas, *The Hiram Key: Pharaohs, Freemasons and the Discovery of the Secret Scrolls of Jesus*, London 1996; Tim Wallace-Murphy and Marilyn Hopkins, *Rosslyn: Guardian of the Secrets of the Holy Grail*, Shaftesbury 1999. The exaggerated nature of these analyses may be characterised by Dan Brown's desire to embody the mystery and legend of the Chapel in the 17-million bestselling thriller *The Da Vinci Code* (2004).

2. INSPIRED BY LIGHT

2.1. Gandy's Visions

1. See John Summerson, 'Gandy and The Tomb of Merlin', *The Architectural Review*, vol. LXXXIX, no.532, April 1941, pp.89-90.

2. According to Ludovico Ariosto (1474-1533), Merlin had been imprisoned and killed by the Witch of the Lake, who had stolen his magic powers. Merlin's body and spirit, the latter being still alive, were kept inside 'un'arca di pietra dura,\ lucida e tersa, e come fiamma rossa;\ tal ch'alla stanza, ben che di sol priva,\ dava splendore il lume che n'usciva'. See Ludovico Ariosto, *Orlando Furioso* (1516), canto III-XV, Verona, 1963, p.47. Summerson refers to *Orlando Furioso in English heroical verse* by John Harington (London; printed by G.Miller for I.Parker, 1634) when he quotes: 'The very marble was so clear and bright, \ that though the sun no light unto it gave, \ The tomb itself did lighten all the cave'. See also the Exhibition Catalogue, *Joseph Michael Gandy 1771-1843*, London 1982.

3. John Summerson, 'The Vision of J.M.Gandy', *Heavenly Mansions and Other Essays on Architecture*, New York 1963, p.129.

4. Brian Lukacher, *Joseph Michael Gandy: The Poetical Representation and Mythography of Architecture* (Ph.D. University of Delaware, U.M.I. Research Press 1987), p.170. By the same author see also, 'Phantasmagoria and emanations: lighting effects in the architectural fantasies of Joseph Michael Gandy', *AA Files,* vol.4, 1983, pp.40-48.

5. Walter Scott, 'Ballad of Rosabelle', *The Lay of the Last Minstrel: with Life and Notes*, Edinburgh 1805, canto VI, xxiii, p.148.

6. Robert William Billings, 'Rosslyn Chapel Description', *The Baronial and Ecclesiastical Antiquities of Scotland*, vol.IV, Edinburgh 1845-52, pp.2-3.

7. *Ibid.*, p.3.

8. *Ibid.*

9. For a fuller explanation of Gandy's survey of the building, see Angelo Maggi, 'Poetic stones: Roslin Chapel in Gandy's sketchbook and Daguerre's Diorama', *Architectural History*, vol.42, 1999, pp.263-283.

10. *The Gentleman's Magazine*, vol.LXXXVII, part II, September 1817, p.209. Annie Wilson is wonderfully described and depicted by the correspondent of the journal as follows: 'Annie Wilson recites the Latin Epitaphs with apparent facility; but her pronunciation is so harsh and discordant, that for an English ear it is quite unintelligible: – if any thing in the way of interruption comes across her, she commences once more her elegant demonstration, her narrative of the Apprentice's Pillar, with "his head bearing the scar just aboun the brow that his master made upon it, his mother's head represented as if bewailing the death of her son, and the apprentice's maister's head, just before he was hangit," and finishes with her recitation of the Latin Epitaphs'.

11. Dr Antony Todd Thomson (1778-1849), a well-known physician, during his visit to the Chapel in 1823 notes in his journal the same 'divining-rod': 'After Breakfast, we proceeded to the chapel of Roslin, which is now shewn by the landlord of the inn, since the old lady, who for so many years used to repeat the story of its faded glory, had been gathered to her fathers. Mr Wilson, for that is the name of the present shewman, has too much understanding to believe one half of what he is obliged to detail. He uses a staff to point to the carvings and other features of the chapel, and told us that it was a present from Sir Walter Scott, having been the rod of office which the worthy baronet filled when the king visited Edinburgh'. I am indebted to Dr Ian Gregg for giving me permission to quote from Thomson's *Journal of a Vacation in Parts of England and Scotland* (1823) in his possession.

12. National Library of Scotland, Edinburgh, Adv.MS. 29.4.2, f.229. The author of this manuscript clearly states that the words used in the quotation are transcribed from the 'Monthly Retrospect of the Fine Arts, Monthly May–July 1809.' George Shepherd's copy of Gandy's painting is in the Print Room of the Victoria & Albert Museum in London (Press-mark: 3031.76).

13. For the collaboration between Soane and Gandy, see Brian Lukacher, 'John Soane and his Draughtsman Joseph Michael Gandy', *Daidalos*, vol.25, September 1987, pp.51-64.

14. See J.Mordaunt Crook, 'John Britton and The Gothic Revival', in John Summerson (ed.), *Concerning Architecture, Essays on Architectural Writers and Writing presented to Nikolaus Pevsner*, London 1968, pp.98-119. On Gandy's contribution to Britton's works of medieval topography and Rosslyn Chapel see also Brian Luckacher, *Joseph Gandy. An Architectural Visionary in Georgian England*, London 2006, pp.74-75.

15. See John Britton, 'An Essay Towards an History and description of Roslyn Chapel, Scotland' in *The Architectural Antiquities of Great Britain; represented and illustrated in a series of views, elevations, plans, sections and details of various Ancient English Edifices: with Historical and Descriptive accounts of each*, vol.III, London 1812, pp.47-56. For the connections of the Chapel and Scottish Freemasonry, see: Robert Brydon, *Rosslyn. A History of the Guilds, the Masons and the Rosy Cross* Rosslyn Chapel Trust, 1994; Robert Cooper (ed.), *An Account of Roslin Chapel 1778*, Edinburgh 2000.

16. It is also important to note that many of the architectural details represented in the painting are clearly inspired by Gandy's visit to Durham Cathedral.

17. Beyond the plates published by Billings, Gandy's influence can be seen in the designs of John Lessels and E.F.C.Clarke published in *The Transactions of the Architectural Institute of Scotland*, session 1862-63, in which we are presented with a series of architectural details in a portion of the work entitled 'Roslin Chapel, shown in some of its more peculiar characteristics' (RCAHMS: National Monuments Record of Scotland, RIAS Engraving Books 1.12).

18. Britton, op.cit., p.47.

19. Gandy's sketchbook, purchased at Sotheby's, 15 July 1999, is now kept at Sir John Soane's Museum as vol.161.

20. In reference to this, Gandy, in his sketchbook, clarifies the origin of this detail, writing: 'This one [related to the circular finial] remain[s] at North Door', f.20. verso [London, Sir John

Soane's Museum, vol.161].

21. Gandy was not the only architect to distort the original appearance of Rosslyn Chapel and the functionality of all its parts. George Meikle Kemp (1794-1844), the architect of the Scott Monument, made a watercolour view of the Apprentice Pillar seen from the south aisle. This image goes well beyond the architectural truth: a panelled loggia, for which there is, and never has been, any evidence, is inserted in the final part of the Lady Chapel above the entrance to the Crypt. Another architectural fantasist, enthralled by the mediaeval beauties of Rosslyn, is the English painter George Cattermole (1800-1868), who worked for John Britton producing finely worked views of many extant British churches. His oil painting Rosslyn Chapel [see fig.74], provides a new hypothesis, not previously noted in the history of the building, for the existence of some form of screening between the nave and the aisle. The masonry wall on which the artist adds a piscina, taken either from the west wall or from one of the entrances to the Chapel, is part of his fictional depiction.

22. In addition to the evidence of the crease line on the building, a series of engravings published immediately before and after Gandy's views make it clear that the aisles and Lady Chapel were covered in the eighteenth and early nineteenth century by a high pitch roof rising to a peak in the front of the East window of the clerestory. The most important are: the engravings of Sparrow published in Francis Grose's *Antiquities of Scotland*, 2 vols., London 1790; and the lithographs of Thomas Mann Baynes in *Twenty Views of the City Environs of Edinburgh*, London 1823. Edward Blore, in his plates of Rosslyn Chapel for Walter Scott's *Provincial Antiquities and Picturesque Scenery of Scotland* (2 vols., London 1826), shows clearly how the roof covered more than half of the clerestory windows.

23. All of the drawings in the sketchbook were originally made in pencil. Later on Gandy chose the most interesting drawings to trace over in pen. In this way, his first impressions, recorded on site, were filtered through a radical selection process that he later used for his published images.

24. J. Britton, *Architectural Antiquities*, op.cit., p.49.

25. In the same sketch, Gandy provides notes on the colour of the stone which assumes a 'General tone of Colour Bronze Green mixed with, tints filled with Brown and Black': Gandy's Sketchbook (London, Sir John Soane's Museum), f.23 verso.

26. The date when the album was offered for sale is not clear. From the *List of catalogue of English Book sales 1676-1900* (London, 1915), at p.277, it seems that soon after John Britton died his literary and manuscript collections were offered for sale on 4 May 1857 – viz: 'John Britton's, Library. Autograph and other Manuscripts Collection. Priced – 4 May 1857. S. Leigh Sotheby & John Wilkinson – 3 Wellington Street, Strand'. The British Library holds a copy of the sale catalogue in which appears the following description: '263 – Britton J. His collection towards a separate publication on the History and Antiquities of Roslyn Chapel, *prepared for binding*. This interesting collection is accompanied with several original sketches, numerous engravings, and autograph letters from David Roberts, W. Burn, Dr Irving and others'. It should be noted however that at this time the material relating to Rosslyn was in a case folder and not in the present binding.

The history of the sale of Britton's books is complicated however by an entry in the web site *www.bl.uk* which records a different sale which was apparently part of a series of disposals made in 1846 when Britton was 75 years old. Nonetheless the British Library catalogue cited above seems to make it clear that Britton retained the Rosslyn material, as a matter of interest to himself, until his death.

An auctioneer's label of a second sale, stuck inside the front cover of the present album, reads as follows: '854. Roslin Chapel – Interesting Collection of MSS (1806-1846) relating to the History and the Structure of Roslin Chapel comprising extensive Autograph Letters (4) by *David Roberts*, *Joseph Gandy*, folio 2pp. *George M. Kemp* folio 4pp. with a sectional sketch. David Irving (2), William Burn (1), John Dundas and notes probably by John Britton; accompanied by 46 original sketches (a few signed by Gandy) and engravings. Bound in folio volume, calf'.

The album was purchased by Sir Hew Hamilton-Darlymple (1814-1887) whose book plate is also attached inside the front cover and carries a number written in pencil, 976. This may refer to the second sale or was perhaps a number relating to Darlymple's library. Later the album was acquired by Canon George Heb[b] Taylor, who was Chaplain at Rosslyn until 1963. Taylor, who had a tremendous interest in the building, is remembered for bringing together a very active congregation at Rosslyn. Mrs Joan B. Taylor recently found the volume in her father-in-law's collection. The essential facts relating to the history and contents of the album are given in Angelo Maggi, 'Documents Relating to Roslin Chapel: a recently discovered collection of papers by John Britton', Architectural Heritage, vol.XIII, 2002, pp.73-98.

27. There is no written evidence in the volume of Britton being the owner of this collection, but we can easily assume, since he was the recipient of most or indeed all of the letters, that it was he or someone on his behalf who collated the material.

28. Ian Goodall and Margaret Richardson, 'A Recently Discovered Gandy Sketchbook', Architectural History, Journal of the Society of Architectural Historians, vol.44, 2001, p.55.

29. 'Documents Relating to Roslin Chapel', letter to John Britton from Joseph Michael Gandy, dated 17 December 1806, f.2. The inscription on the architrave running above the stairs to the crypt is in Lombardic letters. It reads: 'Forte est vinu[m]. Fortior est rex. Fortiores sunt mulieres: sup[er] om[nia] vincit veritas', meaning 'Wine is strong. The king is stronger. Women are stronger still: but truth conquers all'. It is important to note that the quotation is taken from the Latin Bible, or 'Vulgate', which was translated by Eusebius Hieronymus (b.345 AD) from the Hebrew Old Testament and the Greek New Testament. The full translation became the standard version of the Bible used in the Roman Catholic Churches for over one and a half millennia. The Vulgate includes several non-canonical books like 3 Esdras, which inspired the authors of this Latin inscription. The full and original version from the Vulgate reads as follows: 'unus scriptis: fortius est vinum. alius scripsit: fortior est rex. tertius autem scripsit: fortiores sunt mulieres, super omnia autem vincit veritas' (3 Esdras 3: 10-12).

30. Collection Frits Lugt, Fondation Custodia, Paris 1998 A 666 I. The letter is not dated, but we can assume that it was written soon after the publication of the third volume of the Architectural Antiquities in 1812.

31. Ibid.

32. Ibid.

2.2. The Daguerre Diorama

33. Britton, op.cit., p.52.

34. See Angelo Maggi, 'Daguerre e le suggestioni della Rosslyn Chapel', Fotostorica. Gli Archivi della Fotografia, no.3/4, April 1999, pp.32-35.

35. For a discussion of how a Diorama worked, see R. Derek Wood, 'The Diorama in Great Britain in the 1820s', History of Photography, vol.17, no.3, Autumn 1993, pp.284-295.

36. See Wolfgang Schivelbusch, Disenchanted Night: the Industrialisation of Light in the Nineteenth Century, Oxford 1988, p.216.

37. On the Diorama techniques see: G.Bapts, Essai sur l'histoire des Panoramas et des Dioramas, Paris 1891; A.T.Gill, 'The London Diorama', History of Photography, vol.I, January 1977, pp.31-33; Richard Daniel Altick, The Shows of London, Cambridge Mass. and London 1978, chap.IX; Bernard Comment, The Panorama, London 1999, chap.IV.

38. Helmut and Alison Gernsheim, L.J.M.Daguerre, The History of the Diorama and the Daguerreotype, London 1956, pp.176,178.

39. Le Corsaire, 25. Septembre 1824, quoted in Georges Potonniée, Daguerre Peintre et Décorateur, Paris 1935 (reprint 1989), p.82.

40. Blackwood's Edinburgh Magazine, vol. XIX, no.CXI, April 1826, p.467.

41. 'View of Roslyn Chapel, at the Diorama', in The Mirror of Literature, Amusement and Instruction, no.CLXXXV, Saturday 4 March 1826, p.132.

42. Ibid.

43. See Renzo Dubbini, Geografie dello Sguardo, Visione e paesaggio in età moderna, Torino 1994, p.104.

44. From: 'The Diorama' in *The Times*, Tuesday 21 February 1826, p.4.

45. The advertisements for the *Interior of Roslin Chapel* at the Diorama in Lothian Road were placed regularly in the *Caledonian Mercury* between 18 April 1835 and 24 October 1835, when it is recorded that 'the view of the Interior of Roslin Chapel will positively close on Saturday the 31st October instantly'.

46. *Caledonian Mercury*, 12 February 1825, p.3.

47. R. Derek Wood, op.cit., p.293.

48. Robert Forbes, 'An Account of the Chapel of Roslin & c. Most respectfully inscribed to William St Clare of Roslin, Esq. Representative of the Princely Founder and Endower...', *The Edinburgh Magazine*, vol.5, January 1761, pp.2-53. Bell's *Perspective View of the Chapel* is a geometrically correct perspective construction of the building in the taste of the architectural treatises of the time. The way of designing on a plane surface the representations of the vault and the flooring suggests use of a grid as an aid to the composition. This severe application of the principles of perspective projection of shadows and reflections makes the Chapel appear higher than its real dimension. Antiquarians like George Paton (1721-1807) and Richard Gough (1735-1809) collected several copies of this engraving as soon as it was published.

49. The announcement of Delacour's appointment and the establishment of the School of Design is given in the *Edinburgh Evening Courant* for July 12 and 14, 1760: 'The commissioners and trustees for improving Fisheries and Manufactures in Scotland do hereby advertise that by an agreement with Mr De la Cour, painter, he has opened a school in this city for persons of both sexes that shall be presented to him by the trustees, whom he is to teach gratis the Art of Drawing for the use of manufactures... Mr De la Cour is likewise to teach the art of drawing to all persons that choose to attend his school at one guinea per quarter'. Quoted in D.F. Fraser-Harris, 'William De la Cour, Painter, Engraver and Teacher of Drawing' in *The Scottish Bookman*, vol.I, no.5, January 1936, pp.15-16.

50. Julian Halsby, *Scottish Watercolours 1740-1940*, London 1989, p.24.

51. Helmut and Alison Gernsheim, *The History of Photography; from the Camera to the Beginning of the Modern Era*, London 1969, p.66.

52. The title is *Two Views: Ruins of Holyrood Chapel, A Moonlight Scene painted by M. Daguerre and the Cathedral of Chartres by M. Bouton in the Diorama of London, Regents Park*, G. Shulze, London 1825, p.4 (London: British Library 1359.d.6). Regarding the oil painting by Daguerre, *Ruins of Holyrood Chapel by Moonlight* in the Walker Art Gallery of Liverpool, see *A Guide of Pictures in the Walker Art Gallery Liverpool*, Liverpool 1980, pp.50-51; see also Stephen Bann, *The Clothing of Clio. A study of the Representation of History in Nineteenth Century Britain and France*, Cambridge Mass. 1984, p.56.

53. These are the words that Gernshiem uses to describe Daguerre's oil painting of the Holyrood Diorama, in Helmut and Alison Gernsheim, *L.J.M. Daguerre, op.cit.*, p.25.

54. The architect Edward Blore (1787-1879) in his plate of the *Interior of Rosslyn Chapel* for Sir Walter Scott's *Provincial Antiquities and Picturesque Scenery of Scotland* adopted the same point of view. As in Daguerre the view of the interior is drawn in a way that alters the height of the Chapel. This lack of proportion is actually caused by the inclusion of a few visitors, who were drawn to a false perspective scale. It is interesting to note that Blore's plate was published in June 1826, soon after the Diorama was presented in London.

55. David Patterson and Joe Rock, *Thomas Begbie's Edinburgh: A Mid-Victorian Portrait*, Edinburgh 1992, p.15. The complete collection of the original glass plates by Begbie is kept in City Art Centre of Edinburgh.

2.3 Captured Lights of Early Photography

56. The near contemporary article is quoted by John Hannavy in *The Victorian Professional Photographer*, Aylesbury 1980, p.8.

57. According to Stevenson: 'The legal process of taking out a patent was lengthy and expensive,

and although Scotland was officially joined to England by the Act of Union of 1707, it still had a separate legal system, which would require Talbot to pay twice for protection. Since Scotland was a smaller and poorer country than England, it was less likely to repay the cost. In practice, Scottish photography benefited from this useful fact, not simply in terms of commercial profit but because the Scots were free to experiment with a number of processes and inventions patented in England, which included the Daguerreotype'. Sara Stevenson, *The Personal Art of David Octavius Hill*, New Haven and London 2002, p.166.

58. See Sara Stevenson, *David Octavius Hill and Robert Adamson*, *Catalogue of their calotypes taken between 1843 and 1847 in the collection of the Scottish National Portrait Gallery*, Edinburgh 1981, pp.210-211. All the calotypes of Rosslyn Chapel are kept in the Scottish National Portrait Gallery, see 'Landscapes calotypes no.15-25, 96'.

59. *Ibid*. Among recent studies, see Sara Stevenson, *Facing the Light. The Photography of Hill & Adamson*, exhib. cat. Scottish National Portrait Gallery May–September 2002, Edinburgh 2002.

60. Richard Pare (ed.), *Photography and Architecture (1839-1939)*, Centre Canadien D'Architecture/Canadian Centre for Architecture, Montreal 1982, p.14.

61. See John Hannavy, *Thomas Keith's Scotland, the work of a Victorian amateur photographer (1852-57)*, Edinburgh 1981. See also [Charles Sinclair Minto], *Thomas Keith 1827-1895: Surgeon and Photographer*, Edinburgh 1966.

62. See Dorothea H. Fyfe and Charles Sinclair Minto, *John Forbes White, Miller, Collector, Photographer 1831-1904*, Edinburgh 1970.

63. The collodion was a transparent film of gun cotton dissolved in ether and containing potassium iodide spread over a glass negative. Wet collodion was sensitised on the spot and developed immediately giving a high resolution of detail. This idea was successfully utilised by Gustave Le Gray (1820-82) in France, and by Frederich Scott Archer in England, who both made wet collodion negatives during the period 1849-51, although Archer was the first to publish details, in the March 1851 issue of *The Chemist*.

64. See Ina Mary Harrower, *John Forbes White*, Edinburgh 1918, p.30.

65. See Valerie Lloyd, *Roger Fenton Photographer of the 1850s*, exhib. cat. Hayward Gallery London February-April 1988, London 1988; see also John Hannavy, *Roger Fenton of Crimble Hall*, Boston 1976; an essay on the photographer by Richard Pare appears in *Roger Fenton* (Aperture Masters of Photography series, no.4), New York 1987. Among recent studies, see the essays in *All the Mighty World. The Photographs of Roger Fenton, 1852-1860*, Yale University Press, New Haven and London 2004.

66. This historic photograph of Rosslyn Chapel fetched $58,700 at Christie's auction in May 1997 – a world record for a British photo. It was bought by an American art dealer for around four times the original sales estimate.

67. See 'Photography the Instructor of the Architect; and Architecture the best subject for the Photographer', in *The British Journal of Photography*, vol.VII, no.112, 15 February 1860, p.52.

68. Patterson and Rock, op.cit., p.[15].

69. 'The Restoration at Roslin Chapel', *The Builder*, vol.XIX, 29 June 1861, p.443. An anonymous photograph in the NMRS [fig.82] shows Rosslyn Chapel during the restoration with the sculptor Lawrence Baxter (standing) and J. Lawrence Tweedie (on the left) [NMRS no. 39081 copied in 1995].

70. Note that the National Monument Record of Scotland has an album [NMRS Album no.50] of an 'imitator of D.O.Hill' in which the eight albumen prints representing Rosslyn Chapel and Castle are by Begbie. This is evident from a comparison between the images in this album and Begbie's glass negatives collection at the City Art Centre.

71. The albumen paper, the standard printing paper for photographs of the period, was so named after the egg white which was used to bind the light-sensitive chemicals to the paper base.

72. See Patterson and Rock, op.cit., p.[15].

73. For the technical and cultural history of the stereoscope, see Jonathan Crary, *Techniques of*

the Observer: On Vision and Modernity in the Nineteenth Century, Cambridge Mass. 1996, pp.116-136.

74. Wilson's Aberdeen factory, in addition to producing hundreds of thousands of view prints each year, was perhaps the largest producer in Scotland of landscape and architectural *carte de visite* prints, which also found their way into the family portrait album with its specially cut slots for this standard print format. The little *carte de visite* measured only 2½ inches by 4 inches (64 x 100 mm) on its mount and, at prices of only a penny or two pence, became the most popular photographic format of all time. For a general account of Wilson's work see Roger Taylor, *George Washington Wilson, Artist & Photographer (1823-93)*, Aberdeen 1981.

75. Sara Stevenson (ed.), *Light from the Dark Room. A celebration of Scottish Photography: a Scottish-Canadian collaboration*, exhib. cat. Royal Scottish Academy July-Oct 1995, Edinburgh 1995, p.46.

76. George Washington Wilson also contributed to the history of photography with *A Practical Guide to the Collodion Process* which was published in 1855. His description is clear and concise and not only covers the manipulative process of coating, exciting and developing the plate but also gives advice and recommendations, based upon experience, about cameras. For this see a reprint in R. Taylor, op. cit., pp.177-186.

77. George Washington Wilson, 'A Voice from the hills: Mr Wilson at home', *The British Journal of Photography*, vol.XI, no.230, 30 September 1864, p.375.

78. According to the author of the article 'Notice of recently published stereographs. Scottish Gems' in *The British Journal of Photography*, vol.VII, no.109, 1 January 1860, p.7, 'there is nothing inherent in the dry process that should prevent its rivalling the moist one as regards capability of rendering all subjects, the wet process has a considerable advantage'.

79. Archibald Burns (fl.1858-1880), landscape photographer, took over the studio in Calton Hill from David Octavius Hill and Robert Adamson. See Julie Lawson, *Masterpieces of Photography from the Riddell Collection*, Edinburgh 1986, pp.116-118. Unfortunately the photograph in question cannot be located at this present time.

80. The author of the article appears to be in error about the missing pieces of glass from the windows. This is just an effect of light, but a Romantic critic likes the notion of decay.

81. 'Notice of recently published stereographs. Scottish Gems', in *The British Journal of Photography*, vol.VII, no.109, 1 January 1860, p.7.

82. *Ibid.*

83. Marcia Pointon, *William Dyce, 1806-1864: A Critical Biography*, Oxford 1979, p.24.

84. *Ibid.*, p.24. Pointon suggests that William's younger brother Charles Dyce painted Rosslyn Chapel in 1847 and, recalling the glory which restoration again brought to mind, dramatised the scene by the inclusion of two monks and a Cromwellian soldier.

85. See Mary Warner Marien, *Photography and Its Critics. A Cultural History, 1839–1900*, Cambridge 1997.

86. William Donaldson Clark, 'On Photography as a Fine Art', *The Photographic Journal* (Journal of the Photographic Society of London), no.133, 15 May 1863, p.287.

87. Julie Lawson, *William Donaldson Clark (1816-1873)*, (Scottish Masters no.15) Edinburgh 1990, p.14.

88. David Young Cameron as a painter and graphic artist, had many links with photographers. One of his closest friends was the professional photographer James Craig Annan (1864-1946) with whom he travelled to Holland in 1892 and to Italy in 1894. He also wrote an article on his friend's photographic style: 'An Artist's Notes on Mr J. Craig Annan's Pictures now being Exhibited at the Royal Photographic Society', *The Amateur Photographer*, vol.XXXI, 16 February 1900, pp.123-124.

89. In a very different context, John Mitchinson collected photographs of the Chapel accompanied with an account from Mackenzie Walcott's *Ancient Church of Scotland*. The album is titled: *Collection of photographs by John Mitchinson to record the architectural remains of the religious houses in Great Britain, late 19th-early 20th cent. with notes of each foundation from printed sources*. The

collection is kept in the Bodleian Library in Oxford. The Rosslyn Chapel images are in the volume MSS. Top. eccles. b. 32-33. This work is quoted in Mary Clapinson and T.D. Rogers, *Summary Catalogue of Post-Medieval Western Manuscripts in the Bodleian Library*, vol.II, Oxford 1991, p.1226. Mitchinson visited Rosslyn Chapel in 1860.

90. See William M. Ivins, *Prints and Visual Communication*, Cambridge Mass. 1953, p.107. This technique, according to Ivins, was invented about 1860 by the wood-engraver Thomas Bolton who had 'the idea of sensitizing the surface of his wood-block, on which he had a photograph printed from a negative after a relief by Flaxman. He made his engraving through the photograph as though it had been a drawing in tints on the block'.

91. Samuel Gosnell Green, *Scottish Pictures drawn with pen and pencil*, London 1883. The engraving of *Roslin Chapel, with the Prentice Pillar* is on page 20.

92. George Eyre-Todd, *Scotland Picturesque and Traditional*, London 1895. The wood-cut of *Roslyn Chapel* can be seen at page 70. Another engraving taken from a Valentine's photograph of Roslin Chapel appears in Francis Watt and Rev. Andrew Carter, *Picturesque Scotland: Its Romantic Scenes and Historical Associations so described in Lay and Legend, Song and Story*, London 1880, see p.64.

93. Martin Kemp (ed.), *Mood of the Moment: Masterworks of Photography from the University of St Andrews*, St Andrews 1994, p.4.

94. Helmut Gernsheim, *Focus on Architecture and Sculpture, An original approach to the Photography of Architecture and Sculpture*, London 1949, foreword by Pevsner, p.12.

3. FROM ANTIQUARIAN TO PICTURESQUE PERSPECTIVES

3.1. The Gothistic Eye

1. Michael Sadleir, *Things Past*, London 1944, p.176.

2. Iain Gordon Brown, 'Critik in Antiquity: Sir John Clerk of Penicuik', *Antiquity*, vol.LI, 1997, p.203. By the same author see: 'Gothicism, ignorance and bad taste: the destruction of Arthur's O'on', *Antiquity*, vol.XLVIII, 1994, pp.283-287; *The Hobby-Horsical Antiquary A Scottish Character 1640-1830*, Edinburgh 1980.

3. Howard Colvin, *A Biographical Dictionary of British Architects 1600-1840*, 3rd ed., New Haven and London 1995, p.254.

4. For a full account of the different lineage of the Sinclair Families, see Roland William Saint-Clair, *The St Clairs of the Isles. A History*, Auckland 1898.

5. National Archives of Scotland, GD 18 5111/1. See also fig.50.

6. Andrew Kerr, 'The Collegiate Church or Chapel of Rosslyn. Its Builders, Architect, and Construction', *Proceedings of the Society of Antiquaries of Scotland*, vol.XII, 1877-1878, p.223.

7. See Brown, 'Critik...', op.cit., p.204.

8. See GD 18 5010/1-8 at the National Archives of Scotland, Register House, Edinburgh.

9. National Archives of Scotland, GD 18 5010/1. Inscribed: 'London February 22nd'; Sinclair writes: 'I am greatly favoured by Your's containing the Plans for the House at Rosslen, which come pretty near to the amendments I desired Mr Adams to make to the one drawn by himself...'.

10. Sinclair refers to Patrick Lindsay (d.1753); Lindsay's grandfather was a joiner in St. Andrews, and he appears to have learned the same trade, for after leaving the army he settled as an upholsterer in Edinburgh. Prospering in his business he was chosen as a magistrate for the city, and became successively Dean of Guild and Lord Provost of Edinburgh, the latter in 1729, and again in 1733. See Sidney Lee (ed.), *The Dictionary of National Biography*, vol.XI, London 1909, p.1191.

11. Sir George Lockhart (1673-1731), supporter of the Jacobite cause; author of the *Memoirs of the Affairs in Scotland from Queen Anne's Successions to the Commencement of the Union* (1714) and *Papers on the Affairs in Scotland* (posthumous publication).

12. National Archives of Scotland, GD 18 5010/2. Inscribed: 'London, March 15th'.

13. The General refers here to John Sinclair (1683-1750), eldest son of Henry, eighth Lord Sinclair. Being attainted for his share in the Jacobite rebellion, he remained abroad until 1726. Returning to Scotland, he was later to receive back the estates at the hands of his younger brother General James St Clair (d.1762), as had been privately arranged between them. See Sidney Lee (ed.), op.cit., vol.XVIII, pp.298-300.

14. National Archives of Scotland, GD 18 5010/4; inscribed: 'London, April 12th'.

15. Letter from Sinclair to Clerk inscribed: 'London March 18th from St Clair' [National Archives of Scotland, GD 18 5010/3]. In relation to the payment of the repairs he writes: 'I make no doubt of Your taking care of me in the Rosslin bargaine [sic], which I am sorry has allready [sic] given You so much trouble... You may be assured that I will act in that by Your directions, as in every thing else that relates to this affair of Rosslin.

I approve much of Your design of geting [sic] my Brother to lay out the £25 yearly for repairing the Chappell [sic] and am persuaded that if any body can prevaill [sic] with him to do it, it will be You'.

16. Letter from Sinclair to Clerk inscribed: 'London, June 26' [National Archives of Scotland, GD 18 5010/5].

17. Pictorial evidence confirms that during the late eighteenth century and early nineteenth century the aisles were covered by a steeply raked roof. This has left considerable evidence of its presence on the fabric. Against the east wall of the transept there are filled-in crease lines showing where it abutted, and similar filled-in crease lines survive against the lowest parts of the larger pinnacles. Against the east gable there is the outline of filled-in chases for a gable roof at each side of the east window. The roof was high set and would have cut across the clerestory windows, obscuring the lower two-thirds. No horizontal crease line remains between the clerestory windows, and it seems that this has been restored away. The pictorial evidence suggests that the roof had a single slope towards the east and that there must have been a valley between the two eastern pitches, that allowed light into the east window.

18. General Sinclair's use of the word 'Eye' may perhaps suggest that the original arrangement of the tracery of the east window involved some circular 'rose-window' motif. No view of the east elevation of Rosslyn exists before that of Delacour (1761), however an oblique image in Slezer's view of the south side suggests that the window had a large roundel set above the paired lancets. A comparison of Slezer's engraving with the existing south side of the Chapel demonstrates that his record of the pattern of the tracery in the south aisle window – though schematic – is reliable.

19. Letter from Sinclair to Clerk inscribed: 'London, March 3rd' [National Archives of Scotland, GD 18 5010/6].

20. The material used to complete this task was obtained from the demolition of the 'Forecastle', as appears from the recent discoveries made by the archaeologist Tom Addyman during the restoration of the stables attached to the boundary walls. See Tom Addyman, 'Rosslyn Chapel', in Robin Turner (ed.) *Discovery and Excavation in Scotland 1998*, Council for Scottish Archaeology, Edinburgh 1998, p.139.

21. National Archives of Scotland, GD 18 5010/8.

22. John G. Dunbar (ed.), *Sir William Burrell's Northern Tour 1758*, East Linton 1997, p.117.

23. Robert Cooper (ed.), *An Account of the Chapel of Roslin, 1778*, Edinburgh 2000, p.38.

24. Richard Gough, *British Topography*, vol.II, 1780, p.682.

25. Cooper (ed.), op.cit., p.16.

26. See Howard M. Colvin, 'Aubrey's *Chronologia Architectonica*', in John Summerson (ed.), *Concerning Architecture: Essays on Architectural Writers and Writing Presented to Nikolaus Pevsner*, London 1968, p.10.

27. Two volumes selected from the 'Paton corrispondence' are preserved in National Library of Scotland in the Advocates Manuscript Collection. Soon after his death in 1807, Paton's books were sold and his manuscripts, prints, coins and antiquities were dispersed.

28. In one of his letters to Gough, Paton writes: 'you may depend on my assured Inquiry about every printed Account of the Antiquity of this Country'. [National Library of Scotland, Adv. MS.29.5.7.(i) f.78. recto]. This letter is not dated.

29. The second edition of the book was published in 1780.

30. Letter from Paton to Gough dated 26 March 1772 [National Library of Scotland, Adv. MS.29.5.7.(i) f.39v-40r].

31. Gough, op.cit., p.682.

32. Letter from Paton to Gough, dated 20 October 1772 [National Library of Scotland, Adv. MS.29.5.7.(i) f.76 verso]. In the same letter appears a list of material sent to Richard Gough in which is noted one inside view of Rosslyn Chapel, see f.77 verso.

33. See T.I. Rae, 'The Scottish Antiquarian Tradition', *Scots Antiquaries and Historians*, Abertay Historical Society 1972, pp.12-25.

34. Both drawings are preserved in the National Library of Scotland, Adv. MS. 30.5.23. item 86a-86b.

35. For Hutton's notes on Rosslyn Chapel see National Library of Scotland, Adv. MS. 30.5.17. pp.90-91.

36. *Documents Relating to Roslin Chapel*, Letter to John Britton from Joseph Michael Gandy, dated 17 December 1806, f.2. The text transcribed by Gandy from Astle's *Magnates of Scotland* account runs as follows: 'N°XIX is the seal of Sir WILLIAM DE ST CLARE, lord of Roslin, descended from WALDERAM count of St. Clare, who came into England with WILLIAM the First. WILLIAM, the son of WALDERAM, settled in Scotland, and was made baron of Roslin by King MALCOLM CANMORE, and from this WILLIAM all the SINCLAIRS of Scotland are descended (Nesbit's Appendix to his second volume, p.171). WILLIAM DE ST CLARE, the party to the instrument under consideration, was the sixth baron of Roslin; he obtained a charter of confirmation of that barony, and other possessions from king ALEXANDER the Third; he was one of the Scottish chieftains who invaded Cumberland in March 1296, and was amongst the prisoners who were taken by the English on the surrender of the castle of Dunbar to earl WARDEN on the twenty-ninth of April, in the same year. He is said to have been one of the greatest men of his time; was always active, both in the cabinet, and in the field. He died about the year 1300. His lineal descendant Sir HENRY ST CLARE was created earl of Orkney by HACO king of Norway in 1379, which title was confirmed by ROBERT the Second the same year'.

Legend, "✠ S'WILLⱤLMI Dᴱ SCO CLARO MILITIS".

An engraving of the seal appears in Plate III, no.19 of Astle's book [see fig.61].

37. *Ibid.*

38. National Library of Scotland [Acc.11453, vol.II, letter no.123]; letter from Robert Pierce Gillies to Egerton Brydges, dated 25 June 1813.

39. *Ibid.* John Pinkerton, renowned for his collection of 'fabricated' Scottish traditional verses, in his *History of Scotland* refers to a manuscript containing notes by Henry Sinclair, Bishop of Ross, and his nephew Sir William Sinclair of Roslin, including a transcription of Roman inscriptions, which may suggest that these eminent Scotsmen of the sixteenth century may well have had a broader interest in antiquity than purely literary. This was only one of the many manuscripts associated with the legendary library at Roslin Castle which was looted in the seventeenth century. For the Sinclair manuscript manufactory see Professor H.J. Lawlor, 'The Library of the Sinclairs of Rosslyn', in *Proceedings of the Society of Antiquaries of Scotland*, vol. XXXII, 1898, pp.90-120.

40. Robert Pearse Gillies, *Recollections of Sir Walter Scott*, London 1837, pp.107.

41. *Ibid.*, pp.118-119.

42. As Gillies explains in his *Memoirs* the ballad seems to be lost. Unfortunately he cannot recall more then the first two lines which were: 'The gallants laughed and the red wine quaffed, (of olden times the tale)'.

43. Robert Pearse Gillies, *Memoirs of a Literary Veteran*, vol.II, London 1851, p.194.

44. *Ibid.*

45. Gillies, *Recollections,* op.cit., p.106.

3.2. A Highly Picturesque Place

46. Letter from Gandy to Britton dated 17 December 1806 contained in the album 'Documents Relating to Roslin Chapel', see Angelo Maggi, *'Documents Relating to Roslin Chapel*: a recently discovered collection of papers by John Britton', *Architectural Heritage. The Journal of the Architectural Heritage Society of Scotland*, vol.XIII, 2002, pp.73-98.

47. Between 1769 and 1774 Gilpin made a series of tours which he recorded in observations illustrated by his own sketches. These were circulated in manuscript among his friends, who constantly encouraged him to publish them. This he eventually did in 1782, when he started with *Observations on the River Wye, and several parts of South Wales, &c. relative chiefly to picturesque beauty: made in the summer of the year 1770*, which was an immediate success. For the next seventeen years the others followed, eight tours in all as well as *Three essays: On picturesque beauty; On picturesque travel; and On sketching landscape: to which is added a poem On Landscape painting* (1792). The title of each of the eight tours uses the words *Observations... relative to picturesque beauty*.

48. Quoted by Carl Paul Barbier, *William Gilpin: His Drawings, Teaching and Theory of the Picturesque*, Oxford, 1963, p.98.

49. *Ibid.*, pp.102-3.

50. Richard Payne Knight, *An Analytical Inquiry into the Principles of Taste*, London 1805, p.148; Uvedale Price, *Essays on the Picturesque*, vol.I, London 1810, p.44.

51. Christopher Hussey, *The Picturesque. Studies in a Point of View*, 2nd ed., London 1967, pp.1-2.

52. At first Nasmyth ran the school himself, but later his daughters, in particular Barbara and Jane, helped to organise these trips. See Martin Kemp, 'Alexander Nasmyth and the Style of Graphic Eloquence', *The Connoisseur*, vol.173, February 1970, pp.93-100; Peter Johnson and Money Ernlé, *The Nasmyth Family of Painters*, Leigh-on-Sea 1977; J.C.B. Cooksey, *Alexander Nasmyth: A Man of the Scottish Renaissance*, London 1991.

53. Joseph Rock, *The Life and Work of Hugh William Williams*, unpublished Ph.D thesis, University of Edinburgh, 1996, p.47.

54. Helen Rosslyn demonstrates Williams's fluency in watercolour painting which has further developed ten years later in his 1805 view of the Castle from the north. See Maggi and Rosslyn, *Rosslyn Country*, p.38.

55. James Nasmyth Hall, *James Nasmyth Engineer: an Autobiography edited by Samuel Smiles*, London 1897, p.36.

56. Grose relied on antiquarians such as Robert Riddell (d.1794) who lent him drawings by Paul Sandby (1730-1809). Sandby's drawings, mostly produced for the Ordnance Survey of Scotland between 1747 and 1752, were copied by Grose's draughtsman-servant, Tom Cocking. According to Kim Sloan: 'Grose was said to have made most of the drawings supplied to the engravers of his *Antiquities* himself, but there is a question about how much he was assisted in his drawings by Cocking who travelled with him.' Kim Sloan, *'A Noble Art' Amateur Artists and Drawing Masters c.1600-1800*, exhib. cat. British Museum, London 2000, p.128.

57. Britton, op.cit., p.51.

58. See James Holloway and Lindsay Errington, *The Discovery of Scotland: The Appreciation of Scottish Scenery through Two Centuries of Painting*, exhib. cat. National Gallery of Scotland, Edinburgh 1978, p.85.

59. Pennant's visit to Rosslyn was recorded by George Paton in a letter dated 28 September 1772 addressed to the English antiquarian Richard Gough. Paton writes: 'Mr Pennant arrived here safely... Last Monday morning he carried me out with him to Hawthornden & Roslin, was agreeably delighted with both places but more especially the picturesque Rocks & Banks on the *North Esk Water*. The Collection of Sketches, Prospects, Views &.c during this Visit in Scotland

are numerous & fine, I am hope-full the World will be indulged with them in Time' [National Library of Scotland, Adv. MS. 29.5.7.(i) f.71 recto].

60. Following his marriage in 1797 and well before he built Abbotsford, Scott took a house at Lasswade further down the River Esk. He lived in Barony Cottage, fictionalised as 'Gandercleuch', the residence of the author of *Tales of a Grandfather*, which is still standing.

61. *The Gentleman's Magazine*, vol.LXXXVII, part II, September 1817, p.209.

62. From Burns's poem 'At Roslin Inn', see Raymond Bentham (ed.), *The Poetical Works of Robert Burns*, Boston 1974, p.184. A strange conversation between Annie Wilson and Walter Scott, while on a visit to the Chapel, is wonderfully described by Robert Pierce Gillies in *Recollections of Sir Walter Scott*, London 1837, pp.104-107. For another description of this legendary figure related to the history of the Chapel, see note 10, chapter 2.1.

63. Alexander Murray, *The modern universal British traveller; or, a new, complete, and accurate tour through England, Wales, Scotland and the neighbouring islands. Comprising all that is worthy of observations in Great Britain*, 'Part III – Scotland and North Britain', London 1779, p.740.

64. Ann Payne, *Views of the Past. Topographical Drawings in the British Library*, London 1987, p.41.

65. Johnson's words quoted in the National Library Catalogue *Boswell and Johnson, The Highland Adventure*, Edinburgh 1973, p.2.

66. James Boswell, *The Journal of a Tour to the Hebrides with Samuel Johnson*, London 1785, p.507.

67. Joseph Farington's 'Account dated Tuesday Septr. 22 1801' in Kenneth Garlick and Angus Macintyre (ed.), *The Diary of Joseph Farington*, vol.V, New Haven and London 1979, p.1630.

68. *Ibid.*, p.1629.

69. Ernest De Selincourt (ed.), *The Early Letters of William and Dorothy Wordsworth (1787-1805)*, Oxford 1935, p.493.

70. Dorothy Wordsworth's 'Account dated Saturday Septr.17 1803' in E. De Selincourt (ed.) *Journals of Dorothy Wordsworth*, vol.I, London 1941, pp.387-388.

71. According to Helen Rosslyn: 'Although this was Dorothy's only visit, William was to make two further Scottish tours in 1814 and 1831. It is probable that, on the latter trip, he revisited Rosslyn with his daughter Dora, as his sonnet 'Composed at Roslin Chapel during a Storm' is dated the same year. The timeless theme of this poem, suggested by the derelict Chapel, is the same as that of his sister's words, written almost thirty years earlier.' See Rosslyn and Maggi, op.cit., p.47.

72. They constitute a small volume in folio which she gave to several friends. See Elisabeth Leveson Gower, Duchess of Sutherland and Countess of Stafford, *Views in Orkney and on the North-Eastern Coast of Scotland, taken in 1805 and etched in 1807*, published by the author in 1807; see also, William Fraser, *The Sutherland Book*, vol.I, Edinburgh 1892, pp.493-494.

73. Britton, op.cit., p.51. On lady amateurs' drawing classes at Rosslyn, see Helen Rosslyn's essay: 'Rosslyn: "That Romantic Spot"' in Rosslyn and Maggi, op.cit. p.45.

74. See *Views of Edinburgh and its vicinity, drawn and engraved by J. and H.S.Storer, exhibiting remains of antiquity, public buildings, and picturesque scenery*, Edinburgh 1822.

75. Cuitt's Jr. miniature painting of the interior of Rosslyn Chapel is part of a collection of drawings at the Victoria and Albert Museum of London [Print Room press-mark: E.2554-1919].

76. See *Views of the city and environs of Edinburgh. Drawn on stone by T.M.Baynes*, London 1823.

77. Renzo Dubbini, *Geography of the Gaze. Urban and Rural Vision in Early Modern Europe*, Chicago 2002, p.132.

78. See William Baird, *John Thomson of Duddingston, Pastor and Painter; A Memoir*, Edinburgh 1895, p.53. The development and significance of the artists' illustrations for Scott's project are explored by Katrina Thomson in *Turner and Sir Walter Scott. The Provincial Antiquities and Picturesque Scenery of Scotland*, exhib. cat. National Gallery of Scotland December 1999–March 2002, Edinburgh 1999.

79. Turner's 'Dunbar and Edinburgh Sketchbooks' in the Tate Gallery of London, contain six pencil drawings of the Castle and the Chapel. These books were apparently carried by Turner on all his sketching excursions during his visit to Scotland in 1801. In the 'Dunbar' Sketchbook on f.44 verso appears a sketch of Rosslyn Castle and Chapel as seen from the north east, which is very similar in composition to the view of this subject in the *Provincial Antiquities*.

80. It is important to note that a number of preparatory sketches for, or related to, Blore's drawings are in the British Library, London (MSS. 42000-42047). Unfortunately none of them represent the three Rosslyn plates for the *Provincial Antiquities*.

81. On the importance of 'steel facing' prints in the history of printmaking, see William M. Ivins, *Prints and Visual Communication*, New York 1969, p.73.

82. See William Beattie, *Scotland Illustrated in a Series of Views by T. Allom, W.H. Bartlett and H.M. Culloch*, vol.II, London 1842.

4. Victorian Restorations and Controversies

4.1. The Unmaking of Pictorial Beauty

1. *The Gentleman's Magazine*, vol.LXXXVII, part II, September 1817, p.209.

2. *The Scotsman*, 7 May 1861, p.3.

3. Samuel Dukinfield Swarbreck, *Sketches in Scotland Drawn from Nature and on Stone*, London 1837, caption to Plate I: 'North Entrance to Rosslyn Chapel'. Swarbreck continues, explaining how the stone employed for the restoration works was 'fortunately obtained, as is supposed, from the original quarry'.

4. Letter from James Alexander Sinclair Erskine to William Burn dated 1836 [National Archives of Scotland, document GD 164/1013].

5. *Ibid.* The evidence that John Baxter the elder was the architect for this roof is contained in the Clerk of Penicuik papers [National Archives of Scotland, document: GD.18 5010/6]. The role of Sir John Clerk of Penicuik in preserving the Chapel ruins is discussed in Chapter 3.1.

6. See Ian C. Hannay, *Story of Scotland in Stone*, London 1934, p.192.

7. Letter from Roberts to David Ramsay Hay, London 9 September 1845. [National Library of Scotland, MS.3522.f.16 verso].

8. Letter from Roberts to Christine Bicknell, Rosslyn 1 October 1842. [National Library of Scotland, Acc.7723. no.4].

9. *The Scotsman*, 6 December 1843, p.3.

10. *Ibid.*

11. *Ibid.*

12. Letter from Lord Cockburn to Roberts dated 27 October 1843 in James Ballantine, *The Life of David Roberts R.A.*, Edinburgh 1866, p.157.

13. *Ibid.* This passion and respect for the Rosslyn family is evident when Cockburn records in his *Journal* the death of the 2nd Earl of Rosslyn: 'Yet I never could cease loving and admiring him. His talent, spirit, and long consistency; his gallant, gentleman-like, old soldier-like air, his light erect-looking figure; his grizzly hair; and the very wrinkles around the outer wicks of his eyes, were all admirable'. T. H. Cockburn, *Journal of Henry Cockburn being a continuation of the Memorials of his time 1831-1854*, vol.I, Edinburgh 1874, p.131.

14. Perhaps this was one of the reasons why he chose to be portrayed by David Octavius Hill beside the south porch of this major work of restoration confided to his care.

15. Letter from Roberts to David Ramsay Hay, London 30 October 1843 [National Library of Scotland, MS.3521, f.164 recto].

16. During this phase of restoration Burn carried out plans for a new tracery at the great east window. The newly designed tracery, which can be seen in one of Hill and Adamson's calotypes, was strongly criticised by Hay and Roberts. Around the 1890s there was a lot of

activity at the same tracery and it is possible that during the reworking of the stained-glass the decision was taken to remove Burn's tracery to be replaced with the one in its present form.

17. *The Scotsman*, 8 November 1843, p.3.

18. *Ibid.*

19. *Ibid.*

20. See *The Scotsman*, 22 November 1843, p.3.

21. Letter from Roberts to David Ramsey Hay, London 27 November 1843 [National Library of Scotland, MS.3521, f.170 recto].

22. David Roberts wrote to the editor of *The Scotsman* about the publication of two letters to Lord Cockburn regarding the state of Rosslyn Chapel. The name of Lord Cockburn is never mentioned in the paper. Evidence that the 'eminent and learned personage in Scotland' to whom these letters were addressed was Cockburn is contained in Roberts's letter to his Scottish friend David Ramsay Hay, London, 27 November 1843 [National Library of Scotland, MS.3521, f.170 recto].

23. Letter from Roberts to Hay, London 2 December 1843 [National Library of Scotland, MS.3521, f.172 recto].

24. See letter from Roberts to Lord Cockburn in *The Scotsman*, 6 December 1843, p.3.

25. John Ruskin, *Modern Painters*, vol.I, London 1898, p.127.

26. *Ibid.*

27. Robert William Billings, 'Economy in Scottish Architecture', *The Architect*, vol.XXXIII, 21 March 1885, p.177.

28. Letter from Roberts to Hay, London 29 December 1845 [National Library of Scotland, MS. 3522, ff.25r-25v].

29. See letter from Roberts to Hay, London 29 March 1846 [National Library of Scotland, MS. 3522, ff.35r-36v].

30. A preliminary watercolour sketch dated 1845 of this frontispiece is in the V&A Print Room [Mus. No. FA 540].

31. Letter from Roberts to Hay, only dated 1846 [National Library of Scotland, MS. 3522, f.41 recto]. In the list given by Roberts to Hay, Melrose actually appears first, but a combination of brackets and underlining makes it clear that Roberts's intention is to put Rosslyn's plate first.

32. *Ibid.* f.41 verso.

33. Ballantine, op.cit., p.236.

4.2. Britton's RIBA Lecture

34. At the lecture Britton reads the following lines from Hay's *Genealogie*: '…he built the church walls of Rosline, haveing rounds with faire chambers, and galleries theron… he builded the bridge under the castle, and sundrie office houses. In the south-east side therof, over against the chapell wall, he made plaine the rock on which the castle is builded, for the more strength therof, and he planted a very fair fruit orchard; but his adge creeping on him, made him consider how he had spent his time past, and how to spend that which was to come. Therfor, to the end he might not seem altogither unthankfull to God, for the benefices he receaved from him, it came in his minde to build a house for God's service, of most curios worke, the which, that it might be done with greater glory and splendour, he caused artificers to be brought from other regions and forraigne kingdomes, and caused dayly to be abundance of all kinde of workemen present, as masons, carpenters, smiths, barrowmen, and quarries, with others…. The foundation of this rare work he caused to be laid in the year of our Lord, 1446, and to the end the work might be more rare; first, he caused the draughts to be drawn upon Eastland boards, and made the carpenters to carve them according to the draughts thereon, and then gave them for patterns to the massons, that they might therby cut the like in stone; and because he thought the massones had not a convenient place to lodge in near the place where he builded

this curious colledge, for the towne then stood half a mile from the place where it now stands, towitt, at Bilsdone burne, therefor he made them to build the towne of Rosline, that now is extant, and gave every one of them a house, and lands answerable therunto; so that this towne, att that time, by reason of the great concourse of people that had recourse unto the Prince, (for it is remembered of him that he entertained all his tennants that were any way impoverished, and made serve all the poore that came to his gates, so that he spent yearly upon such as came to beg att his gates 120 quarters meale,) became very populous, and had in it aboundance of victualls, so that it was thought to be the chiefest towne in all Lothian, except Edinburgh and Hadingtone. He rewarded the massones according to their degree, as to the master massone he gave 40 pounds yearly, and to every one of the rest he gave 10 pounds, and accordingly did he reward the others, as the smiths and the carpenters with others'. From Hay, op.cit., pp.26-27. It is important to note that the author of the transcription of Hay's text in the *The Builder* (vol. IV, January 1846, pp.27-28) modernised the quotation into Victorian English and omitted the punctuation of the 1835 edition of the *Genealogie*.

35. Samuel Joseph Nicholl, 'On the collegiate church or chapel at Roslyn [Roslin, Rosslyn] by John Britton read on 12 January 1846 (7 p., ill.)' in 'Notes made by Nicholl, while a member of the RIBA in the session 1845-1846'. See Angela Mace (ed.), *Architecture in Manuscript, 1601-1996: Guide to the British Architectural Library Manuscripts and Archives Collection*, London 1998, p.296. Nicholl's manuscript and sketches are kept at the RIBA Library [shelf mark Ref. RIBA/MS.SP./2/4].

36. In HenryVII's Chapel there is an ornament which was introduced in late Perpendicular Gothic style, and which is very characteristic in Rosslyn Chapel. This is sometimes called the 'Tudor flower', not because it was introduced in the time of the Tudors, but because it was very much used at that period. It generally consists of the fleur-de-lis, alternately with a small trefoil or ball. At Roslin this feature is used as a stone cresting of the battlements on the east end walls. See Jill Lever and John Harris, *Illustrated Dictionary of Architecture 800-1914*, London and Boston 1993, pp.41,90.

37. The Manuscript Collection at British Library has two large anonymous drawings of Rosslyn Chapel: one of *The Lady Chapel Boss* [size 830 x 620 mm., shelf mark 31323 L4 (LLLL)] and another one representing *The Last three bays on the South side* [size 500 x 930 mm., shelf mark 31323 K4 (KKKK)]. The are both no doubt copied from Gandy's plates published in Britton's *Architectural Antiquities*. These watercolours are subdivided (the first one in four parts, the second one in six) and are mounted on canvas like the backing for an old map. Since these are 'easy to fold' drawings there is a strong possibility that they were used as lecture diagrams by Britton in 1846.

38. Nicholl, op.cit., p.3. Donaldson in the year of Britton's lecture on Rosslyn was honorary secretary of the RIBA.

39. *The Builder*, vol.IV, 1846, p.28.

40. G.P.H. Watson, 'The Church in Medieval Scotland', in George Scott-Moncrieff (ed.), *The Stones of Scotland*, London 1938, p.47.

41. The Dance of Death motif (French: *danse macabre*; German *Totentanz*) originated no later than the early fifteenth century, and seems to have appeared first in France, before spreading to Germany, Italy, the Swiss cantons and even in Spain. In its original form it was an elongated mural painting, either in a church or on the walls of a churchyard or burial ground. It depicted a series of figures, both living and dead, in procession. The living figures are generally presented in the order of their social precedence on earth, and there is usually an alternating series of living forms and cadavers or skeletons. It has been suggested that the subject is really a dance of the dead, rather than a dance of death, which seems to be a valid distinction. See J.M.Clark, *The Dance of Death in the Middle Ages and Renaissance*, Glasgow, 1950. According to Clark: 'The medium employed for the forms of the work varies considerably. There are poems and prose works, manuscripts and printed books, paintings on wood, stone, or canvas, stained glass windows, sculptures, embroidery, tapestry, metal work, engravings on stone or metal, and woodcuts'. Clark's Appendix A, pp.114-118, offers a chronological list of paintings and sculptures, and a list of persons represented in each major surviving cycle, as part of his

attempt to compare the principal examples with one another. In the introduction of *The Baronial and Ecclesiastical Antiquities of Scotland* (1845), Billings refers to the *Dance of Death*. He cites comparisons with Vincent de Beauvais as a (much earlier) iconographic source for this imagery, which may otherwise be found in Amiens Cathedral.

42. *The Builder*, op.cit., p.28.

43. The tone of the criticism infuriated Roberts, who sent a long and petulant account of the meeting to Hay, using phrases such as 'far worse, miserable imposters such as Burn'. See letter to Hay from Roberts, dated 30 January 1846 [National Library of Scotland MS. 3522, ff.31-33].

44. Letter from Roberts to Hay, London 30 January 1846 [National Library of Scotland, MS. 3522, ff.31r-32v]. 'B–' is how Roberts usually refers to Burn in his letters to Hay.

45. See, Andrew Kerr, 'The Collegiate Church or Chapel of Rosslyn, its Builders, Architect, and Construction', *Proceeding of the Society of Antiquaries of Scotland*, vol. XII, 1878, p.225.

46. Letter from Roberts to Hay, London 30 January 1846 [National Library of Scotland MS. 3522, f.32 verso].

47. According to Roberts, in a letter to Hay dated 30 January 1846, he received a reply only from John Britton: 'I rec.d a very civil but I must say guarded note expressing his regret that in having *ventured* to differ in my opinion from me he had given me cause of offence – But offering to forwarded [sic] them to the Secretary and / – together *with any farther* communications I might wish to make bring them before the Institute at their next meeting –

In reply to this I wrote to thank him for his kind offer and accepting it – at the same time stating that after his courtesy I should have the whole explanation in his hands' [National Library of Scotland, MS. 3522, ff.32v-33r]. John Britton in his letter of apology, London 20 January 1846, wrote: 'Thanks, my dear Sir, for your Communications about Roslyn, & for the interest you take in such works. – I hope nothing will occur to prevent my attendance at the next meet[in]g of the Architects Instit[ute] when I hope an opportunity will be afforded for me, & Mr Burn, to enter into some explanation, for the purpose of doing you justice. – Such a *discovery* is worth fighting for, & I regret that you did not come forward on the former evening, when the drawings were present –

You may be assured that I will take some opportunity of bringing the subject before the Instit[ute]' [National Library of Scotland, Acc.7967/1, Mf. MS. 381, 1846].

48. *The Builder*, vol.IV, 1846, p.64.

49. Letter from Roberts to Hay, London 30 January 1846 [National Library of Scotland, MS.3522, f.31 verso].

50. In this case Roberts refers to the following passage in Father Hay's *Genealogie*: 'When my goodfather was buried, his corps seemed to be intire att the opening of the cave, but when they came to touch his body it fell into dust: he was laying in his armour, with a red velvet cap on his head on a flat stone: nothing was spoild except a piece of white furring that went round the cap, and answered to the hinder part of the head. All the predecessors were buried after the same manner in their armour'. Hay, op. cit., p.154.

51. Letter from Roberts to Hay, London 30 January 1846 [National Library of Scotland, MS.3522, ff.33v-34r].

52. *The Builder*, op.cit., p.51. The member of the Institute refers humorously to the following lines of a celebrated poem by Samuel Taylor Coleridge (1772-1834): 'The Knight's bones are dust, / And his good sword rust; – / His soul is with the saints, I trust.' See *The Knight's Tomb* in Samuel Taylor Coleridge, *The Poetical Works of S.T. Coleridge*, vol.II, London 1834, p.65.

53. *Ibid.*, p.64.

54. *Ibid.*

55. *Ibid.* Britton continues the letter with the following words: 'Let it not be imagined by the reader that I make these remarks with any ungenerous or unkind feelings towards the author of the inimitable 'Waverley Novels', whom I had the pleasure and honour of knowing and corresponding with in life, and whose memory and merits I revere, in death. His works

have been read and admired by millions of people, and have afforded me, with other readers, indescriable [sic] gratification and delight. The youthful reader should, however, be warned against errors, mis-statements, and misrepresentations even of popular authors'.

56. Letter from Roberts to Hay, London 23 March 1846 [National Library of Scotland, MS. 3522, f.35 recto].

57. Album 'Documents', p.7.

58. *Ibid.*, p.3.

59. It is important to note that Kemp's survey drawing shows two existing flying buttresses which are not recorded by Cresy in his North to South section of the Chapel.

60. According to Cresy: 'From a view of these sections, it is apparent that the principal upon which they are set out has its origin in the equilateral triangle; it determines the height and the breadth, the mass and the void'. See Edward Cresy, *A Practical Treatise on Bridge Building and on the Equilibrium of Vaults and Arch, with Professional Life and Work of John Rennie (1761-1821)*, London, 1839, p.3.

61. John R. Thomson, the custodian of the Chapel between the 1840s and 1860s, had a very strong interest in all the architectural aspects of the building. He was also an amateur photographer and compiled a photograph album with many views of the building for Hezekiah Merrick of Eskill House, owner of the Roslin Gunpowder Mills. The photograph album by Thomson is kept in the RCAHMS.

62. The outline of the section corresponds to plate 68 published by Cresy in his *Practical Treatise*. A copy of Cresy's *Roslyn Chapel Section through the Nave* is contained in the album 'Documents'.

63. Kerr, op.cit., p.226.

64. Album 'Documents', p.18.

4.3. The 'Antique Replicas' Controversy

65. An article published in May 1861 states, on the authority of two young Episcopalians, that the Chapel was to 'be opened at Whitsunday'. See *The Scotsman*, 7 May 1861, p.3. In a later communication this is contradicted: 'It has been stated that it was intended that Roslin Chapel should be opened for divine service at Whitsunday. We learn, however, that such has not been the intention, and that it will yet be five or six weeks before the service is commenced. We are also informed that the restorations which for some time past have been going on, have nothing to do with the arrangements for the occupation of the edifice as an Episcopalian place of worship'. See *The Scotsman*, 18 May 1861, p.2, IV. The Chapel was rededicated on Tuesday, 22 April 1862, by the Bishop of Edinburgh.

66. National Archives of Scotland, GD 164/1014/1.

67. It is the amount of restored masonry at the base which leads to the conclusion that it has largely been replaced. It is also important to note that around the base are intertwined eight dragons which in the later photograph appear re-carved.

68. National Archives of Scotland, GD 164/1014/6.

69. The relevant references are: *The Scotsman* from May to July 1861; 'The Restoration at Roslin Chapel', *The Builder*, vol.XIX, 29 June 1861, p.443; 'Roslin Chapel', *The Building News*, vol.VII, 5 July 1861, p.560; and *The Times*, 20 June 1861, p.12.

70. *The Scotsman*, 7 May 1861, p.3, I. All quotations given below are from this source.

71. *The Scotsman*, 9 May 1861, p.3, II.

72. *The Scotsman*, 28 May 1861, p.2, IV.

73. Houston was a Scottish historical genre painter and watercolourist. The painting in question titled 'Sir Walter Scott in Roslin Abbey' was on display at the Royal Scottish Academy in 1855.

74. *The Scotsman*, 7 May 1861, p.3, I. This letter is published under the pseudonym of 'An Artist' with Randolph's letter to the editor.

75. *Ibid.*

76. *Ibid.*

77. *The Scotsman*, 28 May 1861, p.2, IV.

78. *The Scotsman*, 9 May 1861, p.3, II.

79. *The Scotsman*, 28 May 1861, p.2, IV.

80. *The Scotsman*, 9 May 1861, p.3, II.

81. In another letter to the editor of *The Scotsman* (30 May 1861) an anonymous author seems to be very pleased with the new shape of the Pillar. He writes: 'May I hope to be pardoned if I dare to say that I think the Prentice Pillar itself actually improved by the cleaning it has undergone? It is to be seen now for the first time for centuries in the colour and proportions and in the sharpness of outline, in which its architect and carver intended it to be seen. And it looks no longer squat and clumsy, as it did in its dingy coat of white, but shows us a fair, well-fashioned column, rich to excess in its ornateness perhaps, yet chaste in proportion and effect'.

82. *The Scotsman*, 28 May 1861, p.2, IV.

83. In response to the problem of damp, Bryce informed Lord Rosslyn that: 'I desired him [the workman] to give the Roof another coat of oil with little Whitelead, as there was one or two drops, but I am told the Chapel is now all but dry' [National Archives of Scotland, document GD 164/1014/6]. Enquiries to Stained Glass manufacturers were made and replies to the Earl survive from John Hardman & Co. and Stained Glass Works in London, see National Archives of Scotland, documents: GD 164/1014/15, GD 164/1014/13. The stained glass windows above the altar are from a later stage of replacement. The following inscription, which is not clearly visible, dates from 1896: 'To the Glory of God: in most affectionate remembrance of his only sister Harriet Elisabeth Sinclair, daughter of James Alexander, third Earl of Rosslyn, and wife of George Herbert, Count Munster of Derneburgh in Hannover, this window was entirely restored and filled with stained glass, November 1896 by Francis Robert, fourth Earl of Rosslyn'.

84. *The Scotsman*, 22 June 1861, p.6, III.

85. *The Scotsman*, 30 May 1861, p.2, VI.

86. *Ibid.* According to him: 'They are clearing off from the beautiful carved work with which the whole interior is enriched, bit by bit, and with the utmost reverence and care, all the mosses, lichens, lycopodiums, ferns, and other vegetable matter, which, from the Chapel being exposed to the effects of the external atmosphere through unglazed windows and open doors, have gathered over it'.

87. *Ibid.* Ignoramus, the pseudonym of the author of this letter, continued his defence in this way: 'The anti-restorers are somewhat vague in their loud yet sentimental outcry, and one requires to ask how far their objections carry them. If they say – 'Do not lay a hand, or a chisel, or a brush, even though dipt [sic] in pure water only, on a single stone; leave it to time and sure decay; leave us to enjoy it as we have enjoyed it, and let future generations take their chance of something being left; we can only regard them as unreasoning, if not selfish, in their love of the venerable building. But if they admit restoration at all, even as a necessary evil, how could they have it carried on more prudently and cautiously than it is being carried on at Roslin? I for one cannot see that the clearing away of the lime and whitewash with which the tracery was thickly clotted, is anything but the reverse of a desecration. Nor do I recognise the sacredness of the ferns and lycopodiums over whose fall your corespondents mourn. The Chapel was not intended to be a huge fernery, a pretty toy for ladies young or old, and if the rain and the damp of the external atmosphere were properly excluded, these plants would of course disappear. The lycopodiums, I believe, are harmless, except as they give a foreign colour to the walls; the ferns are positively mischievous, their roots widening the interstices into which they dig, and gradually affecting the stability of the building. Perhaps the horror of the stove expressed by 'Randolph' is on account of those delicate plants, which would persist stove-dried'.

88. I am extremely grateful to Jane Thomas of the Royal Commission on the Ancient and

Historical Monuments of Scotland for this information. The notice that Laurence Baxter was Bryce's carver for the restoration works at Rosslyn appears in Colin McWilliam, *Lothian, except Edinburgh* (Buildings of Scotland), Harmondsworth 1980, p.416.

89. *The Scotsman* 18 June, p.2, VII. The article was republished in *The Times*, 20 June 1861, p.12.

90. *Ibid.*

91. *Ibid.*

92. *Ibid.*

93. *The Scotsman* 21 June 1861, p.2, VI.

94. *The Scotsman* 22 June 1861, p.6, III-IV.

95. *Ibid.*

96. *Ibid.* On the same subject see J. Cumming, 'Sandstone as a Building Material', *The Architect*, vol.XL, 3 August, 1888, p.63.

97. *Ibid.*

98. *The Times* 20 June 1861, p.12.

99. *The Scotsman* 22 June 1861, p.6, III-IV.

100. *Ibid.*

101. Sir George Gilbert Scott (1811-78), as the most successful Victorian architect, was one of the principal protagonists of the restoration debate in England. He was appointed Surveyor to the Fabric of Westminster Abbey in 1849. Scott's approach to restoration was based on the original design of the building, not the use of original materials nor for the form acquired by the building through history. In practice he often broke his own conservation principles, published in *A Plea for the Faithful Restoration of our Ancient Churches* (1851).

102. *The Scotsman*, 22 June 1861, p.6.

103. *Ibid.*

104. *The Scotsman*, 21 June 1861, p.2, VI.

5. CONCLUSIONS

5.1. The Visual Interpretation

1. Robert William Billings, 'Rosslyn Chapel Description', *The Baronial and Ecclesiastical Antiquities of Scotland*, vol.IV, Edinburgh, 1845-52, p.3.

2. See Thomas Ross, 'Rosslyn Chapel, a paper read at Rosslyn', *Transactions of the Scottish Ecclesiological Society*, vol.IV, part III, no.12, 1914-1915, pp.238-247. Ross in his text quotes another architect who made the same kind of suppositions of how the crossing was intended to be finished: Thomas Kemp (1833-1853), son of the well known architect of the Scott Monument. The only surviving record of Kemp's *Collegiate Church of St. Matthew's at Rosslyn in its (supposed) finished state* appears in John Thompson, *The Illustrated Guide to Rosslyn Chapel and Castle*, Edinburgh 1934, p.2.

3. *Ibid.*, p.240.

4. The Rosslyn cast retains much of the original detail subsequently obscured by the cement that was applied in the nineteenth century. Unfortunately, there is limited information concerning details of acquisition other than that it was purchased from the well-known reproduction business of Giovanni Franchi in 1871, for £75,5s. The cast (inv.no. 1871-59) is displayed in gallery 46A of the V&A.

BIBLIOGRAPHY

Manuscript Sources

National Archives of Scotland, Edinburgh

'Letters from General James Sinclair to Sir John Clerk of Penicuik (1738-1742)' [GD 18 5011/1-8].

'Letter from James Alexander Sinclair Erskine to William Burn (1836)' [GD 164/1013].

'Letter from David Bryce to Lord Rosslyn (16/3/1859)' [GD 164/1014/1].

National Library of Scotland, Edinburgh

'Hay's Memoirs. Or a Collection of several things relating to the most famed families of Scotland, c.1700' [Adv.MS.34.1.9 (i)].

'Letters from George Paton to Richard Gough (1772)' [Adv. MS. 29.5.7. (i)].

'Letter from David Roberts to Christine Bicknell (1/10/1842)' [Acc.7723 no.4].

'Letters from David Roberts to David Ramsay Hay (1843-1846)' [MS. 3521-3522].

'Letter from John Britton to David Roberts (20/1/1846)' [Acc.7967/1 Mf. MS.381, 1846].

Sir John Soane's Museum, London

'Gandy Sketchbook', Sir John Soane's Museum, London [vol.161].

Private Collections

'Documents Relating to Roslin Chapel', a collection of papers (1806-1846) by John Britton.

[Antony Todd Thomson], 'Journal of a Vacation in Parts of England and Scotland, 1823'.

Printed Sources

Altick, Richard Daniel, *The Shows of London*, Cambridge Mass. and London, 1978.

Anderson, Robert, 'Notice of working drawings scratched on the walls of the crypt at Roslin Chapel', *Proceedings of the Society of Antiquaries of Scotland*, vol.X, 1872-4, pp.63-64.

Ariosto, Ludovico, *Orlando Furioso* (1516), contemporary reprint, Verona, 1963.

Baird, William, *John Thomson of Duddingston, Pastor and Painter; A Memoir*, Edinburgh, 1895.

Ballantine, James, *The Life of David Roberts, R.A.*, Edinburgh, 1886.

Bann, Stephen, *The Clothing of Clio. A Study of the Representation of History in Nineteenth Century Britain and France*, Cambridge Mass., 1984.

Bapts, G., *Essai sur l'histoire des Panoramas et des Dioramas*, Paris, 1891.

Barbier, Carl Paul, *William Gilpin: His Drawings, Teaching, and Theory of the Picturesque*, Oxford, 1963.

Barmby, Beatrice Helen, *Rosslyn's Raid, and Other Tales*, London, 1903.

Barrow, Geoffrey W.S. (ed.), *The Scottish Tradition: Essays in Honour of Ronald Gordon Cant*, Edinburgh, 1974.

Basford, Kathleen, *The Green Man*, Cambridge, 1998.

Baynes, Thomas Mann, *Twenty Views of the City Environs of Edinburgh*, London, 1823.

Beattie, William, *Scotland Illustrated in a Series of Views by T. Allom, W.H. Bartlett and H.M. Culloch*, 2 vols., London, 1842.

Bede, Cuthbert, *A Tour in Tartan-Land*, London, 1873.

Bede, Cuthbert, *The visitors' handbook to Rosslyn and Hawthorden*, Edinburgh, c.1870.

Bénézit, Emmanuel, *Dictionnarie Critique et Documentaire des Peintres, Sculpteurs, Dessinateurs et Graveurs*, 14 vols., Paris, 1999.

Bentham, Raymond (ed.), *The Poetical Works of Robert Burns*, Boston, 1974.

Bermingham, Ann, *Learning to Draw. Studies in the Cultural History of a Polite and Useful Art*, New Haven and London, 2000.

Bicknell, Peter and Munro, Jane, *Gilpin to Ruskin: Drawing Masters and Their Manuals 1800-1860*, exhib. cat. Fitzwilliam Museum November 1987–February 1988, Cambridge, 1988.

Billings, Robert William, 'Economy in Scottish Architecture', *The Architect*, vol.XXXIII, 21 March 1885, p.177.

Billings, Robert William, *The Baronial and Ecclesiastical Antiquities of Scotland*, 4 vols., Edinburgh, 1845-52.

Boswell, James, *The Journal of a Tour to the Hebrides with Samuel Johnson*, London, 1785.

Britton, John, *The Architectural Antiquities of Great Britain; represented and illustrated in a series of views, elevations, plans, sections and details of various Ancient English Edifices: with Historical and Descriptive accounts of each*, 5 vols., London, 1807-1822.

Brown, Iain Gordon, *The Hobby-Horsical Antiquary A Scottish Character 1640-1830*, Edinburgh, 1980.

Brown, Iain Gordon, 'Gothicism, ignorance and bad taste: the destruction of Arthur's O'on', *Antiquity*, vol.XLVIII, 1994, pp.283-287.

Brown, Iain Gordon, 'Critik in Antiquity: Sir John Clerk of Penicuik', *Antiquity*, vol.51, 1997, pp.203-205.

Brydon, Robert, *Rosslyn. A History of The Guilds, The Masons and The Rosy Cross*, n.p., 1994.

Brydone, J., *Guide to Roslin, Hawthornden &c.; by the North British and Peebles Railways*, Edinburgh, 1858.

Bushnell, George Herbert, *Scottish Engravers. A Biographical Dictionary of Scottish Engravers and of Engravers Who Worked in Scotland to the Beginning of the Nineteenth Century*, Oxford, 1949.

Butchart, R., *Prints and Drawings of Edinburgh*, Edinburgh, 1955.

Cameron, David Young, 'An Artist's Notes on Mr J. Craig Annan's Pictures now being Exhibited at the Royal Photographic Society', *The Amateur Photographer*, vol.XXXI, 16 February 1900, pp.123-124.

Cavers, Keith, *A Vision of Scotland. The Nation observed by John Slezer 1671 to 1717*, Edinburgh, 1993.

Caw, James L., *Scottish Painting Past and Present*, Edinburgh, 1908.

Choay, Françoise, *The Invention of the Historic Monument*, Cambridge, 2001.

Clapinson, Mary and Rogers, T.D, *Summary Catalogue of Post-Medieval Western Manuscripts in the Bodleian Library Oxford*, 3 vols., Oxford, 1991.

Clark, James Midgley, *The Dance of Death in the Middle Ages and Renaissance*, Glasgow, 1950.

Clark, William Donaldson, 'On Photography as a Fine Art', *The Photographic Journal (Journal of the Photographic Society of London)*, no.133, 15 May 1863, pp.286-287.

Cobb, Gerald, *English Cathedrals, the Forgotten Centuries. Restoration and Change from 1530 to the Present Day*, London, 1980.

Cockburn, T. H., *Journal of Henry Cockburn being a continuation of the Memorials of his time 1831-1854*, 2 vols., Edinburgh, 1874.

Coleridge, Samuel Taylor, *The Poetical Works of S.T.Coleridge*, 3 vols., London, 1834.

Colvin, Howard M., 'Aubrey's *Chronologia Architectonica*', in John Summerson (ed.), *Concerning Architecture: Essays on Architectural Writers and Writing Presented to Nikolaus Pevsner*, London, 1968, pp.1-12.

Colvin, Howard M., *A Biographical Dictionary of English Architects 1640-1800*, London, 1954, and 3rd ed., New Haven and London, 1995.

Comment, Bernard, *The Panorama*, London, 1999.

Cooksey, J.C.B., *Alexander Nasmyth: A Man of the Scottish Renaissance*, London, 1991.

Cooper, Robert (ed.), *An Account of the Chapel of Roslin, 1778*, Edinburgh, 2000.

Crary Jonathan, *Techniques of the Observer: On Vision and Modernity in the Nineteenth Century*, Cambridge Mass., 1996.

Bibliography

Crary, Jonathan, *Suspensions of Perception: Attention, Spectacle, and Modern Culture*, Cambridge Mass., 1999.

Crawford, Barbara E., 'William Sinclair, Earl of Orkney, and his family: a study in the politics of survival', in K.J. Stringer (ed.), *Essays on the Nobility of Medieval Scotland*, Edinburgh, 1985, pp.234-53.

Crawford, Barbara E., 'Earl William Sinclair and the Building of Roslin Collegiate Church', in John Higgitt (ed.), *Medieval Art and Architecture in the Diocese of St. Andrews*, [Tring] British Archaeological Association, 1994, pp.99-107.

Cresy, Edward, *A Practical Treatise on Bridge Building and on the Equilibrium of Vaults and Arch, with professional Life and Work of John Rennie (1761-1821)*, London, 1839.

Crook, J. Mordaunt, 'John Britton and The Gothic Revival', in John Summerson (ed.), *Concerning Architecture, Essays on Architectural Writers and Writing Presented to Nikolaus Pevsner*, London, 1968, pp.98-119.

Cumming, J., 'Sandstone as a Building Material', *The Architect*, vol.XL, 3 August 1888, p.63.

Cuthbertson, David, *Rosslyn lyrics*, Edinburgh, 1878.

Davey, Norman, *A History of Building Materials*, London, 1961.

De Selincourt, Ernest (ed.), *The Early Letters of William and Dorothy Wordsworth (1787-1805)*, Oxford, 1934.

De Selincourt, Ernest (ed.), *Journals of Dorothy Wordsworth*, 2 vols., London, 1941.

Dubbini, Renzo, *Geografie dello Sguardo, Visione e paesaggio in età moderna*, Torino, 1994.

Dubbini, Renzo, *Geography of the Gaze. Urban and Rural Vision in Early Modern Europe*, Chicago, 2002.

Dunbar, John G. (ed.), *Sir William Burrell's Northern Tour 1758*, East Linton, 1997.

Engen, Rodney K., *Dictionary of Victorian Engravers, Print Publishers and their Works*, Cambridge, 1979.

Eyre-Todd, George, *Scotland Picturesque and Traditional*, London, 1895.

Fawcett, Richard, *The Architectural History of Scotland. Scottish Architecture from the Accession of the Stewarts to the Reformation 1371-1560*, Edinburgh, 1994.

Fitchen, John, *The Construction of Gothic Cathedrals: A Study of Medieval Vault Erection*, Chicago, 1981.

Font-Réaulx, Dominique de, 'Le vrai sous la fantastique. Esquisse des liens entre la daguerréotype et le théâtre de son temps', *Études Photographiques*, no.16, mai 2005, pp.153-165.

Forbes, Robert, 'An Account of the Chapel of Roslin & c. Most respectfully inscribed to William St Clare of Roslin Esq. Representative of the Princely Founder and Endower', *The Edinburgh Magazine*, vol.5, January 1761, pp.2-53.

Fraser-Harris, D.F., 'William De la Cour, Painter, Engraver and Teacher of Drawing' in *The Scottish Bookman*, vol.I, no.5, 1936, pp.12-19.

Fyfe, Dorothea H. and Minto, Charles Sinclair, *John Forbes White, Miller, Collector, Photographer 1831-1904*, Edinburgh, 1970.

Garlick, Kenneth and Macintyre, Angus (ed.), *The Diary of Joseph Farington*, 17 vols., New Haven and London, 1979.

Gernsheim, Helmut, *Focus on Architecture and Sculpture, An Original Approach to the Photography of Architecture and Sculpture*, London, 1949.

Gernsheim, Helmut and Alison, *L.J.M. Daguerre, The History of the Diorama and the Daguerreotype*, London, 1956.

Gernsheim, Helmut and Alison, *The History of Photography; from the Camera Obscura to the Beginning of the Modern Era*, London, 1969.

Gill, A.T., 'The London Diorama,' *History of Photography*, no.1, January 1977, pp.31-33.

Gillies, Robert Pearse, *Recollections of Sir Walter Scott*, London, 1837.

Gillies, Robert Pearse, *Memoirs of a Literary Veteran*, 2 vols., London, 1851.

Glendinning, Miles, MacInnes, Ranald and MacKechnie, Aonghus, *A History of Scottish Architecture: from the Renaissance to the Present Day*, Edinburgh, 1996.

Goodall, Ian and Richardson, Margaret, 'A Recently Discovered Gandy Sketchbook', *Architectural History, Journal of the Society of Architectural Historians*, vol.44, 2001, p.45-55.

Gough, Richard, *British Topography or an Historical account of what has been done for illustrating the topographical Antiquities of Great Britain and Ireland*, 2 vols., London, 1780. [N.B. Rosslyn Chapel does not appear in the 1768 edition of the book].

Gower, Elisabeth Leveson, Duchess of Sutherland and Countess of Stafford, *Views in Orkney and on the North-Eastern Coast of Scotland, taken in 1805 and etched in 1807*, published by the author in 1807.

Grant, James, *Old and New Edinburgh*, London, 1882.

Grant, Maurice Harold, *A Dictionary of British Etchers*, London, 1952.

Grant, Will, *Rosslyn. The Chapel, Castle and Scenic Lore*, Edinburgh, 1947.

Green, Lynne and Walker, Muriel (eds.), *Roger Fenton Photographer of the 1850s*, exhib. cat. Hayward Gallery February–April 1988, London, 1988.

Green, Samuel Gosnell, *Scottish Pictures drawn with pen and pencil*, London, 1883.

Groome, Francis Hindes, *Ordnance Gazetteer of Scotland: A Survey of Scottish Topography, Statistical, Biographical and Historical*, 3 vols., Edinburgh, 1883-1885.

Grose, Francis, *The antiquities of Scotland*, 2 vols., London, 1790.

Guiterman, Helen, and Llewellyn, Briony (eds.), *David Roberts*, exhib. cat. Barbican Art Gallery, Oxford, 1986.

Halsby, Julian and Harris, Paul, *The Dictionary of Scottish Painters 1600 to the Present*, Edinburgh, 1990.

Halsby, Julian, *Scottish Watercolours 1740-1940*, London, 1989.

Hannah, Ian C., *Story of Scotland in Stone*, London, 1934.

Hannavy, John, *Roger Fenton of Crimble Hall*, Boston, 1976.

Hannavy, John, *The Victorian Professional Photographer*, Aylesbury, 1980.

Hannavy, John, *Thomas Keith's Scotland, the Work of a Victorian Amateur Photographer (1852-57)*, Edinburgh, 1981.

Harington, John, *Orlando Furioso in English heroical verse*, London, 1634.

Harrower, Ina Mary, *John Forbes White*, Edinburgh, 1918.

Hay, Richard Augustine, *Genealogie of the Sainteclaires of Rosslyn, Including the chartulary of Rosslyn*, Edinburgh, 1835 [edited and published anonymously by James Maidment].

Helps, Arthur (ed.), *Scottish Diaries of Queen Victoria. Leaves from the Journal of Our Life in the Highlands from 1848 to 1861*, London, 1868.

Herdman, William Gawin, 'Linear Perspective', *The Art Journal*, 1st November 1849, pp.329-331.

Historical and Descriptive Account of Rosslyn Chapel and Castle with Engravings, drawn and Engraved by J. & J. Johnstone, Edinburgh, 1827.

Holloway, James and Errington, Lindsay, *The Discovery of Scotland: The Appreciation of Scottish Scenery through Two Centuries of Painting*, exhib. cat. National Gallery of Scotland, Edinburgh, 1978.

Hussey, Christopher, *The Picturesque. Studies in a Point of View*, London, 1967.

Hyde Ralph, *Panoramania! The Art and Entertainment of the 'All-Embracing' View*, London, 1988.

Irwin, David and Francina, *Scottish Painters at Home and Abroad 1700-1900*, London, 1975.

Ivins, William M., *Prints and Visual Communication*, Cambridge Mass., 1953 (reprint 1969).

Johnson, Peter and Ernlé, Money, *The Nasmyth Family of Painters*, Leigh-on-Sea, 1977.

Johnson, Ronald, *The Earl and the Architect*, Edinburgh, 1986.

Jokilehto, Jukka, *A History of Architectural Conservation*, Oxford, 1999.

Kemp, Martin, 'Alexander Nasmyth and the Style of Graphic Eloquence', *The Connoisseur*, vol.173, February 1970, pp.93-100.

Kemp, Martin (ed.), *Mood of the Moment: Masterworks of Photography from the University of St Andrews*, St Andrews, 1994.

Kerr, Andrew, 'Rosslyn Castle, its Buildings Past and Present', *Proceedings of the Society of Antiquaries of Scotland*, vol.XII, 1878, pp.412-424.

Kerr, Andrew, 'The Collegiate Church or Chapel of Rosslyn, its Builders, Architect, and Construction', *Proceedings of the Society of Antiquaries of Scotland*, vol.XII, 1878, pp.218-244.

Kirk, James (ed.), *The Records of the Synod of Lothian and Tweeddale, 1589-1596, 1640-1649*, Edinburgh, 1977.

Knight, Richard Payne, *An Analytical Inquiry into the Principles of Taste*, London, 1805.

Langmuir, Erika, and Lynton Norbert, *The Yale Dictionary of Art and Artists*, New Haven and London, 2000.

Lawlor, H. J., 'The Library of the Sinclairs of Rosslyn', in *Proceedings of the Society of Antiquarians of Scotland*, vol.XXXII, 1898, pp.90-120.

Lawson, John Parker, *Scotland Delineated in a Series of Views by C. Stanfield. W.L. Leitch, T. Creswick, D. Roberts and others,* London, 1847-54.

Lawson, Julie, *Masterpieces of Photography from the Riddell Collection*, Edinburgh, 1986.

Lawson, Julie, *William Donaldson Clark (1816-1873)*, (Scottish Masters no.15), Edinburgh, 1990.

Lee, Sidney and Stephen, Leslie (eds.), *The Dictionary of National Biography: From the Earliest Times to 1900*, 22 vols., London, 1921-1922. [Different editions and later supplements]

'Letter to the editor', *The Times*, 20 June 1861, p.12.

'Letters to the editor', *The Scotsman*, (7 May 1861–22 June 1861).

Lever, Jill, and Harris, John, *Illustrated Dictionary of Architecture 800-1914*, London and Boston, 1993.

Lukacher, Brian, *Joseph Gandy. An Architectural Visionary in Georgian England*, London 2006.

Lukacher, Brian (ed.), *Joseph Michael Gandy 1771-1843*, exhib. cat. Architectural Association November-December 1982, London, 1982.

Lukacher, Brian, 'John Soane and his Draughtsman Joseph Michael Gandy', *Daidalos*, vol. 25, September, 1987, pp.51-64.

Lukacher, Brian, 'Phantasmagoria and emanations: lighting effects in the architectural fantasies of Joseph Michael Gandy', *AA Files*, vol.4, London 1983, pp.40-48.

Lukacher, Brian, *Joseph Michael Gandy: The Poetical Representation and Mythography of Architecture* (Ph.D. University of Delaware, U.M.I. Research Press, 1987).

Mace, Angela (ed.), *Architecture in Manuscript, 1601-1996: Guide to the British Architectural Library Manuscripts and Archives Collection*, London, 1998.

MacGeorge, A., *William Leighton Leitch, Landscape Painter*, London, 1884.

MacGibbon, David and Ross, Thomas, *The Ecclesiastical Architecture of Scotland*, 3 vols., Edinburgh, 1896-1897.

Macmillan, Duncan, *Painting in Scotland: The Golden Age*, Oxford, 1986.

Maggi, Angelo see also Rosslyn, Helen.

Maggi, Angelo, 'Poetic stones: Roslin Chapel in Gandy's sketchbook and Daguerre's Diorama', *Architectural History, Journal of the Society of Architectural Historians*, vol.42, 1999, pp.263-283.

Maggi, Angelo, 'Daguerre e le suggestioni della Rosslyn Chapel', *Fotostorica. Gli Archivi della Fotografia*, no.3/4, April 1999, pp.32-35.

Maggi, Angelo, '*Documents Relating to Roslin Chapel*: a recently discovered collection of papers by John Britton', *Architectural Heritage. The Journal of the Architectural Heritage Society of Scotland*, vol.XIII, 2002, pp.73-98.

Maggi, Angelo, 'Insolite prospettive: l'architettura nelle fotografie di Roger Fenton', in Nico Stringa (ed.), *Fotologie. Scritti in onore di Italo Zannier*, Padova 2006, pp.211-216, 402-405.

Mallalieu, Huon L., *The Dictionary of British Watercolour Artists up to 1920*, 3 vols., Woodbridge, 1976-90.

Marien, Mary Warner, *Photography and Its Critics. A Cultural History, 1839–1900*, Cambridge, 1997.

Mattingly, Harold; Burnett, Ian Alistair Kendall and Pollard, A.W.(eds.), *List of Catalogues of English Book Sales 1676-1900 now in the British Museum*, London, 1915.

McEwan, Peter J.M., *Dictionary of Scottish Art and Architecture.* Woodbridge, 1994.

McMillan, William, *The Worship of the Reformed Church of Scotland 1550-1638*, Dunfermline and London [1931].

McWilliam, Colin, *Lothian, except Edinburgh* (Buildings of Scotland), Harmondsworth, 1978.

Muir, Thomas Smyth, *Descriptive notices of some of the ancient parochial and collegiate churches of Scotland*, Edinburgh, 1848.

Murray, Alexander, *The modern universal British traveller; or, a new, complete, and accurate tour through England, Wales, Scotland and the neighbouring islands. Comprising all that is worthy of observations in Great Britain*, 'Part III – Scotland and North Britain', London 1779.

Nasmyth, James Hall, *James Nasmyth, engineer an autobiography edited by Samuel Smiles*, London, 1897.

Pare, Richard (ed.), *Photography and Architecture (1839-1939)*, Centre Canadien D'Architecture / Canadian Centre for Architecture, Montreal, 1982.

Pare, Richard, *Roger Fenton* (Aperture Masters of Photography, no.4), New York, 1987.

Patterson, David and Rock, Joe, *Thomas Begbie's Edinburgh: a Mid-Victorian Portrait*, Edinburgh, 1992.

Payne, Ann, *Views of the Past. Topographical Drawings in the British Library*, London, 1987.

Pennant, Thomas, *A Tour in Scotland*, 2 vols., London, 1790.

Pointon, Marcia, *William Dyce, 1806-1864: A Critical Biography*, Oxford, 1979.

Potonniée, Georges, *Daguerre Peintre et Décorateur*, Paris, 1935 (reprint 1989).

Price, Uvedale, *Essays on the Picturesque*, London, 1810.

Rae, T.I., 'The Scottish Antiquarian Tradition', *Scots Antiquaries and Historians*, Abertay Historical Society, 1972, pp.12-25.

Ray, Gordon N., *The Illustrator and the Book in England from 1790 to 1914*, Oxford, 1976.

Riches, Anne, and Stell, Geoffrey, *Materials and Traditions in Scottish Building*, Edinburgh, 1992.

Rock, Joseph, *The Life and Work of Hugh William Williams*, unpublished Ph.D thesis, University of Edinburgh, 1996.

'Roslin Chapel', *The Building News*, 5 July 1861, p.560.

Ross, Thomas, 'Rosslyn Chapel, a paper read at Rosslyn', *Transactions of the Scottish Ecclesiological Society*, vol.IV, part III, no.12, 1914-1915, pp.238-247.

Rosslyn, Helen and Maggi, Angelo, *Rosslyn Country of Painter and Poet*, exhib. cat. National Gallery of Scotland April-July 2002, Edinburgh, 2002.

Rosslyn, Peter, *Rosslyn Chapel*, n.p., 1997.

Ruskin, John, *Modern Painters*, 6 vols., Orpington and London, 1898.

Russell, Ronald, *Guide to British Topographical Prints*, London, 1979.

Sadleir, Michael, *Things Past*, London, 1944.

Saint-Clair, Roland William, *The St Clairs of the Isles. A History*, Auckland, 1898.

Schivelbusch, Wolfgang, *Disenchanted Night: the Industrialisation of Light in the Nineteenth Century*, Oxford, 1988.

Schnapp, Alain, *The Discovery of the Past. The Origins of Archaeology*, London, 1996.

Scott, Sir Walter, *Provincial Antiquities and Picturesque Scenery of Scotland*, vols.2, London, 1826.

Scott, Sir Walter, *The Lay of the Last Minstrel: with Life and Notes*, Edinburgh 1805.

Scott-Moncrieff, George (ed.), *The Stones of Scotland*, London, 1938.

Sim, Katharine, *David Roberts R.A. 1796-1864, A Biography*, London, 1984.

Slezer, John, *Theatrum Scotiae*, London, 1693.

Sloan, Kim, *'A Noble Art' Amateur Artists and Drawing Masters c.1600-1800*, exhib. cat. British Museum, London, 2000.

Stevenson, David, *The Origins of Freemasonry: Scotland's Century 1590-1710*, Aberdeen, 1998.

Stevenson, Sara, *David Octavius Hill and Robert Adamson, Catalogue of their calotypes taken between 1843 and 1847 in the collection of the Scottish National Portrait Gallery*, Edinburgh, 1981.

Stevenson, Sara (ed.), *Light from the Dark Room. A Celebration of Scottish Photography: a Scottish-Canadian Collaboration*, exhib. cat. Royal Scottish Academy July–October 1995, Edinburgh, 1995.

Stevenson, Sara, *Facing the Light. The Photography of Hill & Adamson*, exhib. cat. Scottish National Portrait Gallery May-September 2002, Edinburgh, 2002.

Stevenson, Sara, *The Personal Art of David Octavius Hill*, New Haven and London, 2002.

Summerson, John, 'Gandy and The Tomb of Merlin', *The Architectural Review*, vol. LXXXIX, no.532, April 1941, pp.89-90.

Summerson, John, *Heavenly Mansions and Other Essays on Architecture*, New York, 1963.

Swarbreck, Samuel Dukinfield, *Sketches in Scotland Drawn from Nature and on Stone*, London, 1837.

Tasker, Edward G., *Encyclopedia of Medieval Church Art*, London, 1993.

Taylor, Roger, *George Washington Wilson, Artist & Photographer (1823-93)*, Aberdeen, 1981.

Bibliography

'The Restoration at Roslin Chapel', *The Builder*, 29 June 1861, p.443.

The Transactions of the Architectural Institute of Scotland, session 1862-64.

Thomas, Jane, *Midlothian. An Illustrated Architectural Guide*, Edinburgh, 1995.

Thompson, John, *The Illustrated Guide to Rosslyn Chapel and Castle*, Edinburgh, 1934.

Thomson, Katrina, *Turner and Sir Walter Scott. The Provincial Antiquities and Picturesque Scenery of Scotland*, exhib. cat. National Gallery of Scotland December 1999–March 2002, Edinburgh, 1999.

Turner, Jane (ed.), *The Dictionary of Art*, 34 vols., London, 1996.

Turner, Robin (ed.), *Discovery and Excavation in Scotland 1998*, Edinburgh, 1998.

Two Views: Ruins of Holyrood Chapel, A Moonlight Scene painted by M. Daguerre and the Cathedral of Chartres by M. Bouton in the Diorama of London, Regents Park, London, 1825.

'View of Roslyn Chapel, at the Diorama', *The Mirror of Literature, Amusement, and Instruction*, vol. CLXXXV, Saturday 4 March 1826, pp.129-132.

Views of Edinburgh and its vicinity, drawn and engraved by J. & H.S. Storer, Exhibiting Remains of Antiquity, Public Buildings, and Picturesque Scenery, 2 vols., Edinburgh, 1822.

Views of Roslin Castle and Chapel from drawings by J.M.W. Turner, E. Blore and Thomson of Duddingstone; with a Descriptive Letter, Edinburgh, 1828.

Watson John, 'St. Matthew's Collegiate Church, Rosslyn' in *The Transactions of Edinburgh Architectural Association*, vol.9, Edinburgh, 1928, pp.105-115.

Watt, Francis and Carter, Andrew, *Picturesque Scotland: Its Romantic Scenes and Historical Associations so described in Lay and Legend, Song and Story*, London, 1880.

Williamson George Charles (ed.), *Bryan's Dictionary of Painters and Engravers*, 5 vols., London, 1903-4 [and later reprints].

Wilson, Daniel, *The Archaeology and Prehistoric Annals of Scotland*, Edinburgh, 1851.

Wilson, George Washington, 'A Voice from the hills: Mr Wilson at home', *The British Journal of Photography*, vol.XI, no.230, 30 September 1864, p.375.

Wood, Christopher, *Dictionary of Victorian Painters*, Woodbridge, 1976.

Wood, R. Derek, 'The Diorama in Great Britain in the 1820s', *History of Photography*, vol.17, no.3, Autumn 1993, pp.284-295.

INDEX

Within each entry to this index, page references to the text are listed first, followed (in italics) by a separate sequence of plate references to the illustrations.

Index

PHOTOGRAPHIC CREDITS

The plates in the book are reproduced with the kind permission of the following:

Plate 72 © National Museums Liverpool, Walker Art Gallery,

Plates 34-36 © Rouen, Musée des Beaux-Arts. All rights reserved.

Plate 60 © Sir Robert Clerk of Penicuik.

Plates 26-28, 30, 31, 33 © The British Library Board. All rights reserved.

Plates 25, 38-41, 52, 77, 78, 100 © The Trustees of the National Galleries of Scotland.

Plates 9, 45, 79, 83 © V&A Images. All rights reserved.

Plate 82, Blackburn Museum and Art Gallery.

Plates 16, 17, 20, 22, 23 by courtesy of the Trustees of Sir John Soane's Museum.

Plates 12, 43 courtesy of Edinburgh City Libraries and Information Services, Scottish Library.

Plate 7 National Portrait Gallery, London.

Plate 6 RIBA Library Photographs Collection.

Plates 70, 71 Ruskin Library, University of Lancaster.

Plates 37, 46-50, 103 The Cavaye Collection of Thomas Begbie Prints. City Art Centre; City of Edinburgh Museums and Galleries.

Plate 56 The Royal Commission on the Ancient and Historical Monuments of Scotland.

Plates 4, 5, 109 Trustees of the National Library of Scotland.

Plate 96 Writers Museum, Edinburgh.

Every attempt has been made to obtain permission to reproduce copyright material. If any proper acknowledgement has not been made, copyright holders are invited to inform the publisher of the oversight.